# WRITING REVOLT

D1340002

# WRITING REVOLT

## An Engagement with African Nationalism, 1957-67

### Terence Ranger

WEAVER
W
PRESS

JC JAMES CURREY

James Currey
is an imprint of Boydell & Brewer Ltd
PO Box 9, Woodbridge, Suffolk IP12 3DF, GB
www.jamescurrey.com
and of
Boydell & Brewer Inc.
668 Mt Hope Avenue, Rochester, NY 14620-2731, US
www.boydellandbrewer.com

Weaver Press
PO Box A1922
Harare
Zimbabwe
www.weaverpress.co.zw

Frontispiece: Cover of the first edition of *Revolt in Southern Rhodesia, 1896-7*
(London: Heinemann, 1967)
Other photographs from the author's private collection.
The publishers would also like to thank George Kerekwaivanane who compiled the list of
names and the bibliography.

Published in paperback in Zimbabwe and Southern Africa by Weaver Press and in the
rest of the world by James Currey.

British Library Cataloguing in Publication Data
A catalogue record for this book is available from the British Library

ISBN 978-1-84701-071-1 (James Currey paper)

Papers used by Boydell & Brewer are natural, recyclable products
made from wood grown in sustainable forests

Typeset in ATC Laurel Book 10.2/14 by Weaver Press , Harare
Printed and bound in Great Britain by CPI Group (UK) Ltd, Croydon, CR0 4YY

# Contents

# LIST OF ABBREVIATIONS

| | |
|---|---|
| CACBA | Citizens Against the Colour Bar Association |
| CAP | Central Africa Party |
| ICU | Industrial and Commercial Workers' Union |
| NDP | National Democratic Party |
| PCC | People's Caretaker Council |
| SRANC | Southern Rhodersian African National Congress |
| SRLAWF | Southern Rhodesia Legal Aid and Welfare Fund |
| TANU | Tanganyika African National Union |
| TUC | Trade Union Congress |
| UCRN | University College of Rhodesia and Nyasaland |
| UFP | United Federal Party |
| UNIP | United National Independence Party |
| UPP | United People's Party |
| URP | United Rhodesia Party |
| ZANU | Zimbabwe African National Union |
| ZAPU | Zimbabwe African People's Union |
| ZNP | Zimbabwe National Party |

To Shelagh

and to the memory of John Reed

# REVOLT IN SOUTHERN RHODESIA 1896~7

# T.O. RANGER

# PREFACE

When I published *Bulawayo Burning* in 2010 I had exhausted my primary material. There was nothing left to do but to devour myself and to make use of the 'Ranger Papers'. These consist of a large amount of material deposited at Rhodes House when I retired in 1997, together with letters to my parents, and the transcript of my friend John Reed's daily diaries for the period when we lived in the same place and shared in the same political activities. Taken in all this material amounts to a very large archive for the years between 1957, when I first went to Southern Rhodesia, and 1967 when I published my first book, *Revolt in Southern Rhodesia*. I therefore devised a title under which I could write about two different things. *Writing Revolt* might mean producing a record of the African awakening which I had witnessed during those ten years. And it might mean the process which led me to write that first book. This book is therefore intended both as history and as historiography.

I revealed these plans to the participants at a workshop on my work at the University of Illinois in September 2010. To my relief they agreed that it would be useful to possess an account of the ten years to 1967 and that I need not go on to my career in Dar es Salaam, and UCLA, and Manchester, and Oxford, and back again to the University of Zimbabwe after retirement. After 1967 I possess much less material. But to my surprise they insisted that I provide some information about my life before I went to Rhodesia in 1957. The reader needed to be prepared – or at least as prepared as I had been myself – for my responses to Rhodesia.

I have been very anxious, however, that this book should not take the form of the classical Africanist autobiography – the golden years of discovery of Africa under the benevolence of late colonialism followed by a steady disillusion, as theory wars raged among Africanists, as Africa itself collapsed into chaos, as the grind of teaching and examining replaced inspiration. I am not claiming that we made great discoveries in those ten years. Indeed, some of the ideas we had about African history were inoperable and others were frankly ridiculous. I am very aware that the golden age of Zimbabwean historiography is now, with more than a score of Zimbabwean historians researching and publishing. This book is about a primitive stage of Zimbabwean historiography.

It is also about the ways in which politics and history interacted. The men I discussed Zimbabwean history with were the leaders of African nationalism; my seminar papers were sent to prisons and restriction areas. Both they and I were making political as well as intellectual discoveries. I had previously worked on Irish history. Now I found again a context in which history was much too important to be left to historians.

In writing this book my main debt is to my wife, Shelagh, who shared all these adventures and to whom this book is dedicated. After that it will be obvious to any readers of this book how much I owe to John Reed. John used to confide to his diary that he could never possibly have been friends with me except in Rhodesia – since I was not a socialist – but we are still close friends today, nearly sixty years later. John's generosity in making his daily diary available to me has been an enormous source of strength for this book. I owe a very great deal to my late mother, Anna, first for believing in me and then for preserving my letters to her. I am very grateful to the librarian and archivist of Rhodes House, Lucy McCann, for allowing me full access to the 'Ranger Papers' and for making it possible for me to work on them at home. My ex-student and now colleague, Professor Jocelyn Alexander, has helped greatly with the selection and transport of these papers. Professor Diana Jeater has drawn me to reflect on my career. Professor Terri Barnes organized the conference on my work at the University of Illinois at which I was able to present my first ideas for this memoir. In Zimbabwe Professor Ngwabi Bhebhe and Dr Gerald Mazarire have shown great enthusiasm both for historiography and for discussion of the nationalist past.

And over and above these men and women there is the great cloud of the dead – students, colleagues, political activists, comrades – whose names are recorded in the book. I have survived almost all of them and I intend this book as a memorial to them as well as to me.

# CHAPTER ONE

# 1929-57

# A Very Ordinary Boy

My old friend, Michael Utidgian, who keeps up much better than I do with our school fellows, tells me that he met the other day another Highgate boy who has become a university historian. 'I can't understand why Ranger has become so radical,' he said. 'He was such an ordinary boy.' Indeed, there was only one person who would not have accepted this description – my mother. Nothing would shake her faith that I was extraordinary. I failed maths; my termly report for French said I was out of my depth and quite content to drown; I failed Latin so often that I had to go to Oxford a term late; I was no good at the sciences which might have equipped me to play a role in my father's electro-plating firm. The only sports I was good at were those that were too vulgar for my school, like table tennis, or too posh, like croquet. All in all I was very unlike these African schoolboys and schoolgirls whose brilliance gave rise to the myth that they had two brains. Except for literature and history I might as well not have had a brain at all.

My mother, however, was convinced that I was exceptional. She even believed that like dogs I could sense a person's moral worth. If I did not like one of my father's business associates that was more or less proof that he was dishonest – a reasonable enough surmise in the sleazy business of war profiteering. My father, the most obliging of men, was content to accept these judgements – and my mother's equally positive views of my younger brother Jim. Meanwhile my parents gave me what I needed to feed on – countless holiday visits to cathedral towns and castles, and a reasonably well stocked library at home (which contained most of Dickens, for example). I was never made to feel that I had failed.

Of course Africa was not part of this education. There were no slave trade museums in those days. It was from my father's books that I derived my ideas of Africa – Kipling, Haggard, Buchan, and a little later, Conrad. I have often thought about the odd effects of such a literary education which has left no trace on my adult responses to Africa. We did not know any Africans personally; there were no African boys at Highgate School, though there were Greeks and Armenians and German Jews.

My family was very apolitical. Or at least this was true once it was accepted that they would always vote conservative and read the *Daily Telegraph*. (Years later, when I was in Rhodesia, my mother wrote to the *Telegraph* to say that she could not understand why they got Rhodesia wrong and everything else right.) My father's one political choice was to break the bus pickets during the general strike. My mother's defining political moment was her moral disgust at British failure to stand up to Hitler and her admiration for Antony Eden. This led to the only rupture I can recall between my mother and me over my own political awakening and disgust at Eden's policy over Suez. Both of us were taking moral positions rather than political ones – and in this at least I was being prepared for my responses in Rhodesia. The only quarrel I had with my father was over the use of the atomic bomb, which appalled him but which with the cynicism of youth I saw as just another weapon.

My parents were not members of any party branch; my brother was a member of the Totteridge Young Conservatives, but more for social than political reasons. I was not a member of anything. The family's moral politics was contained within a bourgeois life style which varied in elaboration according to my father's prosperity. At the height of his success we rented a fine mansion in Bishop's Avenue, ran a model steam engine round the garden, and kept a New Forest pony – which to everyone's surprise gave birth one morning to a foal. My father kept a barrel of beer in the garage as a reward for the police who brought our pony back when she had roamed. On that side of the great divide – whether one trusted the police or feared them – we were firmly trusters. I think that this contributed to my intense disgust when I found that in Rhodesia one could not trust the police at all.

I don't think I became wedded to wealth or to bourgeois interests during my father's palmy days. For one thing his prosperity was always visibly in flux. We moved from house to house and flat to flat. By the time I got to Oxford nothing was left of my Savings Certificates and I contributed to the family budget out of my £300-a-year State Scholarship. For another thing his successes were dependent on that most elusive quality – charm. My aunt Gladys – mother's downright, left-leaning sister – told me once that in his youth my father was the most charming man in the world. 'You are not nearly so charming as your father,' she told me, 'but you wear better.' And in one way I suppose I do. I am writing this aged 82 and he died at 63, chain-smoking and full-English-breakfast eating to the end. But when my father had become fascinated by an idea he could sell it to anyone. Many of these ideas were in advance of their time – under-soil football pitch heating, flower baskets hanging from lampposts – but all had an air of provisionality.

Moreover, my father was a great gambler. He bet on horses and dogs; he bet on chess games at the Gambit Club. Years later my mother told me what had happened to my Savings Certificates – broken out of their metal box with a poker, they funded an afternoon's gambling. At the time I enjoyed it. If he won he would invariably spend the winnings at once, taking my brother and I and our school friends out to a restaurant. This wasn't good for the family economy but it was fun for my friends, and he was easily the most popular father around. (Many of the others were stiffly conventional.)

The result of all this was that I grew up in horror of gambling and this was reinforced later by the very similar sto-ry of my wife, Shelagh's, father – also a charming salesman and gambler. But I was deeply grateful to my parents for taking me to the theatre, and particu-larly the Royal Opera House. And I am deeply grateful to them for sending me to Highgate School and keeping me there when times became hard.

*Terence Ranger, aged 17.*

There were some odd teachers at Highgate. With many away at the war, men had been brought back from retirement, some of whom were truly eccentric. There was Doc Martin, for instance, who ran a secret society – 'buckets of gore, is what we're here for' – complete with an axe and executions. But there were also some brilliant teachers. One of these was the senior history teacher, T.N. (Tommy) Fox, back from army intelligence, with his bottle deep spectacles and one wisp of hair wrapped around his head. Fox was a brilliant Socratic teacher and a radical Fabian. He purified my literary style, which tended to imperial purple. But he did not spot my elusive radicalism and I was not a member of the inner group whom he gathered in Highgate cafés for mildly socialist talk. Indeed his greatest influence on me was to convert me to his belief that Oxford was the only university worth considering.

When I got a scholarship to Leeds I was deeply mortified and determined to win an Oxford scholarship and transfer. Years later, when I had been deported from Rhodesia in 1963, Fox invited me to a Fabian Society meeting in his Kentish village. But by that time I had become much too radical and adventurist for Kentish Fabians. In short, I left Highgate and Oxford as I had entered them – unformed by any political ideology.

My 18 months of National Service did not take me to Africa. I was an Education Corps sergeant because I wanted to discover whether I could teach. My 'overseas' service was performed on the Isle of Wight, where in the glorious summer of 1949 I caught the bus along the coast from one artillery base to another, teaching the gunners mathematics. Before that I was with the Coldstream Guards in Aldershot, where I discovered that I *could* teach – even the band-boys who were little younger and much more worldly-wise than I was. I also learned something about racism, since the Guards had recently returned from Egypt and conversation in the Sergeants' Mess was unashamedly contemptuous of 'the wogs'. It did not occur to me then that I would find myself confronting such attitudes in Africa itself.

Oxford did nothing to educate me about Africa either. The core of the History Honours syllabus was a continuous knowledge of English history. I heard about Africa only in the context of Prince Henry the Navigator. Nor was I political. Faced with producing two critical essays a week I had no time for politics or girls. I worked obsessively hard. A great moment came when my tutor, John Prestwich, told me that he thought I should aim to do research and become a university historian. My idea of history – unlike my idea of Africa – was formed by Oxford. In those days, before the rise of the History Workshop, we paid no attention to oral tradition or personal reminiscence. Oxford made me a rigorous archival historian, which I remained throughout my years in Rhodesia.

But I did make at least one important Africanist connection during my graduate work. I was working on seventeenth-century English and Irish history under the supervision of Hugh Trevor-Roper, who later became notorious among Africanists for dismissing the possibility of any meaningful African history whatever. My thesis was about the first Earl of Cork, the richest man in Britain, and, as I came to appreciate later, a classic example of 'settler' history. Cork had the fullest set of diaries and correspondence and estate papers of any man in Britain, but the native Irish only flitted about its margins. I had joined Oxford's first graduate college, St Antony's, and there I met and spent hours talking with Carl Rosburg, who was working on Mau Mau. Like all proper young Englishmen I regarded Mau Mau as the height of barbarity, and I was astonished when Rosburg insisted that it was instead a rational nationalist movement. A few years later it was Rosburg who introduced me to the Southern Rhodesian African nationalist leaders.

At St Antony's too I met my wife, Shelagh Campbell Clarke. Highly intelligent, Shelagh was a victim of the prevailing gender attitudes. Her brother, Bryan, was at Magdalen College, Oxford, and became a distinguished geneticist. Shelagh's father had been killed during the war – in the Café de Paris bombing. Her mother had survived by industry and pluck. Shelagh felt that she had to contribute to the family finances and so she did not go to university but instead trained as a shorthand typist. It was twenty years later when she finally took her degree, in Politics and Religious Studies at Manchester. When I met her, Shelagh was working as the Bursar's Secretary at St Antony's. She was much more travelled than I was. She had been evacuated to Canada, the Bahamas and New England during the war, while I was sleeping in my bedroom at home near Northolt aerodrome and trying to detect which planes were British and which German. She had visited post-war Germany and France and Italy, while I was working my way through English cathedral towns and deploring the effects of the German air-raids. She spoke good French and some German. At this point she was much more internationalist than I was and her British patriotism was mitigated by her experience of the devastation of post-war Germany. She had also encountered in the Bahamas late imperial society and her father had envisaged migrating to the West Indies after the war. Unknowingly she was preparing for our as yet unforeseen Rhodesian experience.

We were young, but the Warden's wife, 'Pussy' Deakin, was romantic. She liked the idea of a College wedding and ensured that afterwards we were allocated a flat in Winchester Road. St Antony's was a small and sociable society. But my three happy years there drew to a close without my doctoral thesis being completed. Of course, I wanted to remain in Oxford. I sat the All Souls examination twice. I competed for the Post-Mastership fellowship at Merton. I have often reflected on my good fortune in not succeeding. But meanwhile I had to find a job which Oxford would not take seriously as a long-lasting competitor. I went to Lancing school to be interviewed for the post of sixth-form history teacher and was lent *Lucky Jim* to read overnight so that I could appreciate the horrors of provincial universities. But I realized that Lancing could easily become a life-time project. And I wanted to become a university teacher.

My great friend in Oxford – and at school – was Peter Dyson, with whom I shared digs. His mother, Connie, was Principal of Hillcroft College, where I spent many nights listening to music and debating philosophy. I remember Connie Dyson fondly foreseeing our future. Peter, it was taken for granted, would become a famous professor. For me Connie foresaw a successful career as a comprehensive school headmaster. Had this been my fate I should have been better off economically than I am now. But even then I realized that Connie was casting me in a secondary role. I wanted to become a famous professor too.

I chose an apparently odd route towards this end and joined Dartmouth Royal Naval College. Dartmouth was aspiring to become the university of the Royal Navy and I was one of the first of a new type of lecturer. ('Must you come to work in your bedroom slippers?' the senior master asked me when I appeared proudly wearing my new suede shoes.) Dartmouth was, and is, a most beautiful place. We were paid a pittance, but it sometimes seemed that we should be paying a subscription ourselves for membership of an exclusive club, There were boats to mess about in on the river; there were beagles to follow; there was rugby, which has remained an enthusiasm ever since; there were bookshops and restaurants and beaches. There was a constant competition between the naval officers and the lecturers for first access to the cadets. In the summer term I would leave the house at 7 a.m. and walk across the fields to give my first class before a fine breakfast, and an ironed copy of *The Times* in the wardroom.

It was all very different from life in Rhodesia. But it also led us towards that. At Dartmouth there were cadets from Pakistan and Sri Lanka, and they were very homesick. I helped them open bank accounts; Shelagh cooked them curries from recipes sent by their mothers. This was one part of our political awakening. The other was the coincidence of Suez and Hungary in 1956. Not surprisingly Dartmouth turned out to be a bad place to launch petitions against the invasion of Egypt. We began to think that it would be useful to go and work overseas – to 'do good' in a post-imperial world. I wrote to the British Council offering my services and had an enthusiastic response. I was offered a lectureship at a University in Malaysia. I can still remember the information sheet which told me that the University was close to town – provided the road was not shut by guerrilla activity. I was very close to going to Asia, rather than to Africa.

But then I read an article in *The Times* by Basil Fletcher, Vice-Principal of the new University College of Rhodesia and Nyasaland. Fletcher painted an idyllic picture. The College, its copper roofs gleaming in the sun, was a beacon of hope between the white nationalism of South Africa and the black nationalism of East Africa. It stood for partnership and multiracialism. At once I decided that this was the place for me. Its working language was English and it seemed to stand for ideals I could enthusiastically embrace. I wrote to Kenneth Kirkwood, who had recently become Professor of Race Relations at St Antony's, to ask if he thought it a good idea for me to apply. He replied with an enthusiastic assent. So I applied for a lectureship in history in Salisbury and was offered the job. I still knew very little about Africa, having read only Trevor Huddleston's *Naught for Your Comfort* and John Gunther's *Inside Africa*. But the Principal, Walter Adams, was misled by my Dartmouth experience into thinking that I was an officer and a gentleman. He appointed me Warden of the Halls of Residence.

My Oxford patrons were displeased. John Prestwich told me that I had destroyed my chance of appointment to any British university, let alone Oxford. (When I gave the Inaugural Lecture for my Oxford Chair in 1987 it gave me great pleasure to reserve a seat for John in the front row.) I did not set out for Rhodesia as a radical. The most assiduous Rhodesian Intelligence man could not have found any reason to exclude me from my new post. But my political morality had been formed by the Britain of the Second World War. It seemed to me the worst civic crime possible to jump a queue. I firmly believed in the equality of classes and races. Shelagh often used to say that we were economic migrants to Rhodesia, and it was true that my pay improved enormously. But almost all British migrants were going to Rhodesia to escape from the ethos of wartime Britain. As I wrote to my parents on 10 February 1957, 'it is extraordinary to read in the papers and to hear in conversation so much about the decline of Britain – how she is losing all her best blood by emigration and getting coloured immigrants in return; how the resignation of Eden is a final and mortal blow to all the decencies, how the Colonial Office is conspiring to surrender to all anti-British groups. People commiserate with you for having lived in such an atmosphere.' By contrast, Shelagh and I went to see the fulfillment of contemporary British ideals in the Colonies. This made all the difference.

I was 27 when I arrived in Southern Rhodesia. I already knew quite a bit about myself – that I could work hard, teach, make friends. I was a married man with two thirds of a doctoral thesis written. But there was a lot I did not know. I did not know whether I had physical or moral courage; whether I could bear being widely unpopular; whether I could take – or follow – a lead; whether I could throw myself into a cause; whether my historical imagination could expand to embrace a whole new civilization. Had I been one of the slightly older generation of Africanists who commanded African troops during the Second World War I should already have found some of this out. As it happened it was my years in Southern Rhodesia which were to give me the answers.

I had read hardly anything academic about Southern Rhodesia before going to teach there. After all, not long before I had thought I might go to teach in Indonesia! Southern Rhodesia was soon to become the subject of three major studies by the London Institute of Race Relations – Philip Mason's *The Birth of a Dilemma: The Conquest and Settlement of Rhodesia*, 1958; Richard Gray's *The Two Nations*, 1960; and Mason's *Year of Decision: Rhodesia and Nyasaland in 1960*, 1960. This trilogy showed the centrality of the Rhodesias to the discussion of race, but none of these books had been published in 1957 when I arrived in Salisbury. Richard Gray had been a candidate for the post of first lecturer in history at the University College of Rhodesia and Nyasaland and had he been appointed UCRN would have had from the beginning the leading researcher on Rhodesian history. Instead it had to make do with me, whose ideas about Rhodesia had been gathered from Rider Haggard and Baden-Powell and more recently – and very differently – from the novels of Doris Lessing.

I arrived in Southern Rhodesia deeply ignorant and this book itself is really a year by year record of what I discovered about its realities and of what I tried to do about them. But it may be helpful to sketch the essentials of the Southern Rhodesian situation and of its place in the world as I understood them when I arrived there.

I knew that Southern Rhodesia – as its name suggested – had been the creation of Cecil John Rhodes and his British South Africa Company. I knew that the new colony had been established by violence, in the 'Matabele War' of 1893 and with the suppression of the 1896-7 uprising. I knew that the Company had continued to administer the territory until 1923, when a referendum of the white settlers de-termined that it should be governed by them in what was called Responsible Self Government rather than join the Union of South Africa. Britain had retained pow-ers to veto Rhodesian legislation, though these had never been used. Nevertheless Southern Rhodesia aspired to independence and to Commonwealth status. There was a popular image of the white Rhodesian, which I had absorbed first from boys' stories and then from the novels of Doris Lessing, as a farmer pioneer, seeking to tame the wild. In Rider Haggard and the boys' stories, Rhodesian whites were heroic pioneers, carving civilization out of the bush. In Doris Lessing's novels – *The Grass is Singing*, 1950, and *Martha Quest*, 1952 – by contrast, the male farmer pioneers were shown as burdened by debt and their wives as traumatized by the isolation of the bush. It was only after the Second World War that many Rhodesian farmers prospered. But, as Doris Lessing's novels also showed – *A Proper Marriage*, 1954 and *A Ripple from the Storm*, 1958 – by the 1940s the majority of white Rhodesians lived in the towns, where there was a war-time industrial boom, particularly in Bulawayo, Rhodesia's second city.

What I had read in the press in the 1950s was that Southern Rhodesia had become part of a British experiment designed to prevent the expansion of South

African apartheid northwards and the expansion of an exclusive black nationalism southwards. As part of the Federation of Rhodesia and Nyasaland, created in 1953, tough, segregationist Southern Rhodesia was theoretically committed to a policy of 'partnership', of which the new University College of Rhodesia and Nyasaland was supposedly a shining symbol. In practice, however, the Federation was oddly shaped from the start. Southern Rhodesia had been induced to join it by the promise of markets in Northern Rhodesia and Nyasaland and of flows of labour and raw materials from them. Federation gave a great boost to Southern Rhodesian industry. Salisbury boomed as well as Bulawayo. Salisbury was the site of two parliaments – the Federal and the Southern Rhodesian territorial. It was the site of the Federal University College, the Federal Art Gallery and the Federal Archives. By 1957, when I arrived, one glance revealed a boom city with new buildings springing up to replace the old colonial ones. Its African population had greatly increased and new townships were created to supplement the initial township of Harare. By 1957 every African family and the overwhelming majority of 'single' workers lived in the townships, no matter what their level of education or the nature of their jobs. This replaced an older, more untidy system of discrimination without total residential segregation.

In fact Southern Rhodesian Africans experienced greater white control after Federation than they had before it. I knew that Africans in Northern Rhodesia and Nyasaland had bitterly resisted the expansion of the Southern Rhodesian system northwards and the imposition of the Federation. That maverick Anglican clergyman Michael Scott had taken up the cause of the Nyasaland chiefs and after his deportation had created the Africa Bureau in London, which published material critical of the Federation and of South Africa, some of which I had read. In the years that followed I worked closely with the Africa Bureau.

Because of this African hostility an odd constitutional arrangement had been made for the Federation. The territorial governments within the Federation retained responsibility for African affairs – for African education, African health provision, African agriculture, etc. The Federal Government was responsible for European education, health, agriculture, etc., and for the provision of infrastructure, like roads, railways, power supplies. Hence discrimination was built into the whole Federal system from the beginning. In Northern Rhodesia and Nyasaland African affairs remained the responsibility of Colonial Office Governors. In Southern Rhodesia, however, this arrangement meant that the territorial assembly, in which only white members of parliament sat and for which there were only a handful of African voters, was exclusively concerned with 'Native Affairs'. The Native Affairs Department was the key organ of state and the Minister of Native Affairs represented an authoritarian government to Africans. Its Native Commissioners controlled Africans in the Reserves while white farmers, who possessed much more and much better land, enjoyed Federal subsidies and scientific support. After the passage of the Native Urban Areas Accommodation and Registration Act in 1947 the municipalities each had their own Native Administration Department which controlled the urban townships. City Councils were composed entirely of white councillors. In Salisbury the imposition of this system and of total residential segregation had been bitterly opposed by African leaders.

When I arrived in 1957 I soon learnt that many of the developments which had taken place in Salisbury between 1953 and 1957 were white Rhodesian projects which were now able to draw on Federal – and often British – finance. This was true of the University College of Rhodesia and Nyasaland, which I was going to join. It had originated as a project to provide Southern Rhodesian whites with their own university. In return for Federal government support and for substantial financial aid from Britain it was agreed that the College should offer its services to Northern Rhodesia and Nyasaland as well, and even that African students with the appropriate qualifications could enter. But in the entire Federation there were only a handful of Africans with the required A level passes and in any case the initial College authorities promised Southern Rhodesian whites that residence and social life at the university would be strictly segregated. In 1957 I was met at Salisbury station by the new Principal, Walter Adams – a handsome and charismatic man, who had the difficult task of making this institution, situated in the belly of the Southern Rhodesian beast, a convincing symbol of partnership.

The white Southern Rhodesians I met in 1957 were a very self-confident lot. They believed that they had tamed the bush, establishing profitable capitalist agriculture. They had developed huge energy resources at the Wankie coalfields and had plans for hydro-electric power by damming the Zambezi at Kariba. They had created an industrial revolution in the towns. They were equipping themselves with the amenities of a civilized modern society. At the Federal Archives, a historian – Lewis Gann – had been employed to write a history of the Federation, territory by territory, so as to give the new 'nation' a sense of its heritage. The majority of Rhodesian whites disliked and feared the Afrikaners and their ideology of apartheid. They saw no reason why they themselves should not continue to harness the natural and human resources of Central Africa and to maintain racial segregation under the slogan of partnership. Some Rhodesian whites, particularly veterans of the Second World War, hoped that under the leadership of Garfield Todd partnership could be made more than a slogan. Most were only too happy to continue as they were.

Most of the newly recruited members of staff at the University College of Rhodesia and Nyasaland, hardly any of whom were themselves Rhodesians, accepted this confident vision. The scientists, in particular, were content to serve the needs of white Rhodesian agriculture and industry. Now, fifty years later, it seems incredible that anybody should have supposed that a white minority could retain control of Central Africa. And even at the time there were plenty of signs that the world was changing.

Ten years earlier, in 1947, the bloody independence and partition of India had taken place. Successive Indian High Commissioners to the Federation of Rhodesia and Nyasaland had sought to balance their diplomatic relations with the Federal government with their concern for the Federation's Asian communities and the expectations of black nationalists that India would offer support to anti-colonial movements. In particular, they mediated the influence of Gandhian non-violence on African movements. During my six years in Southern Rhodesia I found myself working with the Indian High Commissioner on a variety of projects which were too sensitive for him to undertake himself.

In Africa itself 1957 saw the birth of the first independent African nation, as the Gold Coast became Ghana. Black Southern Rhodesians working in Ghana, like Robert Mugabe who was teaching there and married a Ghanaian woman, or visiting the new nation for pan-Africanist metings, like George Nyandoro, gained enormous prestige at home. In East Africa the Mau Mau emergency of 1952, of which I had heard so much from Carl Rosberg, had had a tremendous impact on African opinion in Southern Rhodesia, moderates seeking to avoid the rise of such extremism in Rhodesia and radicals copying Mau Mau styles of dress and rhetoric. Northern Rhodesian African leaders were particularly influenced by developing events in the Congo, and especially in Katanga, which seemed to make a natural partner for the Rhodesian Copperbelt, and the name of the Katangan leader, Tshombe, became a synonym for 'sell-out' among African radicals.

In South Africa, 1957 marked the transition from the non-violence of Albert Luthuli to Nelson Mandela's advocacy of selective violence. Shelagh and I, on our passage to Southern Rhodesia in that year, broke our train journey to stay in Johannesburg with friends from St Antony's, Ron and Barry Ballinger. There we experienced both South African political traditions. Barry Ballinger was a member of the Black Sash movement, with its strategy of non-violent symbolic protest. Ron took us to a session of the Treason Trial, with its multiple defendants packed inside their cage, and we heard evidence about seized Marxist literature and Mandela's support of sabotage. In the years that followed, a stream of refugees from South Africa, white, brown and black, passed through Salisbury and many sought the aid of Shelagh and myself. In Britain the anti-apartheid movement campaigned against the South African regime and Canon John Collins organized Christian Action, which gave support to South African ANC prisoners and was prepared to extend that to Southern Rhodesia. Shelagh and I came to co-operate closely with Christian Action.

And, of course, the Treason Trial dramatized the Cold War setting of African anti-colonialism in the 1950s, with the Soviet Union ready to destabilize the West by supporting African liberation movements. Shelagh and I had been politically mobilized in 1956 by the combination of the Suez Crisis and the Soviet repression of the Hungarian rebellion. The first – with its shocking collusion between Britain, France and Israel – fuelled our anti-imperialism. But the second destroyed any belief in the emancipatory potential of Soviet intervention. We came to southern Africa as anti-imperialists but certainly not as believers in Soviet-style Marxism.

We also came to southern Africa, of course, as anti-racists, for as well as global anti-colonialism in the late 1950s there was global anti-racism. Here our greatest influence was the civil rights campaign in the United States, with its non-violent defiance of segregation and its multiracial sit-in campaigns. When we came to launch our own campaign against the colour bar in Salisbury we drew heavily upon this American example.

This, then, was the African and international context of southern Africa in the late 1950s. But what did I know in 1957 about the response of Southern Rhodesian Africans to their own situation and to these global influences? The answer once again is that I had read Doris Lessing, though not this time her novels. In 1956 Lessing had revisited the Rhodesias, being followed everywhere by the CID. Her 1957 account of what she found was published as *Going Home*. Lessing gave a highly sceptical reading of 'partnership' and of the efforts of the Southern Rhodesian Prime Minister, the ex-missionary Garfield Todd, to liberalize the system. She also revisited her old comrades in what in the late 1940s had been a small but active Marxist group. These whites, largely immigrants from Europe and South Africa, had sought to work with both the European working class and the emerging African trade unions. As Lessing thoroughly demonstrated in *Going Home,* they had completely failed. White workers in Southern Rhodesia were the worst enemies of African advancement. The African unions were timid and resentful of white Marxist patronage. In 1948 there was a general strike by African workers, starting in Bulawayo and spreading in ripples to Salisbury and other towns. Later historians have often sought to interpret it as a frustrated and betrayed proletarian revolution. But Lessing depicted its incoherence and the lack of radicalism in its aims. She herself, trying to make comradely contact with African 'socialists' in the Harare township, found instead a terrified refusal to be compromised by white Marxists. (These events were treated more dramatically in her novel, *A Ripple From the Storm*). In 1956 she found her old comrades demoralized and on the sidelines of political development. In *Going Home* she adopts an essentially African nationalist line rather than a Marxist or a liberal one. Southern Africa belongs to Africans, she writes, and the sooner they are in charge the better. She did not yet find in 1956 a radical black nationalist movement, though there were attempts to mobilize African youth. And in fact the revived Southern Rhodesia African National Congress did not emerge until late in 1957, after the publication of *Going Home*. There then soon developed an adoration of Ghana and an admiration for Mau Mau.

Her book had a considerable influence on my immediate responses when I got to Salisbury. Some of the old white Marxists were still around but I regarded them as yesterday's men and women  The choices seemed to me to lie between a more determined multiracial drive for an effective partnership – to contribute to which I had come to Southern Rhodesia in the first place – and a radical African nationalism. This book is a narrative of how Shelagh and I moved from the first position and support for Garfield Todd into membership of the nationalist parties.

# CHAPTER TWO

# 1957

# The University College of Rhodesia and Nyasaland

My new situation as Warden of all three Halls of Residence at the University College of Rhodesia and Nyasaland drew on both my enthusiasm for Oxford and my commitment to egalitarianism. I was determined that the social and cultural life of the students, both black and white, should not follow a South African model. So I introduced echoes of Oxford: gowns and grace at meals; Hall common rooms and libraries; high tables once a week. Once I had become Warden of the mixed-race Carr Saunders Hall in 1958 I deliberately fostered Hall cultures and loyalties. As for egalitarianism I was from the outset committed to the total integration of the Halls no matter what undertakings might previously have been given to maintain the Rhodesian 'tradition' of residential segregation.

My powers were widely resented. I was thought too young to have so much influence on the life of the College and to host the political and intellectual leaders of the Colony at high tables. John Reed in his diaries remarked that the universal criticism of my regime reminded him of the Gospel phrase, 'and they murmured against him' As I explained to my brother Jim on 4 April 1957:

> There are factions based on the English provincial universi-
> ty tradition as against Oxbridge, or on South African tradition
> against all English. My policy in the Halls of Residence comes
> under fire from all sides. The older South African Professors resent

14

*my youth and my 'libertarian ideas'. (South African universities
have students of 16 and are run on school lines); the younger
lecturers wonder why I am doing the job of three Wardens and
so depriving them of office; others think my attitudes to Africans
suspiciously liberal, while a few zealots regard me as a reactionary. Alcohol in rooms; girls allowed to entertain men in bed-sitters;
locking up hours as late as 10.30 – all this has put Old Maidish
Salisbury in a tizzy. The various heresies on the nature of the
university current here would make an Oxford don's hair stand
on end – the dominance of our bogus Social Science departments
and in particular the department of education; the concept of
limited and regulated student societies which are planned so that
their meetings don't clash with each other; more money spent on
tape-recorders and psychological equipment than on books. Of
course one cannot create Oxford in Central Africa nor would one
want to. But I shall attempt to preserve some of its advantages.*

Once we had arrived in Salisbury we soon found that Basil Fletcher's picture in
The Times was untrue or at best misleading. UCRN was funded by the British Government and a Federal government which represented millions of Africans in Northern Rhodesia and Nyasaland as well as Southern Rhodesia. Yet when one was told
one must respect 'public opinion' it was always white Southern Rhodesian opinion
which was meant. The three daily newspapers in Salisbury – the Herald, the Evening
Standard and the Citizen – watched the College like hawks to detect, or invent, any
deviation from the white Southern Rhodesian norm. And that norm certainly did
not represent a middle way between white and black nationalisms.

Salisbury was the most segregated city in southern Africa. I assumed that it had
always been so but I learnt later that it had been made so by ten years' hard labour
since the implementation of the Native Urban Areas Accommodation Act in 1947.
For a decade Salisbury's councillors had worked to ensure that all Africans lived in
townships and not in the city; that African domestic servants should not be allowed
to keep their families with them in the suburbs; that facilities be strictly segregated;
that 'elite' Africans be corralled into small areas on the margin of townships. This
had taken ten years to attain and had been met with fierce African opposition. And
now we came along to propagate residential integration in the College's Halls of
Residence.

The daily papers circled around the Halls of Residence in a feeding frenzy. Race
was titillating enough but an added dimension of sex made UCRN irresistible. So

press photographers laid siege to the girl students, persuading one to be photographed in an imaginary bubble bath and another to strike a pose as a girl singer in a pretend African band that mainly consisted of wall-eyed black guitarists. The girl concerned, a Miss Gentili from Nyasaland, received an anonymous letter addressed to 'the University College for foreigners', telling her that 'you deserve a good spanking. What exactly is your game? The women of Rhodesia are ashamed of you.'

The university administration was also alarmed by all this. The Registrar told staff that they must 'keep some sort of soft drinks for Africans at parties' since 'by Rhodesian law Africans are not allowed to touch European liquor. It will be very bad if it gets out that Africans are being given European liquor here.' John Reed records in his diary that I responded to this by muttering, 'Well, I intend to give it to them.' But to begin with, the six African students were served no wine at high table. In March 1957 a meeting of Hall representatives decided 'that there should be a college dance; they would invite partners, but that no person of one race should dance with anyone of another'. The two African representatives 'took this pretty bitterly'.

And if this sort of discrimination was practised on campus, the African students of course ran into more blatant restrictions and disadvantages off it. UCRN was some way out of town but there was very little public transport and all of it was reserved for whites. City bye-laws provided that no African could be in the town centre after 9 p.m. without a special pass, so John Reed and I issued informal permits as Warden and sub-Warden. And even if an African student could get to town and remain there after 9 no hotel or restaurant or cinema would serve them.

In short, there could hardly have been a worse place to site the Federal University than Salisbury. Africans reacted in two different ways. Despite everything, some welcomed the prospect of university education with joy. The African Cultural Association gave a great reception in March 1957 which, as I told my parents, was 'tremendous fun'. 'There were lots of speeches intermixed with hot jazz from an admirable band and some astonishingly good singing – also of the hot variety – by four wine-tuxedoed Africans called the City Quads. A chief spoke with great dignity of his joy that his people were proved capable of European education. "We have two sorts of education in Southern Rhodesia," he said. "European education and native education. But what is native education? Before the Europeans came we had no education at all."' In May, John Reed learnt from one of the Nyasa students 'of the intense interest the Africans in Harare take in the university; how he was picked up by an African taxi driver as he was walking towards the university … The man knew his name, what he was studying, where he had studied before, and he had the particulars of all the African students in a notebook. "We are noticing you very closely," he said.'

On the other hand there were the handful of black students themselves. They had experienced enough of Rhodesian society not to believe in the sincerity of 'partnership'. But as John Reed noted in March, 'I am half ashamed to be so glad that these Africans who actually suffer have a very wry and humorous rather than the rhetorical sense of their wrongs that the African in England often shows. Style counts. It is almost as if they demonstrate the enormity of the injustice by the sophistication with which they can regard it.'

But one issue strained sophistication. There were three Halls of Residence – and four sexes. There was my own particular charge in that first year – Swinton Hall, the white women's residence. There was a Hall for European men – Manfred Hodson – and one for African men, Carr Saunders. But there was no Hall for black women. And yet there *was* a black woman – and one of the most remarkable students at that. She was Sarah Chavunduka, queenly, beautiful, cultivated – an example of a superior race if ever there was one. Many years later I heard Sarah accept nomination as Woman of the Year at a ceremony at the Harare International Book Fair. Her introducer had emphasized that she was the first African woman student, but Sarah said that she had certainly not wanted such a role. She would have been much happier if there had been ten other black women so that she could just be a student. Still, she said, she had to accept the invidious honour and come to terms with it in memory, just as she had to come to terms with it in life.

What was to be done in 1957 with Sarah? She began by living in our spare bedroom at the Swinton Warden's house, surrounded as all the other early buildings were by mud and building waste. But the Principal, Walter Adams, came to think this was unacceptable. It was certainly no long-term solution, much though Sarah and we enjoyed it. (And I think Adams may have been influenced by driving down to see me one day and finding Sarah pushing a perambulator around the house. Whose it was I never discovered.) Above all, Adams believed he could use Sarah's individual case to establish the general point of integration. As John Reed noted on 19 March, I told him that 'Adams reckons to have mixed hostels in a year. I am not sure that Adams' game is entirely fair. None of us know where we stand – and if in bringing mixed hostels about he disregards individuals, then the resentment of the Africans against the set up will overset the point gained. The idea of reducing segregation to an absurdity in order to do away with it is likely to be quite painful while it is going on. Ranger suggests that Adams was acting on this plan in insisting that Sarah went down to Carr Saunders. It was so patently absurd that she should go that the girls in Swinton would get together and agree to have her with them.' And this strategy *was* quite painful while it was going on, especially for Sarah.

For months she became the personal object of a struggle over principle. The girls in Swinton swung to and fro. There was first a majority vote – 16 out of 18 – that Sarah should be invited to join them – though even then only in her own separate corridor and with her own separate toilet facilities. So Sarah joyfully moved in. But then there was a visceral reaction. Parents expressed outrage. Girls came to weep in my study and told me they knew it was wrong but that they could not bear the thought of living in the same building as an African. By 20 July a counter-petition had been organized by the Hall reactionaries asking that Sarah be removed and that a promise be given that there would be no desegregation at UCRN for the next ten years. On 21 July the *Sunday Mail* carried the story. Sarah, reading the paper over breakfast in Hall, burst into tears. Feeling terrible, some girls began to change sides. Meanwhile the reactionaries overplayed their hands.

Inspirer of the reaction was a parent, a Mrs Gladys Parker, through whose daughter Anne the gutter press learnt of everything that was happening in Swinton. Mrs Parker made me a symbol of wicked integrationism. She attended every event at College and noted my misconduct. After a buffet lunch on 4 July in Carr Saunders Hall to celebrate the Queen Mother's visit she complained to Adams that 'it was full of ragged and smelly Africans … ragged and smelly rogues and houseboys', and how 'the Warden was talking only to Africans, men, the whole time'. Our confrontation reached an absurd climax in December when Sarah was invited to be bridesmaid at a European wedding in the Anglican Cathedral in Salisbury. I was of course there and vainly tried to prevent Mrs Parker and her photographer from taking intrusive pictures of this scandalous event. There was a moment of chaos when bride, groom and guests were popping in and out of every cathedral door and Mrs Parker and I were squaring off. 'Mrs Parker affects me in a curious way,' I admitted to my parents, 'as almost the palpable presence of evil – flabby, eccentric, dyed.' I was very rude to her and for her part she pursued me through the Cathedral 'hissing "Nigger Lover" in a penetrating tone'.

More serious as an attack was a motion presented to the Southern Rhodesian parliament by the leader of the opposition, Aitken-Cade, whose daughter was also a student in Swinton. Fat, florid and mediocre, he asked the House to deplore integration and all those who worked for it. These could be divided into fifth columnists and traitors. The traitors were Rhodesians prepared to surrender their birthright. The fifth columnists were 'people from England, where no race problems existed, who abused the hospitality given to them by attempting to subvert the Rhodesian way of life. Some of these fifth columnists, who were far from unintelligent, even highly intelligent, exercised in Salisbury an artificial influence over the immature minds of Rhodesian youth. They could, they already had, influenced with their guile, these youngsters that what they were doing was evil.'

Prime Minister Garfield Todd described this motion as the 'most irresponsible' ever put before the House and it was defeated by 18 votes to 2. Still, it was not bad going to have been defined as a major menace within six months of arriving in the country!

By the time of the December wedding, in fact, the cause of segregation had already been lost at UCRN. Sarah at last moved into Swinton Hall on 29 June. Soon thereafter the College Council agreed that rather than seek lodgings off campus the surplus of white students expected in 1958 could opt to live in Carr Saunders. All of them chose to do so. In 1958 I moved down to become Warden of this new mixed Hall and began to implement the time-honoured strategies for building up collegiate spirit. In 1959 all three Halls became multiracial. I was delighted, of course, when the Hall Chairman, the great footballer Cornelius Sanyanga, professed that he felt more solidarity with other members of Carr Saunders, no matter their race, than he did with African members of Hodson Hall. The battle for integration on the UCRN campus had been won. I allowed myself another year or two before taking the campaign against the colour-bar onto the streets of Salisbury itself.

## 'Politics'

None of this 1957 activity was in a strict sense political. But meanwhile politics was happening all around us. On 27 June I learnt my first lesson in the nature of the Rhodesian police. That day there was a strike by African waiters in the Halls. As John Reed notes,

> *They sit down outside drawn up in two rows. The students take gleefully to serving themselves. Professor Rasmussen, who can deal with any situation, is urging, in a tone that suggests that in the past he has tried it dozens of times in dealing with strikes and that it has always worked – that they will be dismissed immediately and then afterwards taken on at lower wages. On the advice of Harvey, the head gardener, the police have been called. Any domestic servant who refuses his duties is breaking the Masters and Servants Act and thus can be prosecuted. … The police arrived. One European with an African policeman as his interpreter. The technique seems to be as follows – to ask what the grievances were. Harvey is in the background pointing out to Terry that those who actually step*

> *forward with grievances are trouble-makers and can be sacked.*
> *When the policeman can get no volunteers he tells his translator*
> *to jeer at them – to tell them they are women, children, not men*
> *… Stung by this, some do come forward … The two complain-*
> *ants are given the sack immediately, and one or two others who*
> *are clearly, by their faces, agitators. Five in all are sacked.*

The first man to protest – at his mother being insulted – was Herbert, who had been with the cook, Mrs Kiley, for years. 'That's your man,' said the white policeman, kneeing Herbert in the groin and throwing him into the Land Rover. I was outraged; Shelagh even more so. 'Shelagh is scornful,' recorded John, 'and not inclined to forgive her husband for failing to assault the policeman with his bare fists.' When I rushed off to complain to Walter Adams, his response began the first crack in his image. Handsome, eloquent, distinguished, Adams had been a leader I was proud to serve, even though his handling of Sarah's case had disturbed me. But now he seemed all too much the Angus Wilson hero, with liberal feet of clay. His own version of radicalism was to favour honest and crudely spoken white workers – foremen in Rhodesia – and the gardener Harvey was a court favourite. 'Do you think they got the right man?' Adams asked me.

I went with Shelagh and John Reed to sit in the gallery of the Southern Rhodesian parliament. We were fascinated and appalled by what John described as 'this strange world of thought, so freakish and unpredictable that it is frightening. That way madness lies. A man will get up and attack the vaunted Western civilization. Did it not produce Hitler? Has it not produced the Atomic Bomb? This will lead him directly to a demand that the voting qualifications for Africans be raised higher. Or he will begin by outlining a theory that only by bestowing responsibility can you mould and expand character to be fit to bear it – and then argue from this that Africans must not be given responsibility.'

Soon after he arrived in Southern Rhodesia John Reed drove out of Salisbury to visit a ramshackle farm. He and his fellow white visitors were greeted with lavish hospitality and with genuine kindness, and then treated to an oration on how the only way to manage Africans was with the fist and the whip. In his diary he asks how one could respond to this contradiction:

> *I have been reading a lot of Marxism so as to work out how to*
> *act in Africa. Things are happening and must happen – so that I*
> *can momentarily forget my profound inability to act … Marxism*
> *provides some kind of framework for contemplating Rhodesia and*
> *especially as it provides a theory for moral neutralization. The*

> *settlers act as on the whole they are bound to act and it is no use*
> *appealing to their hearts or argue with them. The thing to do is to*
> *choose to fight with the Africans for the overthrow of white tyran-*
> *ny – not to spend an hour and a half each morning being angry.*

Neither then nor after did I read much Marxism. I was angry all day. But the problem was to find an African organization preparing to fight. In mid-1957 there was no militant or radical African organization. I looked about for anything that might serve and struck upon the Christian Action Group. In May 1957 Shelagh and I attended a meeting in what John Reed described as 'the non-Conformist atmosphere – a dirty little hall with stone and wooden benches – and terrible biblical pictures, debased pre-Raphaeliteism. Outside trains hoot and pass.' This was Henry Kachidza's Methodist church in Harare, now Mbare. Missionary paternalism suffocated the meeting, together with an awful timidity. The *African Daily News* editor, Nathan Shamuyarira, proposed a paper which 'began with putting the church in order' and went on 'to talk about putting pressure on the Government to pass a bill outlawing racial discrimination in public places'. John thought it 'a careless, shabby document', with the discussion 'demonstrating a complete lack of purpose', and withdraw into gloomy apathy remembering the Mission Sundays of his youth. I irritated the presiding missionary by repeatedly calling for more effective procedures. In the end I was elected to a committee to draw up a new constitution.

I was proud of this since it boiled down to a single clause – that at each meeting the executive should report back that it had carried out the tasks allocated to it at the meeting before. The old missionaries retired, grumbling, to be replaced by the radical Whitfield Foy. I was elected Secretary. The Group gave evidence to public commissions on urban policy. Even John Reed admitted by October that it had become 'a useful group now … a good collection of people – almost as many Africans as Europeans; and Europeans varied: a genuine working man, a printer, gets up to protest about the wages of the Africans with whom he works.' Later, my 'takeover' of the Christian Action Group was depicted in Harold Soref's *The Puppeteers* as typical communist infiltration, though no one was less communist than I was. The group was of course no substitute for an African party. But it *was* useful, particularly in its ability to act quickly and to provide immediate relief to political detainees and their families.

And in any case an African party soon appeared upon the scene. This happened in August 1957 when the Southern Rhodesia African National Congress was revived under Joshua Nkomo, James Robert Chikerema and George Nyandoro. I owed my introduction to these men to my old St Antony's fellow student, Carl Rosberg. Carl visited Southern Rhodesia in August and 'wanted to meet all the leading Africans', so 'I had a busy time contacting them and an interesting time listening to what they had to say. I feel much better informed', I told my parents, 'and have followed up a bit since Carl left. For instance I went to the first meeting of the new Congress, one of only five Europeans bold enough to attend.' I told my parents that 'I was on the whole impressed by their moderation', but this greatly understated matters. The Congress meeting was not much larger and hardly any more radical than a Christian Action gathering. It too was shrouded in timidity and did not give the impression of a group of men fighting for the overthrow of white tyranny.

But my attendance began my formal connection with nationalism. As John noted in his diary for 19 September, I told him that I had been meeting African leaders and had attended the inaugural meeting of the revived SRANC. '[Guy] Clutton-Brock, who seems in an indefinite but real way somewhere behind the Congress, has suggested that Terry should do work for it – pointing out that they need good propaganda which will have to be taken seriously by Europeans.' On the same day I received a letter from Guy:

> *Dear Ranger, it was good to see you at the meeting last Thursday. I hope as many people as possible will join the Congress. I propose to if, as I think, they have fully accepted the provisional policy. It is a risk, of course, but I think it worth taking in the present unyielding set-up. The new organization will need a lot of help in research and publication … After the meeting Josias Maluleke, who is organizing secretary of Mashonaland region of the TUC, which is of course a lot less than it sounds, asked me if I knew of anyone who would help a group of about 70 strong to study Trades Unionism and I wondered if there was a chance that you would be able to go, or Reed … They could probably get one of the class rooms in the Community Centre … I have given them some books and pamphlets on Trade Unionism in the past. But they clearly need someone to lead a simple study group based on a particular pamphlet or book.*

I went with John Reed to meet the Congress leaders in their little office, in a room behind a business agency. As John noted, 'they seem more patently delighted by Shelagh's offer to do typing for them', but 'their main concern at the moment is agricultural policy. They have deleted the original passage in the programme which merely called for the repeal of the Land Apportionment Act and are now in doubt. They invite Terry and myself to consider the matter. It is hard to conceive anything more remote from our meagre competence, but we agree to look into it.' In fact I proposed that John should undertake work with the trade unions and that I should do research on land. And that was how we were drawn into the nationalist movement.

Guy himself had strong views on agriculture. He urged that 'the repeal of the Land Apportionment Act would still leave the Reserves entrenched in the Constitution, allow Africans to buy land elsewhere and thus relieve the overcrowding in the Reserves'. Clutton-Brock says 'there is no shortage of land, and most European farmers realize they have too much to deal with and would sell, only there are no buyers. European farming should be controlled – and farmers farming badly or neglecting their land should be forced to relinquish it. Africans aided to buy land. Collective farms (under some other name of course) should be organized, for traditional African farming was largely collective. He claims that the African farms well – better than the European – that he produces food more economically.' So I undertook to explore these ideas and John wrote to Maluleke offering classes on trade unionism.

My initial paper on land was ready by mid-October 1957 and was 'received with enthusiasm'. I settled down to write a longer version. Meanwhile John undertook the more hands-on task of penetrating the townships. It was a revelation to him – 'I am amazed at the size of Harare,' he noted on 8 October, 'and the rows upon rows of these square, bleak rather sinister buildings. Through the windows there is in each room a density of things – the whole of the volume inside seems filled with clothes and bicycles hanging from the ceiling.' At his first meeting there were 20 or so men 'with expressive, intelligent faces'. These meetings were 'exciting and moving', and John accurately suspected that I envied him a little his 'lone and less frustrated expeditions into the African world proper'. After one meeting John noted: 'A wonderful day – I am quite tight and superbly happy.'

Soon the Congress and trades union leaders were penetrating our space, too. Late in October George Nyandoro, Moses Ayema and two branch secretaries came to dinner in Carr Saunders. 'The Congressmen are obviously very pleased to be able to get at the students and the students at Congress. Nyandoro is distributing *Chapupu* (the Congress journal), snatching a word with the waiters, and all of the others engaged in close conversation with a student or groups.' Mrs Parker's worst fears were being realized! John's impression of Nyandoro was as 'small, wiry, rather light-skinned'; he talked about

> ... *police raids and what he said to the detective, about his persecution, difficulty in getting jobs – laughing uncontrollably at every pause. A mad, Lucky Jim world, of phoning employers and recommending themselves as good natives in affected European*

> *voices – phoning stores, ordering brandies which they collected*
> *posing as their own cookboy… Nyandoro is a disturbing, gay,*
> *vigorous personality. A demagogue. But they need a demagogue.*
> *Intelligent, I think perhaps capable of vindictiveness. He speaks*
> *laughingly of the 'deviationists'. Sincere I think. Dumbutshena*
> *a quiet, wry man, one of the brains of the outfit … Ayema is*
> *the rough working man, not without humour, direct and naive*
> *in his hopes. He sees the revolution round the corner, the world*
> *turned upside down, the African trampling on the European.*

On 22 October John went again to Harare, this time entering a house 'with no ceiling, only the underside of the corrugated iron and bleak', where lives Mangwiro, 'the man in the bow tie'. John spoke on the history of trade unions in Britain to the blare of the township loudspeakers. The TUC leader, Reuben Jamela, in his ancient car, drove John back to UCRN. In view of what was to come, there was poignancy in Jamela's view – recorded by John – that 'the present leaders of Congress were sound and sincere and he expects they will remain in place for a good while. He is clearly willing to trust them himself.'

From then on John continued to give trade union classes and both of us attended with Shelagh all the Congress meetings, as these grew larger and more confident.

# History

While all this was going on I had little time to do any history. The Earl of Cork remained incomplete and I did not begin any African research project. But history was all around us in a rather odd way. There was white history, whose relics dated back no further than the late nineteenth century and were thus by my Oxford definition hardly history at all. These were celebrated in annual rituals like 'Occupation Day'. And there was legendary, monumental history – the Great Zimbabwe ruins, Khami, what were then called 'the slave pits' in Inyanga, and so on. These were very much on display as proof of a glorious past. But no one was quite sure how glorious or how past. It was official doctrine that none of them had been built by Africans, and the Southern Rhodesian government used to insert 'causeries' in the African press to prove that Great Zimbabwe had not been constructed by the Bantu. (I did not know it then, because I refused to read the *Bantu Mirror* as a paper for 'good boys', but its missionary editor was fending off demands from younger readers for some African history by telling them that they would have to make it first.) Whites gloried in archaic speculation; Africans simmered with the frustration of the history-less.

And yet a good deal of Federal money was being spent on history. There was a first-rate National Archives which among other things was employing Lewis Gann to write the history of the Rhodesias and so contribute to a sense of national identity. The leading archaeologist, Roger Summers of the Bulawayo Natural History Museum, was preparing for a major excavation at Great Zimbabwe in 1958. In many ways this was all too accessible to us. By mid-1957 John and I were helping excavate sites near Salisbury as training for the Great Zimbabwe dig, where it was thought we might lead a team of university students. During our first long vacation we visited Zimbabwe and the Inyanga pits and forts, for which I prepared myself by reading the innumerable fantastic legends and speculations published in that bible of the antiquarian tradition, the *Native Affairs Department Annual*. I went out into the countryside with Professor George Fortune as he collected praise poems to the High God, Mwali.

All this, of course, should have enlarged my notion of what history was. But I did not imagine that I could become an archaeologist or an oral historian. So what I was looking for was a major archival project. As early as 10 February 1957 I went with Professor Eric Stokes to visit the National Archives. 'It is really very well equipped though there is not much stuff prior to 1850,' I told my parents; 'it seems as if I shall have to learn Portuguese in order to do anything on the earlier period. The great collection is of Livingstone material and my Professor says that there is need for a definitive biography. Either project is alarmingly large-scale.'

I did not learn Portuguese and I did not begin work on Livingstone. What fascinated me instead was the question of how a real African history might be written. In September I spoke to some ten earnest inquirers in Harare – 'very third programme stuff on whether an African history was possible, in which I have become very interested'. In the context of Rhodesia this arcane material earned headlines in both the black and white press. 'Historian asserts that Zimbabwe was built by Bantu', they blared out.

This alerted the *African Daily News* which reported on 8 October that I was to write the history of the empire of Monomatapa. I wrote to my parents that 'as a result I have received a very Rider Haggardish letter from Bulawayo, all about a map of 1620 with a French story or legend on the back which my correspondent had half translated "with the aid of a French woman".' But I was no nearer knowing what I wanted to work on.

Meanwhile speeches at Congress meetings were drawing on a remembered history. One exhorted Africans not to eat oranges from the Mazoe Valley since they were sustained by the blood of Africans killed there during the 1896 and 1897 risings. But it did not occur to me at the time that this was a topic for historical research, and I did not question the speaker about his sources.

# Echoes of the Future

Still, the record for 1957 does contain echoes of my future historical work – oddly enough mainly of my most recent (2010) urban social history, *Bulawayo Burning*. In December, 'I went out to Harare with Simpson Mtambanengwe to see a boxing tourney organized for the College funds. It was a splendid occasion. Jazz bands playing between rounds; innumerable diversions as pick-pockets were chased around the streets; gaudy dressing-gowns, at al. Actually it was all very restrained, almost tame, with strict observance of the rules and fights stopped as soon as blood was drawn. The only frisson came when the heavyweight idol of Harare was knocked stone cold by his Joburg opponent and the crowd came swarming in from the cheap seats towards the ring, shouting "We want our money back!" in Shona.'

In December too John made his first day-time trip to Harare on a Sunday afternoon, 'from the deserted streets of Salisbury, to the crowds who might be at a fairground. Stretches of newspapers and coloured magazines laid out for sale – and inspection – and by the side, also laid on the ground, rows of second-hand jackets. The beer gardens full of people – people gathered around to talk, to mend broken down cars, people walking hand-in-hand, men in shirt-sleeves leaning on their elbows at the balconies of the men's hostels … To me it seems better to be like this than like Salisbury.'

At the end of our first year we knew almost nothing about the rural areas. But we had a keen sense of the vitality of African urban culture.

# CHAPTER THREE

# 1958

# The Southern Rhodesia African National Congress

By the end of 1957 the issue of segregation at UCRN had been more or less settled and we did not yet take it onto the streets of Salisbury. For us 1958 was a year of crisis in our relationship with Congress and a year of discovery of the rural areas. It was also for me a year of historiographical breakthrough in which the Earl of Cork was finished and I at last determined what African topic should succeed him. And there were, of course, constant reminders of the inequalities of Salisbury life. On the first of June, for example, John and Shelagh and I went down to Harare Hospital to visit Simpson Mtambanengwe who had had an operation. As John recorded, 'There are long queues of Africans outside the doors and we join one of these but some relatives of Simpson's who know us by sight greet us and somehow we get ushered forward and a way opens before us, and we go in before the rest. "It's just like being born rich," says Terry, hating it.' My welfare state values still prevailed.

## Politics

By this time, however, Shelagh, John and I had gone through a major crisis in our relations with Congress. While John was away in West Africa at the end of 1957, I had several meetings with Congress leaders: 'We ranged over nationalism and democracy. I tried to persuade them that they must do some serious thinking about minority safeguards and that democracy is about the rights of minorities.'

New Year's eve we spent in Highfield, driving around 'for hours looking for our rendezvous', as I wrote to John Reed, 'and finally guided there by a ridiculously intoxicated man on a bicycle. The sitting room of Paul Mushonga's house (he is the Vice-Treasurer of Congress) is fortunately quite large because he had knocked two houses into one. But it was very full. Mr Ayema was there; so was Chikerema, Dumbutshena, Nyandoro and Mushonga, plus wives. George Nyandoro's political vocabulary is becoming increasingly immoderate. Cyril Dunn [the *Observer* journalist] was there; Stanley Moore, the Quaker, was there en famille, so that the room seemed to be overflowing with white babies, a jolly Marxist couple from Joburg who were hitch-hiking around the world, another Quaker, George Loft and his wife – and as guest of honour, Lawrence Vambe, Nathan Shamuyarira's superior, who had just returned from America. It was a jovial scene – everyone, except I suppose the Quakers, drinking beer or spirits out of bottles. At a strategic moment Dumbutshena called the meeting to order. Vambe spoke about the United States and England – the usual rather touching stuff about how splendid the ordinary Englishman was at home and how he changed on crossing the seas; Dunn told us about Tom Mboya [Kenyan politician] and discussion became general.'

In mid-January 1958 I attended a course on nationalism and democracy at St Faith's Mission: 'the bishop of Mashonaland graced the whole proceedings with his presence, as did the local chief loaded with medals and paraphernalia'. Over lunch, Chief Makoni confided in me that he found such occasions difficult. 'I can serve you or I can kill you but to sit and have a meal with you ...' There were lectures on liberal democracy and totalitarian democracy; on European nationalism and nationalism in Africa. As I wrote to my parents, 'I expected a fairly rough passage because I was taking a line critical of the idea of nationalism as such, and warning them to avoid the excesses of European and Asian nationalism. The Congress leaders were there and I anticipated a lively debate. In fact I escaped very lightly and afterwards Robert Chikerema asked whether he could meet me in Salisbury to talk in more detail about how the nationalist movement could be controlled and employed constructively.'

In fact it was Chikerema who precipitated our crisis. John Reed, writing from Nigeria in late January 1958, thought that with the overthrow of Garfield Todd by his cabinet, 'all hope of a constitutionalist gradualist career for Congress is over. It might be worth Congress's while to start formulating policy on long term and revolutionary lines.' So it was with lively anticipation that on 2 March 1958 we all went to a Congress meeting in a Harare cinema with pictures of British film stars around the walls. It was packed, with all the doors blocked by eager crowds. Seeing us, George Nyandoro signaled for us to come up on the stage. Joshua Nkomo was chairing. As John wrote: 'They began by singing 'Ishe Komborera Africa' – strongly, superbly. Looking down on the packed heads – feeling the sound as it lifts up – is an experience of great richness.' Nkomo spoke at length in English, insisting that the revolt against Todd was an attempt to prevent African advancement. Then Chikerema made 'a strange and disturbing speech, in which he first told how before he went into politics Sir Patrick Fletcher was a tax collector and was charged with misappropriation of public funds'. Chikerema laid a solemn curse on Fletcher: 'May the curse of Judas Iscariot fall upon him and may he be tormented by all our ancestral spirits, grant this O Lord.' Afterwards Chikerema sought me out to tell me that if I were asked by anyone to give evidence, on what he had said I should do so. 'I really meant it and I can prove it.'

It was doubtful whether this attack on Fletcher amounted to long-term and revolutionary politics, though it certainly gained Chikerema prestige and popularity. Joshua Nkomo told me afterwards that neither he nor any of the other speakers knew Chikerema was going to make this charge against Fletcher. Nkomo was inclined to attribute it to Zezuru hot-headedness. 'One can never tell what they are going to say.' Even George Nyandoro was shocked! The regime was not going to lose a chance to exploit these divisions, nor to expose white sympathizers with Congress.

By this time Rhodesian Intelligence was regularly reporting our activities. When Garfield Todd came to high table on 19 March, before addressing a political seminar attended by more than the total number of students in the College, he gestured towards John and said to me, 'that fellow Reed. He was giving lectures to Trade Unionists. I thought I'd seen his name on the list. And you attended both the open meetings of Congress. But you needn't worry now. Though if that gang had got in there might have been trouble.' I noted that Todd spoke 'with the utmost contempt of Fletcher and the others, curtly, as "the gang"'.

Their power to harm, however, had certainly not been destroyed. They determined to prosecute Chikerema and to call all the whites who had attended the 2 March Congress meeting as witnesses to his words, starting with me. I said I would not testify unless subpoenaed to do so. The others said the same. On 12 May Shelagh and I, together with John, Eileen Haddon and Eleanor Glynn-Jones – who had attended the Congress meeting with her infinitely respectable Oxford supervisor, Margery Perham – were subpoenaed, and the press had a field day reporting that we had been questioned about subversive (even 'communist') activities without indicating what these were. Panic ensued. The mere fact that we had been at a Congress meeting – a legal meeting of a legal party – was enough to terrify our associates and employers. Eleanor was made by her headmistress at Chisipite school to swear that she would not indoctrinate the girls; UCRN appointed a lawyer to defend its and our interests; Todd's revived United Rhodesia Party, for which John and I had been canvassing, took steps to expel us.

Meanwhile we had continued to meet and talk with Chikerema and with Nyandoro, who was just back from Ghana. On 29 March I had them together with Ayema and Paul Mushonga as dinner guests. John noted that 'it is suddenly no longer possible to take these men seriously. After Nkomo, after the Congress meeting, it is obvious that these are not men of much significance. Ayema – a sound working class politician perhaps. But the others don't seem up to the level of the Trade Union people. Chikerema may be something; but if he is, he is something wholly ruthless and cynical … The talk after dinner rather wild and at times directly revolutionary. Chikerema says there will have to be bloodshed and, for a long time, any blood is bound to be African blood. They must know that, yet I am not quite sure they do.'

On 20 April we went to what the *Daily News* called 'a glamorous and colourful tea party' given by the trade unions in Bhika Brothers Hotel. Nyandoro was 'received tumultuously'. John sat next to Chikerema. 'He interests, fascinates me. Mushonga seems a weak man and George perhaps no more than a demagogue. But Robert Chikerema is the intellectual, the lean sardonic man. He is not the pedantic, learned African nor the cold puritanical African – but the passionate intellectual. Such men are dangerous. His character can be seen in the matter of the attack on Sir Patrick Fletcher, which now appears to me in a quite different, though still puzzling, light. He expects to – and almost certainly will – lose the case. And McDonald Stuart, the lawyer Shelagh works for, says he could be jailed for criminal libel and then broken financially by Fletcher, after that, in a civil case. I think he is looking for martyrdom – perhaps as a bid for the ultimate leadership of Congress. This is a very different kind of man from the comfortable, moderate Nkomo or the demagogic Nyandoro or the weak, harassed Mushonga.'

Then we prepared to be questioned. The first session was on 16 May. Shelagh vowed to adopt 'an obstructionist policy of bovine imbecility'; she would tell the magistrate more than he wanted to know about everything Chikerema had said – except what he had said about Fletcher. The rest of us reluctantly told all. But we were given a hard time. I was accused of conspiring with Eleanor so as to protect Chikerema and asked whether I preferred the company of Africans to Europeans. John recorded that I was 'truculent' in my replies. 'Shelagh was at the witness stand very demure and shy, was very gently used, and gave them absolutely nothing.' The next day Chikerema was arrested and given bail on condition that he did not attempt to meet any of us.

The scandal raged throughout May. Colonel Pardy, organising secretary of Todd's United Rhodesia Party, was phoned by the Federal Party office 'saying that Reed was a dangerous character; he was a member of Congress, had given talks on trade unionism to Congress, and had said that Southern Rhodesia really belonged to the Africans.' Pardy heard that Congress was controlled by six Europeans, of whom we were two, and that Walter Adams was about to dismiss us both. Pardy thereupon wrote to expel us from the URP. On its side Congress collected money for Chikerema's defence. Enoch Dumbutshena told us there had been 'a tremendous response to the Defence Fund and Africans are coming a long way to be present at the preliminary hearing on June 9th.' Leopold Takawira told Eleanor that Congress leaders were going about saying, and had said to him, 'these Europeans, look at them, they come to meetings and pretend to be on our side – and then they turn and give evidence against us.'

It was an embarrassing position to be in. The African crowd on 9 June was indeed very big. Shelagh told the prosecutor 'in great detail Nkomo's views on the Todd crisis and the iniquity of the Land Apportionment Act'. The court adjourned, the UCRN-appointed lawyer told Shelagh that she must 'remember' Chikerema's speech; back in court she was asked if she now recalled anything else and replied, 'Well, this lawyer says I have to say …' and was promptly dismissed by the judge. At the end of the day Chikerema was carried out shoulder-high; George Nyandoro harangued the crowd and they marched off singing 'Ishe Komberera'. Congress had come a long way in defiance from its first meeting in August 1957.

The final decision came on 10 July. Chikerema was fined £100 or 6 months; we were complimented as witnesses by the judge – intelligent and honest, with a proper bias towards Chikerema as our host. Chikerema was again carried off in triumph. Three days later Shelagh and I lunched with Eileen and Michael Haddon. Herbert Chitepo, who had defended Chikerema, was also there. Relaxed with wine he said that 'he had expected to be instructed to plead truth and justification and would have liked to do so'. But he thought that since 'the trial and verdict were political we might have stretched a point or at least been less pedantically honest'.

In the outcome we did not seem to be too damaged by all this. The URP and UCRN recovered from their panic. African leaders continued to consult us. My statement on land was published as Congress policy in the *Central African Examiner*. In August, John and I and Shelagh attended a conference on African trade unionism at St Faith's at which 'every vaguely disaffected element' made an appearance. For most whites, though, politics in 1958 was a matter of Todd's struggle with Whitehead. Both came to talk under my chairmanship at the political seminar at UCRN. On

13 August, Whitehead, who had annihilated Todd's URP in the election, spoke on urbanization. He came over, John noted, as

> *most unprepossessing, yet at the seminar he impresses. Grasp,*
> *and strong delivery – he speaks as a strong man. 'I intend' not*
> *'we' or 'the government', cutting right down on migrant labour,*
> *forcing the employers of cheap labour to mechanise. But practical,*
> *recognizing the reactionary nature of the Salisbury Council, the*
> *difficulty of getting them to budge on anything. He is determined*
> *to by-pass what cannot be shifted and have something to show*
> *after five years … Europeans must start learning to do without*
> *domestics – already only the less competent Africans are taking*
> *this up – and he has no intention of making the job more attrac-*
> *tive. As things are Europeans will soon find that the Africans*
> *who are willing to do a job like this are of such low quality that*
> *they might as well do without and start putting in labour saving*
> *devices. Simpson, very properly, gets up and challenges him on*
> *his election pronouncement that there would be job reservation for*
> *Europeans. His reply is interesting. He says of course this is not*
> *justifiable on any principled or moral grounds. But rather than see*
> *his whole scheme for African advancement threatened by a few*
> *hundred out of work Europeans, who will attribute their failure*
> *to African advancement and spread panic through the Europe-*
> *an community, he would rather 'hide them away in some job' to*
> *keep them quiet. What does it matter to African advancement if*
> *waiters on European railways are all Europeans – they can still*
> *become head waiters in the best hotels … He enjoys the evening.*

We watched with fascination as an increasingly radicalized Congress confronted this tough-talking Prime Minister.

## Penetrating the Countryside

But first Congress had to be sure that it had rural support. Among the Congress leadership in Salisbury there was intense debate. Where would radical action be more likely? And what was needed to organize it? Some people looked to urban strikes, and if workers wanted to strike only for higher wages rather than demand political claims then this meant breaking the autonomy of black trade unions and taking them over. Others believed that state authority could best be challenged in the Reserves, where there was widespread protest against destocking and the impo- sition of agrarian rules. This meant launching campaigns of impudent insult against

Native Commissioners and Chiefs.

During 1958, Congress made several efforts to introduce foreign journalists and sympathetic whites to the inequities of the Native Land Husbandry Act, which initiated a process of the survey and allocation of ploughing land and grazing rights, and enforced conservation rules. George Nyandoro hailed the Act as 'the best recruiter Congress ever had', and he tried hard to organize tours of the Reserves so that sympathizers could see people's hostile reactions to it.

One of these took place on 26 October 1958 when John and I, Eileen and Michael Haddon, Eleanor Glynn-Jones and the anthropologist Kingsley Garbett, were escorted by Nyandoro and by the government supporting Jasper Savanhu, into Seke Reserve. It was a Sunday, which was a bad day for serious inquiry. Indeed the whole expedition had that atmosphere of farce which sometimes accompanied Nyandoro's enterprises. It turned out that Land Husbandry had not yet been implemented in the area. And everyone was drunk. As John recorded, 'the next village we find in gay uproar, in the middle of a beer drinking party. Not a single person in the village is sober and some of the women are not able to stand. But we are made very welcome and everyone wants to shake hands with us and talk to us.' At Sadza village the headman turned out to have twelve acres, and an angry commoner complained that he had been given only three. Nyandoro 'harangued the booze-dazed Headman's son with his wickedness'. The interplay between Nyandoro and Savanhu was bewildering in its jovial brutality. 'Jasper, we shall have to lynch you one day,' said George, slapping him on the shoulder.

In the end perhaps the most important thing for us was our introduction to Shona prophetic myth. We passed the home of the great Chaminuka, 'who told the Shona that they must prepare by giving their daughters to the Matabele and thus making a firm peace with them, but his advice was not followed'. Another expedition to Chinamora on 8 November was more productive. The chief himself appeared. The Land Development Officers suggested we go to a 'good' village, with 'fertile looking soil and healthy crops'. We saw at first hand the Congress technique of systematic disrespect. 'George and Paul Mushonga nag and jeer at the officials all the time,' wrote John. 'I am impressed by the steadiness with which they take it all and their readiness to argue dispassionately against what are little more than taunts.' And we encountered another great form of Shona religiosity. The Congress leaders were annoyed to find that most of the farmers were Vapostori (Apostolics), 'a sect which turns them away from worldly things and makes them content with a very simple life – and hence less useful for Congress purposes'.

Neither of these expeditions did as much to convince us of rural unrest as Herbert Chitepo's regular reports of his court activity in the countryside, where he managed to defend herders and peasants successfully against breaches of agricultural rules. When we got back on 8 November I met Herbert at a party given by the Harare Cultural Club. He told me that he had succeeded with an appeal on behalf of Sipolilo tribesmen fined for refusing to produce grazing permits. 'This decision may make it virtually impossible for the authorities to continue administering the Land Husbandry Act.'

# History

For me the great event of 1958 was the completion and examination of my doctoral thesis. In February I told my parents that I had had 'a real blitz' on the thesis. Professor Stokes had given me a light teaching load. By June the writing was finished. By August it was nearly typed by the departmental secretary. By the end of October it was posted off to Oxford. It was examined on 30 November. It was a great relief to have finished it after so long and in the middle of so many Rhodesian preoccupations. Now I could at last turn to what I might do in African history.

My thesis was a considerable scholarly achievement. It drew on an enormous range of seventeenth-century sources. It discovered how, after three centuries, the Earl of Cork became the richest man in Britain. It established that his wealth did not derive from Protestant entrepreneurship – from iron mines and improved agriculture – as the Puritan myth had it. The production of iron, from ore imported into Ireland, using the extensive forests of Munster for fuel without any re-planting, was important as a means of moving capital around Europe rather than as laying the foundations of a sustainable industry. Cork was not a large-scale farmer or animal herder. He was a rentier. His wealth depended on gaining land from the crown and church and then over decades improving the terms on which he held it – from short leases to freehold grants. This was done by buying up parts of land grants made by the king to court favourites. Cork's name never appeared in these transactions and I had to trace them ploughland by ploughland, from grant to grant. Cork's was a classical colonial fortune dependent on the manipulation of surveys and land grants, and on membership of the minority but dominant religion and race.

The thesis impressed its examiners and I was given a congratulatory viva – 'Have a glass of sherry. Where are you going to publish?' But I was already very dissatisfied with it. It was relevant enough at one level to colonial African history – to the accumulation of Kenyan or Rhodesian agrarian fortunes. But the 'native population' hardly appeared at all in it, until they rose up in 1641 and the whole edifice of Cork's fortune was swept away. It did not explore Cork's ideology and sense of self justification. He had the most remarkable sons and daughters in Britain and he educated them expensively and effectively on the Protestant Grand Tour, in Holland and Switzerland and Venice. His children emerged as scientists, philosophers, playwrights, politicians and blue-stockings. Yet there was not a word about them in the thesis. It was the study of a man with all his humanity drained away. I learnt from this when I published *Are We Not Also Men?*, a study of the Samkange family, and paid adequate attention to religion, wives and families. Meanwhile I had a doctorate. Trevor-Roper had persuaded the Clarendon Press to publish it. I told my parents that I would revise it. And then nothing happened.

This was not because I had already begun African research, but because it was becoming increasingly necessary for me to do so. As I told my parents on 9 September 1958: 'I am frantically reading up African history at the moment – all very odd and hard to remember.' 'I am lecturing on early African history this term,' I told them on 28 September: 'very interesting but hard work since it is all more or less new to me'.

Earlier in the year I had undergone two experiences which had shown me what *not* to try to undertake as an African historian. The first was taking part in the excavations at Great Zimbabwe in May 1958, which I did while my thesis was being typed up. As I wrote to my parents, this was 'a welcome relief' from politics and the Chikerema panic. John Reed and I drove to Great Zimbabwe on 18 May, the same day that the *Sunday Mail* reported that Chikerema had been given bail provided he did not seek to see us. Had he done so during the next week it would have to had been at the bottom of a trench.

John reported our time at Zimbabwe:

> *Very early in the morning on 19 May African convicts in striped suits begin filling up a water wagon at our tap … At 8 am to the door of the Temple – which is duly opened by Summers and Whitty. Talk from Summers – then we climb to the Acropolis to view an exceedingly deep pit by a man named Robinson who has made his pottery sequence. Back at the Elliptical Building Terry and I begin a hole inside the 'sacred enclosure'. We lift a rough pavement put down about 1950 and then begin removing the humus down to what may be a dagga floor or may just be the surface of the pre-cultural soil. Our trench is against the walls, at a point where the two walls meet, and our operation is by uncovering the foundations to find which wall is earlier. Tea is laid on at Shepherd's Hotel, with the manager, immaculately dressed, dancing attendance. Then back to an afternoon of dirt removing.*

On 22 May we moved to Trench 5 'which is already 8 or 9 feet deep in places. Digging out quantities of muddy midden, rich in potsherds. Terry had discovered a six inch length of stick at the bottom which may be useful for carbon dating.'

We had brought with us one of the African students, Tranos Makombe, who had a trench and tent of his own and felt like a hermit. Tranos had got me to talk on the evening of 22 May in Mucheke township to the multicultural society. I said I would talk again about 'the writing of African history'. As John recorded, we arrived about 8.45 p.m. at a hall,

> *full of Africans sitting on rows of benches. A European with a*
> *round face and high pitched voice is conducting a discussion about*
> *a proposal that Africans when travelling through regions where*
> *there are no beer halls should be allowed to buy beer at European*
> *stores. … Terry gets up and comes over to me in the front row*
> *and says quietly 'I can't give my talk on History to this audience'*
> *(I think he is right. The talk is really an elaborate attack on the*
> *anthropologists). 'I think I will just talk about the University.' I*
> *would have felt quite embarrassed for him but I know how well*
> *Terry can manage in these corners. Terry talks about the time*
> *when there will be more Africans than Europeans. The chairman,*
> *an African, concludes by comparing Terry and myself to Jesus*
> *Christ, in order to teach poor mortals, coming down to their level.*
> *Terry full of self contempt all the drive back through the night.*

On 25 May we drove Makombe back into Bikita Reserve and John contrasted our romantic vision of the landscape to its realities: 'round about wooded hills and rocks of deep romantic loveliness … In the eye of romance it is a landscape for knights errant, anchorites and enchanters. It is the landscape of a poor people on a poor soil.'

Great Zimbabwe had been an escape. We learned a good deal about what archaeologists do. We had learned enough, perhaps, for me to teach about it. But we certainly hadn't learnt how to be archaeologists. *That* wasn't the way forward. In June another route was closed. The history department had drawn up a simple strategy to begin its assault on Zimbabwean history. We would each take our period. I had been a seventeenth-century man – I would take the seventeenth-century. Our new recruit, Richard Brown, had been an eighteenth-century man, working on the history of parliament. He would take the later modern period. Eric Stokes had been a nineteenth-century man, working on the Utilitarians in India. He would take the colonial period. And indeed Brown went on to work on the Ndebele state and Stokes on colonial Barotseland. The plan was publicized in the *African Daily News*.

That evening there was a knock on the door of my flat. There was a legless man in a wheelchair. It was the remarkable Donald Abraham, a linguist turned ethno-historian. Although he had lost the use of his legs from some degenerative disease, Abraham travelled through the Reserves collecting Shona oral traditions. He collected them from elders, from chiefs and especially from spirit mediums, who were believed to be possessed by the spirits of dead kings. In a state of trance these mediums spoke with the voice of the spirit, presenting extraordinary first person narratives of the remote past. Abraham wasted no time on either historiography or social niceties but bombarded me with questions about language. Did I speak Arabic, Portuguese or Shona? With each negative he visibly relaxed. I took him to dinner.

John recorded this visit from 'a learned though amateur historian…':

> … A Jew, slightly over-anxious to be pleasant and polite, with a
> vast learning on the subject of Shona history, an extraordinary
> memory, the marks of indiscipline upon everything he says outside
> his subject, and now and then a glint in his eyes. Over dinner he is
> boring and I think showing off on the metaphysics of African history
> and so on. Later, after dinner, talking about his own researches he
> is fascinating. Fluent Shona speaker. Reads Portuguese and has
> been working on the documents, also reads Arabic. He reckons to
> know within 10 miles where the original Zimbabwe is – for the
> Fort Victoria Zimbabwe is a replica double the size of the original,
> built by a megalomaniac of which he has collected traditions.

Even on his own research, then, there were 'the marks of indiscipline'. These later became more evident and in the end disabling. Abraham believed that the most ancient tradition, articulated by the medium who represented the founding chiefs, was 'correct'. He made no allowance for the social dynamics of tradition. But although from that first meeting I did not believe that he was the man who would write the history of Mutapa, it became increasingly clear that I was not going to be.

What I still needed was a great body of archival material – but one which illustrated African responses and initiatives rather than colonial policies. In the end it was Eleanor Glynn-Jones' mentor, Professor Perham, who determined my choice. After she had attended the March 1958 Congress meeting, Perham announced that African nationalism in Southern Rhodesia was a typically rootless, fly-by-night affair. It did not connect with a deep past or promise a long future. I had myself been very wary of unconstrained nationalist emotion. But as nationalist rallies grew in size and fervour, I began to wonder. Where had all this come from? What were the antecedents of African nationalism in Southern Rhodesia?

I knew there was some material about this in the National Archives. So when I was in Oxford for my doctoral viva I sounded people out about a possible research project on African politics. The response was enthusiastic – though I don't think Hugh Trevor-Roper or John Prestwich endorsed it. Most enthusiastic was George Shepperson in Edinburgh, who adjured me to realise that I was living through a moment of history. I must keep notes on all the meetings I attended, he said, and record what I could of their background and consequences. By the time I returned to Southern Rhodesia, I had 'an African politics project'. I wrote to John about it on 20 January 1959:

> *I shall return, I warn you, full of enthusiasm and energy. I shall at once embark on some great research project. I see Abraham has Monomatapa buttoned up. I am toying with the idea of doing African politics in Southern Rhodesia as a research subject (historical not sociological) and thought I might write to Doris Lessing asking her whether she could give me any useful lines ... What do you think of such a project? Abraham has scooped Monomatapa and it seemed a good idea to me to combine my general and academic interests. Besides it would mean meeting a lot of jolly old Africans and travelling about a bit. Also since there have not been very many African political movements in Southern Rhodesia the subject is do-able (I think) in a couple of years. Journalism, I know, and no doubt suspect to all parties ... I am in a position to get some information from Africans. I think, for instance, that Nkomo might co-operate within the obvious limits and that he will appreciate that the study would be sympathetic. At any rate in the sense of taking African politics as a serious subject. But I do not suppose that I could get access to the Security files!*

John replied enthusiastically: 'I think the scheme to work on African political movements is excellent. You can become a sort of G.D.H. Cole of Central Africa. As you say, good fun too. It could become a history of the people of this country rather than its rulers.' And Eric Stokes wrote to say that my way was clear:

> *Abraham is in London. We booked him to a research grant from Anglo American to go into the Portuguese records in London and Lisbon. His latest article in Nada on the Monomatapa dynasty is quite sensational if true. He claims there is a live oral tradition reaching back to 1420 and verifiable by Portuguese sources. So you can make a graceful bow of exit in the matter.*

# CHAPTER FOUR

# 1959

# The Central African Emergencies

In 1959 I had been in Southern Rhodesia for two years. Quite a lot had been achieved. I had finished my doctorate and found an African research project. At UCRN there had been progress with integration. It looked as though my life was set fair. In 1958 I had moved from the women's residence at Swinton Hall and joined John Reed in Carr Saunders which was to become the first male integrated residence. I carefully selected European students to join the Africans. The Hall was a great success. In September 1958 I had written to my parents:

> *Carr Saunders is going so well that I feel reluctant to leave it*
> *to someone else. This is especially so at the moment since both*
> *the other Halls are in violent revolt with petitions and protests.*
> *Carr Saunders is completely immune. A full Hall meeting sum-*
> *moned by the Hall Committee have voted unanimously that they*
> *have full confidence in the Warden and sub-Warden and wish*
> *for no change. I find this very touching and very pleasing that*
> *the Cinderella of the halls should be so much happier than the*
> *others. The students are very proud now of being in Carr Saun-*
> *ders instead of being in Hodson which has no Common Room, no*
> *corporate spirit, no morale, but plenty of noise and disaffection.*
> *To achieve this in a multi-racial hall is doubly valuable since it*
> *gives the Africans no chance for feelings of discrimination and since*
> *it makes Europeans think of Carr Saunders not as the 'mixed hall'*
> *but as an enviably contented society. I have applications from*

> *present Hodson occupants to be allowed to come into Carr Saun-*
> *ders next year and race has not affected the decision either way.*

This situation continued through 1959 despite all the other storms of that year. Sir Alexander Carr Saunders himself was an active patron and allowed us to use his coat of arms – three white elephants – for a hall tie. On 23 September 1959 John recorded:

> *Tonight is Carr Saunders guest night though Carr Saunders is*
> *unwell and there is an empty chair next to Terry. The compa-*
> *ny are all the present members of the hall, with those former*
> *members who have been able to come. All those still at College*
> *but now at Hodson come down. There are of course no ladies*
> *at all. There is one large table running round three sides of a*
> *square Before the dinner, sherry in the Common Room. Then*
> *with dinner, wine. And afterwards port. Terry makes an ex-*
> *cellent speech and we toast absent founder and present friends.*
> *The students seem very pleased and interested and afterwards*
> *a group of about seven come upstairs to the lounge with Terry*
> *and myself – talk mostly about politics but very intelligently.*

John noted in September 1959 after dining with Shelagh and I, Richard and Lyn Brown, and the translator Clive Wake, that 'this is a pleasant comfortable society, as good perhaps as any I have known.'

I am very glad to find among my papers a letter of February 1960 from Tony Hawkins, still today serving the University of Zimbabwe. 'The atmosphere in the History Department and also in Carr Saunders was always very friendly. I hope that in the coming years you will be able to maintain this distinctive atmosphere in Carr Saunders because I feel that in this way some traditions can be built up.'

My academic life seemed as promising as my social. At the beginning of 1959 I turned to my new research project on African politics. I wrote to my parents in February that I had 'sounded various Africans about my research project, so far with encouraging success. I may get access to an imposing collection of papers belonging to one of the first African leaders with a bit of luck.' Meanwhile Trevor-Roper was canvassing publishers to take my doctoral thesis. In April 1959 he wrote to say that Clarendon Press would take it and I allowed myself to dream of rapid publication in two fields. 'If I can get something out on African politics fairly rapidly and get it accepted by a good commercial publisher, I may get two books in one year which would be a good demonstration of versatility.' By June I had signed the Clarendon contract and told my parents, 'I am waiting until the long vacation to really begin with the African politics stuff.' In November I hoped 'to complete revision of my thesis by Christmas; my article on the Strafford book after that and then get down to some African research'. John expressed envy in his diary: 'Terry without ever seeming to exert himself at all in history keeps the material turning out.' In August he noted that I was organising a panel at the History Teachers' Conference on 'The Value of the African Past'. Solomon Mutsvairo, who took part, came to tea and told us 'about Chaminuka and his prophecies and spirits and visitations'.

Despite John's envy, however, I did not produce much. The doctoral thesis was never revised and it was a long time before I began to publish on African politics. I found the thesis narrow. As for African politics, I did not see the 'imposing collection of papers' until forty years later, when I was able to work on Thompson Samkange's manuscripts in the Samkange castle. The result of that was *Are We Not Also Men?* In 1959, though, I was a long way from being able to pull the African political material together.

But I *was* very busy with contemporary politics. In February 1959 the clash between an increasingly assertive nationalism and an increasingly aggressive Prime Minister exploded. After the Emergency of February I found myself enormously busier.

# The Emergency of February 1959

Federation was threatened with break-up, particularly because of violent discontent in Nyasaland. The Colonial Office did not possess enough soldiers and police to control the situation and would have to rely on men from Southern Rhodesia. In early February 1959 I wrote to my parents: 'Things are getting tense as troops are flown to Nyasaland and threatening noises made. The situation is rather panicky – there was a tremendous run on guns and ammunition on the strength of a rumour (totally untrue) that there was to be an African general strike.' On 26 February I wrote to them again: 'Our troops are out and we are in state of emergency: all the African leaders have been arrested and charged with a "plot". There is no violence here or any sign of it. The government's action is a complete bluff and an irresponsible one at that. There is not even a state of emergency [yet] in Nyasaland! I am so furious and ashamed that I can hardly write about the situation here.'

In early March I explained to them at unusual length 'my own attitude to the crisis':

> *The emergency in Southern Rhodesia is a nonsense. We have no*
> *violence or even an effective strike. The Congress here could not*
> *have launched any dangerous riots or 'rebellions' partly because*
> *many of its members are non-violent and respectable men, partly*

> *because the government has so firm a control on the instruments*
> *of discipline, partly because in any case even the extremist leaders*
> *realize that there is no immediate future in Southern Rhodesia*
> *for a violent resistance movement … The government have given*
> *a variety of reasons for the emergency but none of them seem to*
> *me to justify it, still less to justify the new laws which are being*
> *introduced. These new laws are immensely severe. One bans all*
> *African National Congresses, including the Northern Rhodesian*
> *one which is not banned in Northern Rhodesia … and including*
> *the South African one which is not even banned in South Afri-*
> *ca. It gives the police power without warrant to search premises*
> *for evidence that a person is a member of any of these banned*
> *organizations and to make arrests on suspicion. It indemnifies*
> *all public servants from any suit in a court of law … Another*
> *provides for the detention of persons. This enables the Governor,*
> *on the advice of the Minister, to make a detention order against*
> *any person with no cause shown. The detainee can then be put*
> *in a prison camp and kept there for five years without trial.*

There was a good deal of protest against these laws but none at all against the emergency itself. Indeed, as I told my parents, 'the only public protest against the declaration of the emergency came in a letter from your intrepid son to the *Central African Examiner* which it was almost impossible to get that timid journal to publish'. And that was putting it mildly. The *Examiner,* supposedly a 'liberal' paper, sent my letter to the censor and to Sir Edgar Whitehead himself so that he might immediately reply. And even then the *Examiner's* editor, Cole, heavily cut and edited my letter. I refused to have it appear in that version. The *Examiner's* own reaction to the emergency was to compare Whitehead to Abraham Lincoln, a noble patriot fighting against secessionist extremists. (They did not mention slavery).

As John Reed and I listened to Whitehead's speech on the radio at 8 a.m. on 26 February in my flat at Carr Saunders Hall, Abraham Lincoln did not come to mind. Most of the speech, as John wrote in his diary, 'is a fulsome congratulation of the police swoop. A positive writhing in delight at its sheer virtuosity; its extent, the long patient planning, the secrecy, the smooth success. 88% of the listed people were under arrest within 12 hours of the police descent.' On 1 March he wrote again after the revelation that Sir Roy Welensky, the Federal Prime Minister, had joined Whitehead in the police operations room in the small hours of 26 February closely following every detail of the arrests. 'It is this loathsome gloating over the police action which fills me with more repugnance than the action itself … They boast over what is shameful.'

And yet we learned that the arrests had not been so efficient after all. Non-members of Congress – and some office bearers in multiracial parties – were arrested while significant Congress figures escaped. Police were led into the Salisbury townships by prominent African supporters of Whitehead who pointed out their personal enemies for arrest. Our friend, the heroically-bearded Daniel Madzimbamuto, escaped arrest by 'being out at some shebeen. When he returned home quite drunk he was told that the police had raided – and he went off to the *African Daily News* office to find out what was going on. Someone in the office reported him to the police who came and arrested him there.' Guy Clutton-Brock had left St Faith's co-operative and active participation in Congress to go to work in Botswana. He and Molly had just returned and were holidaying in the Maleme Rest Camp in the Matopos when he was arrested.

John and I knew Guy well, of course. John had been working with African trade unionists in the townships, many of whom were detained. I had been giving classes in the townships. We had both attended Congress meetings. We had many friends among the detainees and knew that they were not the thugs and criminals being portrayed in the press, We knew the men who had been arrested at St Faith's and some of the African Advisory Board members who had been arrested in Bulawayo. We were not surprised when the very conservative priest in charge at St Faith's, Father Lewis, said that the detainees from there were 'good Christians', or when the Native Administration Department of Bulawayo Municipality described the detainees there as responsible and co-operative men. A sense of astonishment, shock and shame filled the townships. No lists of those arrested were published for weeks. Families were left to fend for themselves before welfare systems were set up.

## Legal Aid and Welfare

A few days after the Emergency I wrote to my parents: 'Shelagh has had a great deal of work in sitting with Molly Clutton-Brock [who was staying with Eileen and Michael Haddon], driving her to [Highlands] prison to see her husband. Shelagh has also organized car trips to Bulawayo to take the wives of detainees imprisoned there to see their husbands. She has found out where the families are and bullied the relevant authorities. And I have been asked by the Africa Bureau to administer a welfare fund set up in England'. From then on Shelagh's reputation grew. 'I am widely known among Africans as Mr Shelagh Ranger,' I told my parents in April.

In responding to the Africa Bureau I followed my customary tactic and made use of the Salisbury Christian Action Group to begin relief, but as usual it was my intention to create a specialized committee. This led to some confusion. On 11 May, the Bureau's Jane Symonds wrote to say that since 'the liberals of SR have been rising to the occasion so well we do not want to create some additional committee'. To this I replied on 27 May:

> With typical perversity we have waited until you have decided not to form a Committee to form one ourselves. The reason for this is that Herbert [Chitepo] has had offers of funds from Justice and Christian Action and feels most strongly that all funds should be co-ordinated here. So Guy [Clutton-Brock] and Michael Haddon and I have banded together to form a Salisbury Committee. In addition there will be a local appeal here made by us in co-oper-ation with Stanlake Samkange and other African members of a committee he has established. In addition to these committees yet another is rumoured in Bulawayo which I am going to investigate in two days time so as to establish amicable relations between this mushroom crop of committees. Herbert has just been briefed by a firm of Bulawayo solicitors to interview all the remain-ing 110 detainees on behalf of this mysterious committee. The first hearings are scheduled for 2 weeks time and there is much preparation to do. The procedure is that the Government send a summary of their case against each detainee who then has 7 days in which to say whether he is to be legally represented or not.

The Southern Rhodesia Legal Aid and Welfare Fund Committee subsequently met every week in the Methodist church in Mbare. I later summarized its development. I described how the original two Salisbury committees – one consisting of Guy, Michael and myself, the other consisting of Stanlake, Nathan Shamuyarira and other elite Afri-cans – had agreed to amalgamate. In response to the joint committee's appeal £1,567 was contributed locally and £2,041 from overseas. The committee struggled to retain control of legal aid and welfare. On 11 July 1959 I wrote to Jane Symonds:

> This is for your private ear and not to be flaunted at Christian Action, though they deserve it to be flaunted. They have sent out an English barrister – one Dold. They did so against the advice of Justice but apparently at the insistence of Collins and Joshua Nkomo. Now Dold is in any case an egoistic old dodderer and likely to put up all backs. Also he is being paid for this trip some-thing like all our legal expenses put together. But worse than that – he did not know before he arrived that the Tribunal had

*already started: that there was a defence team already at work;*
*that all possibilities of appeal had been canvassed and that we had*
*developed a rudimentary welfare system. Now he has discovered*
*these things he finds himself in rather a ludicrous and ridiculous*
*position. I hope he will see sense and go home to recommend*
*that Christian Action send out funds to those already occupied.*

*[Meanwhile] things are going well here. Guy and I and others of*
*our friends were called before the Tribunal as witnesses and could*
*see that it was reasonably run and the defence had the initiative.*
*We think we shall get enough money to pay for the defence of all*
*the detainees and hope to have enough to really launch into welfare.*

John noted my appearance before the Tribunal. He noted on 27 June that 'Herbert Chitepo has called Terry as an expert witness on African political movements, presumably as somebody personally acquainted with the accused to give evidence on the general political atmosphere in which Congress sprang up. Eleanor is also going and George Loft.' He noted on 4 July that I was back from Bulawayo:

*The government has led secret evidence of a general nature on*
*the aims and tendencies of Congress. The Defence has brought*
*witnesses to demonstrate that Congress was not bent on over-*
*throwing the government or a threat to the security of the country.*
*Todd has given evidence and Clutton-Brock, both apparently to the*
*great satisfaction of the defence. Terry is supposed to be a student*
*of African politics and qualified to give an assessment of Congress*
*in comparison with other African movements on the continent. It*
*seems at least possible that the Tribunal will rule that Congress*
*was not in itself a dangerously revolutionary organization. In*
*which case according to remarks made by Beadle before Terry*
*gave his evidence, it will release those detainees against whom*
*there are no charges except that they were members of Congress.*

In September 1959 the Committee issued another appeal. By then all the detainees had appeared before the Tribunal. A committee had been set up in Bulawayo to visit Khami prison and to help with transport for wives and families. When many detainees were moved to Marandellas prison another local committee was formed. The main committee decided to employ a full-time Welfare Officer and in October 1959 appointed Gervase Muchada, of the Christian Action Group, to 'penetrate into the most remote villages to see the families and dependents of the detainees'. Muchada was equipped with a motorcycle, provided with accommodation and paid

£20 a month. He 'soon made himself indispensable to the Committee'. Thanks to him we discovered the needs of the families. 'In many cases it was found that the allowances were not being paid or that dependents were not getting the correct amount.' The Committee wrote letters, made enquiries and sent delegations to government departments. Help was asked for ploughing, the repair and rebuilding of houses, and the provision of clothing and blankets for children and aged parents.

Welfare work had initially been undertaken by Victoria Chitepo. Now most of the work was handed over to Muchada and to Shelagh Ranger. Eileen Haddon joined the Committee to help Michael with the finances. From then on Shelagh was absorbed in welfare work. Native Commissioner's files are full of her letters and the angry responses of the officials. 'Do I have to pay attention to this dreadful woman?' expostulated the Native Commissioner, Sipolilo. But he had and he did. The detailed file on the work of the Committee in the Ranger Papers in Rhodes House is full of case studies of people helped by the Committee. Many involve the problem of hire purchase payments and of foreclosure on furniture and other goods as detainees were unable to pay instalments. Almost all involved the need for school fees, uniforms, etc. The detainees were certainly an upwardly mobile group.

In late July 1959 John went with Jimmy Skinner and Jaap van Velsen to visit Gwelo and Khami prisons. His account gives a vivid impression of prison visiting. John delivered the wives and children he was taking, to 'a gentle, tattered African Salvation Army officer who tells me he has been expecting only one African woman. So many people have come to stay with him he doesn't know how he can manage. I behave apologetically but firmly. Quite clearly, however inconvenient it is, he will have to put up these two ladies and the baby.'

He and Jaap went on to visit a girl Jaap knew in Oxford, now married to a rich Bulawayo businessman. 'She has a huge home, sitting on a sofa, with a bird cage on a green stand beside her and a lapdog in her lap. Jaap is still savage, unkempt, poverty-stricken.' Their hosts could not believe they were ferrying African women, who were taking the detention of their husbands stoically. 'They don't really feel these things,' said their host. 'I don't want to compare with animals but it's rather like a bitch – you know, take away her puppy – and she gets over it. Give her another one – she is just as happy.' This horrified John 'more than anything I have ever had said to me since I came to Rhodesia'.

Next day they went to Khami. John asked to see Maluleke and Mhiza. 'That will be difficult. They are in solitary confinement … These people have been up to mischief.' Rebuffed by the prison director John paced up and down between the inner and the outer gates, 'and dedicated myself to an ever-lasting struggle against this regime. A burning determination that in the end human dignity will be vindicated.' On 13 August the report of the Beadle Commission was published. John wrote that 'the report justifies the government declaration of an emergency and upholds its contentions that Congress had definitely turned to a policy of violence. We would, I suppose, have expected this but for Terry's sanguine reports when he returned from testifying before the Tribunal in Bulawayo … The findings of the Devlin Report raised our hopes, as if the boldness of Devlin in criticizing government action might embolden Beadle. The very contrary. Part of the purpose of the report … is to discredit Devlin.' I responded with a savage assault on Beadle in *Dissent*, a journal John and I founded in March 1959. On 17 August John noted my outline of what I intended to say. 'Even before a word is on paper the mastery is there. Terry's grasp still amazes me. He misses nothing. He forgets nothing.'

So the Committee settled in for the long haul. As *Dissent* disclosed after the Beadle Report, the commandant at Khami made it clear that he would not hold political detainees any more and that Khami would revert to its role as a prison. 'Hard-core' Congress detainees were sent to Selukwe; the rest, including the Nyasas still detained in Southern Rhodesia, were sent to Marandellas open prison under the relatively benevolent eye of Mr Patch. Steps were taken to send the leaders to a restriction in remote Gokwe where they were supposed to rehabilitate themselves with honest toil. My visiting routine changed to trips to Selukwe and Marandellas, while I tried to establish the facts of Gokwe.

It was in Marandellas that I first met David Rubadire, much later Vice Chancellor of the University of Malawi. One day, returning from a visit to the Marandellas detainees, my car shuddered and juddered. I pulled into a garage, where the Rhodesian mechanic made a quick examination and diagnosed 'fuel trouble'. 'What does that mean?' I asked in my ignorance. 'It means someone does not like you very much,' he replied. Some still unknown reactionary student at UCRN had poured sugar into my petrol tank. The engine was cleaned at considerable expense and I continue to drive to Marandellas.

Despite this, and despite my sense of pressure over Dissent, the year ended with festive celebrations. On December 15 1959 I wrote to my brother:

> *On Christmas Eve we are giving a house-warming cum Christmas party in the house at Carr Saunders [which] will also be a party for the Dissent Production team. On Christmas Day we go to the Haddons for a morning party. They have a very nice shaded garden with a swimming pool and Christmas Day here is bound to be very hot. They usually lay on splendid drink and general bonhomie …*

> *[Christmas lunch we spend with Whit Foy] On Boxing Day we go*
> *out to Marandellas prison for a great party for the detainees with a*
> *choir to sing carols and a jazz quartet and plenty of food and drink.*

# Dissent

On March 22 1959 John Reed and I had decided to establish a journal to allow a view critical of the emergency to find expression. We recruited the fiery Methodist minister of Third Street Church, Whitfield Foy, who I knew well through the Salisbury Christian Action Group. Partly because of Whit, the broadsheet came to be called *Dissent*. Whit contributed some cogent articles and gave us moral authority. He was risking more than John or me. When we were threatened with libel and I wanted to refuse an apology, Whit made it clear that as a Methodist minister he could not be involved in a libel case. He involved some of his loyal flock in the production of the broadsheet and eventually was dislodged by the Methodist establishment, though against strong African opposition, and had to leave Rhodesia.

Producing *Dissent* was very hard work. As I told my parents in October:

> Dissent *is really an astonishing operation – the writing,*
> *typing, rolling off on a hand duplicating machine, sort-*
> *ing, stapling, rolling up and addressing a thousand cop-*
> *ies as well as the editorial conferences and accounts.*

Shelagh typed the stencils and usually ran them off. The first page of Per Wästberg's Swedish account of his Rhodesian time begins in translation: 'Shelagh Ranger came into the dining room with ink on her fingers.' John regularly reported her work. 'Shelagh is rattling away in the English Secretary's office on the Dissent stencils,' he noted on 23 June. I conducted the correspondence and wrote most of the articles. John was envious of my newly discovered journalistic facility. On 31 July he recorded 'another day of misery during which Terry writes two more articles in the odd moment he is at home. I toil and grow so nauseated with what I am doing that I have to stop.' On 30 July he noted that I had written 'another excellent piece of journalism ... How well he does this – I can't write Terry's sort of journalism.' John's diary also records the volunteers who came to help staple and package *Dissent*, often members of the NDP or young Asian radicals among whom Hasu Patel was prominent. We sent out some thousand copies – to every Rhodesian and Federal MP, to every British MP – and were sent money by well-wishers. As I go through the *Dissent* correspondence file among the Ranger Papers I am struck by the number of African school teachers and schoolboys who subscribed. Ruth First wrote from South Africa to say that *Dissent* seemed to her to be the most perceptive account available of the Southern Rhodesian situation, a judgement she may have regretted when she later found *Revolt in Southern Rhodesia* to be 'mere vulgar populism'.

*Dissent* was naturally preoccupied at first with the Southern Rhodesian emergency. Its first issue of 26 March 1959 led with a story, 'The Truth About Guy Clutton-Brock'. I remember that as we packed the issues into the boot of my car outside Third Street Methodist Church a very respectably dressed young man came sauntering by. He peered into the car, and became transformed into gibbering fury when he saw the headline, hammering angrily on the windscreen. No doubt subsequent issues provoked the same response. That first issue also contained a critique of the charges against Congress. The second, on 9 April, contained an analysis of the type of intelligence on which the police had been working. A long article I wrote in the third issue was entitled 'The Forgotten Men' and described the fate of the detainees: 495 had been arrested: 492 African men, 2 African women and Guy Clutton-Brock. 307 were members of the Southern Rhodesia African National Congress; 105 of the Nyasaland African National Congress; 83 of the Northern Rhodesia National Congress. 177 men were in Kentucky Prison outside Salisbury, and 315 in Khami Prison outside Bulawayo. The two women – Mrs Mushonga and Mrs Kation – and Guy Clutton-Brock were in Highlands prison. Many of those detained were bewildered, knowing where they were but not why. The fourth issue of *Dissent*, on 7 May, described the 'repatriation' of Nyasa and Northern Rhodesian detainees, some of whom had never lived in those countries.

## *Dissent* in Nyasaland

Up to this point *Dissent* had not said much about Nyasaland. We were aware, of course, that although Whitehead had never mentioned Nyasaland in any of his statements – except to say smugly that he hoped the other two members of the Federation would follow Southern Rhodesia's good example – nevertheless the need to send Rhodesian troops, police and aircraft to Nyasaland underlay the declaration of an emergency. But as news of violence in Nyasaland continued, John and I decided that we must go there to see for ourselves.

We knew well the few Nyasa students who had come to take their post-graduate certificates in education at UCRN. In particular we knew the sardonic George (Gomo) Micongwe, who was now teaching at Domasi. On 22 April I had a letter from Micongwe, which had taken six weeks to reach me from Nyasaland. He told me that he had not been arrested but that his brother and uncle had been. He invited us to come up next vacation, adding 'it is perfectly safe and always has been'.

*Terence Ranger and a student at a*
*UCRN garden party, 1957.*

So in May 1959 Shelagh and I and Eleanor Glynn-Jones drove the long way through Portuguese East Africa to Nyasaland. The drive was quite an adventure in itself and at one point we found ourselves crossing a new bridge only to discover ourselves in the middle of a ceremony conducted on the bridge by the Governor. We passed on the road a car being driven south by Peter Mackay, with his two bull mastiffs beside him – our first glimpse of a man who was to play an important part in our lives. Peter had been caretaking the Mlanje Mountain Hotel, which belonged to his friends, Jimmy and Joy Skinner and where we were booked to stay.

The hotel was on the lower slopes of the majestic Mlanje mountain, with the Likabula river rushing past it and forming pools and waterfalls. It had lovely gardens and the house itself was full of books. All this more than made up for the rather casual catering. I wrote to my parents that it was 'the most lovely place you can imagine … in every way the most satisfactory holiday place we have struck'. Shelagh and Eleanor swam naked in the Likabula pool, watched from the bushes by the Nyasaland CID. I walked up the steep path to the plateau, toiling up as men rushed down it with great planks on their head. In the hotel were staying the Scottish lay missionaries, Albert and Jenny McAdam, Albert the embodiment of frantic energy and Jenny of serene calm. Both had been much involved in the Nyasaland emergency. Albert was Dr Banda's executor and in possession of the sacred Homburg hat. Their house had been searched and Jenny had sat demurely on top of the confidential documents. Albert had written to *The Manchester Guardian* to denounce the emergency and had made himself bitterly unpopular with Nyasaland whites. Intelligence officers drifted casually close to our intense political discussion with them. I handed out copies of *Dissent*. An odd German who frequented the bar announced that 'the more people I know, the more dogs I like'. Jimmy Skinner was debonair; Joy beautiful. There was much discussion of Laurens van der Post, whose *Venture to the Interior* had grossly over-dramatized Mlanje and its foresters. But even in reality the hotel was a magical place, away from the day-to-day grind.

Richard Brown, my colleague in History, and John arrived by car on 14 May. As I told my parents, 'Shelagh has taken a half time job with a Salisbury bookshop so she will have to return after a week but I am staying another week and going to visit an old pupil of mine – an African school teacher and his wife – where I hope to learn what really happened here during the emergency.' I added: 'Dissent has brought me notoriety and I do not relish being type-cast as an extreme liberal any more than as anything else.' But off I went with my extreme liberal reputation and with Richard and John and we drove from Mlanje to stay with the Micongwes. They gave us a tremendous welcome.

On Sunday 17 May we went into Zomba to meet a young white government botanist who had been called in to help the police sort through confiscated Congress documents. He expressed surprise that we were staying with the Micongwes – 'an able man but very unpolished'. He was convinced of the existence of a massacre plot. But he was more interested in private correspondence which he thought illuminated the character of Congress leaders. What they got up to with 'our girls' in Britain was scandalous. They were 'utterly unscrupulous, with no sense of dedication or self sacrifice, merely hungry for power... utterly contemptuous of Europeans, even those sympathetic'. The Church of Scotland was living in a fool's paradise. After African rule it would not be allowed to stay – 'the only church then was to be the African Episcopal Methodists or some such church, which is entirely Negro'.

After this sample of white beliefs we went back to Domasi for lunch, where we met Gomo's brother, Clemens. As John noted in his diary:

> *Clemens was arrested by the police, sent to Kanjedza jail, ques-*
> *tioned and released after 28 days. He answers all our questions*
> *about his treatment carefully and intelligently. He offers to*
> *write something for* Dissent. *But we will have to come back to*
> *George's to collect, as at the moment all his mail is being opened.*

We then went to the Lake for two days, swimming and walking along the shore and watching the fishermen haul in their nets, and staying in the rather fly-blown hotels. On Wednesday 20 May we drove back to Domasi and went to the Micongwes. Mrs Micongwe gave us tea but nothing was said about any paper by Clemens. After a while I asked if there was anything. As John Reed records, 'she said, "Oh, yes, where did he hide it?" It is wedged up above the window behind the pelmet. We climb on a chair and take the papers down. Terry sits down and reads through them. He is impressed. Later I look at them. The account of imprisonment is factual. Clemens describes what happened to him. There is no hearsay. The account ends with a violent and powerful statement of his reaction to the treatment he received. We shall publish this in *Dissent*. We can do nothing else.'

And we did publish the unedited statement in *Dissent* 5 on 4 June:

> *On the second day of my arrest [wrote Clemens] I was packed in a truck together with twenty-five other detainees from Blantyre cell. As soon as the gates of Kanjedza were passed we came to a halt and European guards surrounded the truck. The Camp Commandant, with a pile of detention warrants, appeared and called our names one after the other. We all received warrants and were chained in twos. ... Handcuffed in twos, sitting on the floor, with our hands above our heads for eight hours was our first punishment. All limbs were half paralysed ... After eight hours in this torturing position we were ordered to lie on the floor still chained. When a whisper was heard, or somebody eased his hands from his head, or one tried to look up, the guards used every opportunity to use their baton sticks or the butt of their guns.*

They were stripped and their heads shaved and after interrogation classified as Black, Grey or White. Clemens' account was careful to emphasize how a 'White', or less active member of Congress, was treated. 'Blacks had much worse treatment.' Nonetheless, the effect of his own treatment was to make Clemens a much more passionate nationalist.

On 1 June John noted: 'Terry's piece on Nyasaland very good – also the most outspoken thing we have yet put out.'

> *For those who have in the past few weeks justly criticized the Southern Rhodesian Government's handling of its mock emergency [I wrote] a visit to Nyasaland is at once a stimulating and depressing experience. For everything was, and is, so much worse there. The bungling arrests make our famous dawn sweep seem a very miracle of efficiency; the treatment of those detained makes the conditions inside Khami seem like the rigours of a Boy Scout camp.*

The contrast arose, I said, because the Nyasaland government was so ill-equipped. It depended on white and black soldiers from Southern Rhodesia and these were widely regarded in Nyasaland as the most brutal. And it depended on young, untrained white officials and settlers. 'It has been those warders recruited from the less successful of the European population who have committed the ugliest brutalities in Kanjedza prison camp.'

> *Kanjedza was an artisan training school. Hastily converted*

> into a detention camp it was staffed by the simple expedient of
> seconding all the school instructors to prison duties and supple-
> menting them with other junior government officers and unof-
> ficial recruits. Not a single one had experience of prison work.
> No more had the camp commander who is a regular soldier
> with simple notions about the need for discipline. Detainees in
> large numbers were deposited in the improvised camp: the au-
> thorities kept up a continued pressure for more evidence from
> interrogations. It is little wonder that there was chaos ... that
> the prevailing tone was one of harsh discipline and petty humil-
> iation; little wonder that there was violence and intimidation

By contrast, Orton Chirwa was able to give commercial law classes in Khami, and when detainees were transferred to Marandellas they found the regime quite pleasant.

But any suggestions of praise for Southern Rhodesia's more professional police and prison service was soon countered in *Dissent* 6 and 7 on 25 June and 16 July. These reported that 80 Nyasas had been arrested in Salisbury under the Unlawful Organisations Act. They had been collecting funds for the families of detainees in Nyasaland. Police found that they had retained Congress cards 'inside mattresses, under beds, under a pile of grass in the veld'; over 60 of them were sentenced to periods of 12 months to 2 years in prison. At this point the Nyasaland Congress was still legal in Northern Rhodesia and South Africa, where its members had collected large sums of money.

These reports on Nyasaland, and especially the revelations about Kanjedza, created a great storm. On 15 July 1959 the Nyasaland government banned *Dissent*, though by that time it had – together with the Federal government – announced a commission of inquiry into Kanjedza. Meanwhile other publications in Southern Rhodesia banded together to attack *Dissent*'s editors. The *Examiner* announced that, 'if Micongwe's allegation is substantially false it reflects an idiotic irresponsibility on the part of *Dissent*'s editorial board, an unethical confusion of liberty with licence'. The Salisbury *Evening Standard* of 22 June wrote that the Kanjedza report 'is enough to make one's hair curl. Belsen, it would seem, could not have been much worse.' Returning to the attack on 2 July the *Examiner* dismissed Micongwe's story as 'the lying product of a mind clouded by primitive malice'. Kanjedza had been made to seem 'a kind of Central African Buchenwald'.

John's mood swung to and fro. On 15 June he received a cutting from *The Guardian* which described Clemens' piece as 'written with clarity and restraint'.

'This makes us very pleased indeed.' The next day, John 'got up feeling happy, life interests … I suppose I was pleased about *Dissent*. I was still a fine fighter for a great cause and someone they couldn't overlook. But I can't keep this up for long. A bad morning and I see myself as a foolish idealist, as someone with nothing to lose, who is not committed to Africa and really knows nothing about it, exploiting almost without knowing it, the situation not for self-aggrandisement but in search of a kind of spiritual security.'

On 27 July John reflected on the Devlin Report, which revealed how far Nyasaland nationalism was from a noble cause: 'A narrative filled with the action of strange, violent and unpredictable men … the picture of the struggle as it really is. I can remember no moment of humour or generosity in the whole story. Parts are sickening.' But John was not worried by the local press attacks. As he noted about the *Standard* article, 'I do not feel disturbed at all though [it is] intended to frighten us.'

Characteristically, I remained self-confident throughout, though I was astonished that our David-like sling could have brought the Federal and Territorial Goliaths tumbling. On 11 July I asked Jane Symonds if she could discover 'anything about the Kanjedza inquiry and why it was ordered. We are in a mystery here and cannot believe that it was *Dissent* alone that did it.' Tom Kellock, a lawyer who had helped collect evidence for the Devlin Commission, assured us that Clemens' account was the most moderate he had seen of Kanjedza. He had been in the gallery during the Commons debate on Nyasaland and wrote to me on 7 July to say that he had been disgusted by the 'braying' of the Tories. 'Fenner Brockway said that *Dissent* was edited by moderate Europeans and the Tories howled.'

In July we received many expressions of support from Nyasaland. On 3 July, Colin Cameron, the Congress lawyer, wrote to me. I had asked him whether he could obtain further signed statements to back up Clemens' account. In his first enthusiastic reaction to the Commission he thought these were now not needed. 'By now the news of the Commission has come to light and our thanks to *Dissent* for its great help. I have a good few men who can assist there. I spoke to some lads in detention (actually they had been removed to hospital for sickness) and they had read your article and agreed in toto with the facts as stated.' On 8 July, Aleke Banda wrote to me. He had been the youngest detainee arrested in the Southern Rhodesian emergency, having been picked up at Inyati school and taken to Khami. He was then deported to Nyasaland and was just beginning his meteoric rise to influence among the founders of the Malawi Congress party:

> I have read a number of the copies of *Dissent* [he wrote] and have
> found them awfully good. I should especially like to express my

*appreciation to you for publishing the article on the conditions in Kanjedza. You have drawn the attention of the world to all the brutalities which were being done. Please stand firm in defence of that article. Nearly every person who comes out of Kanjedza testifies to those horrible conditions. Three times, when I was at Ryalls Hotel with Mr Dingle Foot, people from Kanjedza related similar stories to him. The Nyasaland government is only ashamed of all these cruelties. On Saturday the 4th of July Sam Banda appeared in court on the charge of burning some cars early in March. He was acquitted. After leaving the court he was taken back to Kanjedza where he was heavily beaten by an official there for reasons which are best known to the official alone and yet they still deny these allegations. If they need further evidence to this effect I should be willing to collect all the persons who have been released from there and these will all say the same things.*

Telling me that his ambition was to become a journalist, he ended: 'I should be very much pleased if you would be interested that I should be in constant contact with you so that you can help me along in this field.'

Also on 8 July Phil Howard, chairman of the London and Blantyre Company, whose enlightened capitalism led him to hope for a rapid transfer of power, wrote to me. 'I have followed the upheaval *Dissent* has raised over Kanjedza with considerable interest and was heartened to hear on the radio that the British Government has agreed to appoint a Commission of Inquiry ... Before starting to write this letter I questioned one or two ex-detainees and they were all most anxious to go along and give evidence which I had previously established would support the comments in *Dissent* ... I am personally quite sure from the quality of my informants that things were very wrong indeed at Kanjedza and that you have done a public service in publishing the letter you did.'

In the end the Commission failed to collect any significant evidence, but these early expressions of gratitude and confidence did much to maintain my morale. In any case the comparisons with Buchenwald and Belsen were absurd. As I wrote in *Dissent* 8 on 6 August: 'Memories are certainly short if beating and bullying are to be compared with the gas chamber and the firing squad.' The general disbelief that a British colony could engage in such brutalities was extraordinary so soon after the documented atrocities of the Kenyan camps.

We were receiving additional testimonies. One came from Macdonald Chokani, prisoner no. 65. Entitled 'The First Days of the Emergency', it described how he was

> ... *questioned, beaten and then put in a cell for two days by the*
> *police. I was then chained with at least 14-18 friends and off to*
> *Kanjedza prison. Ours was supposed to be the first group to open*
> *the camp. Just as soon as we were dropped at Kanjedza we were*
> *left on an open place for hours and with the terrible heat of the*
> *day I though this would be the last day in life. At very late hours*
> *one by one was called for further inspection and afterwards taken*
> *to a room where the hair was cut short. What a terrible thing this*
> *was – a person not allowed shoes, no underpants and with one*
> *pair of clothes for so many days ... We were then taken from*
> *this house to a dark roomed house and we were provided with*
> *two blankets, mug and a plate. Lastly, cold meal and four tins of*
> *which one was for water and the rest as bucket latrines. We were*
> *locked in this house for two days without going out for sunshine.*

A second came from S. Kamwendo, prisoner no. 57. 'I am very surprised by white settlers stating that we were not putting our hands on the heads which is untrue, so this statement is only to satisfy the UK government. Otherwise the UK government should only come and inquire to the ex prisoners. They will tell them the whole facts.'

But it soon became obvious that the inquiry would get nowhere, and that 'the whole facts' would never be revealed. On 16 July I received a letter from Colin Cameron 'worried about whether Africans will testify before a commission formed by the Federal and Nyasaland governments', though he was convinced that 'beatings are still occurring at Kanjedza'. His anxieties proved fully justified. In September I received letters from him and from Aleke Banda confirming that it had been decided to boycott the Kanjedza inquiry.

Cameron wrote on 11 August that 'a decision will be made to boycott'. He added that he had just received a letter smuggled out of Kanjedza which said that 'interrogation has been re-started and those who have refused have been punished'. Cameron's letter, which had taken a very long time to arrive and seemed to have been opened en route, added that 'ugly things still seem to be going in Kanjedza'. Aleke Banda, writing on 12 September on behalf of the Malawi Congress party, told me that:

> *We have decided to boycott this Commission on Kanjedza. There is*
> *no doubt about the ill-treatment that existed in Kanjedza. The Dev-*
> *lin Report proves that. If these governments have the courage to ig-*
> *nore the Report of the Devlin Commission there is very little cause*
> *for us thinking that they will listen to this 'Federal Commission'. In*

*fact if they accept any report that confirms the allegation that there was bad treatment it will contradict their rejection of the Devlin Report. Moreover, Mr Stevens of the Railways, who is on the Commission, is popularly anti-African. Mr Doig alone cannot do anything to defeat the other two. A Commission set up after these conditions can serve no useful purpose. Folk still in detention in Kanjedza are not giving evidence and we are instructing everyone else not to do so. We hope you will appreciate our reasons for doing this. We have given this matter careful consideration. Colin Cameron, Mr Ross and all other African leaders out of detention think that this is the best move we could take. We cannot expect anything good from this Commission after our experience with the immature piece of work by the Beadle Tribunal Report for Southern Rhodesia.*

The inquiry was a fiasco. Nearly every possible African witness boycotted it. Clemens Micongwe did appear before it but, worried about being associated with a banned publication, told the commissioners that he had not written a statement for *Dissent*, though what was narrated in it was true. The next day he wrote a letter to the commissioners and sent a copy to us. 'I have now learnt that the host in whose house I met the editors of *Dissent* handed over to the editors a copy of the story I typed after they left as a check on their reporting. Now therefore the statement should read that the editor had a true copy of the account.' In the Commission's report he is listed among 'persons [who] appeared but declined to give evidence'. Accordingly the commissioners paid no attention to his published account and did not mention it in their report. Presented with the refusal of African testimony the commissioners found that there was 'no evidence' for allegations of brutality at Kanjedza.

On 22 October in *Dissent* 12 I wrote an indictment of their report.

> *The squalid and chaotic story of Kanjedza prison camp has come to a sad and confused ending. The report of the Commission of Inquiry makes melancholy reading, melancholy for what it reveals, melancholy for what it is unable to reveal. Time and again the report said that the commissioners could find no evidence. Yes, warders carried batons but there was no evidence that they used them; one warder admitted that he had made detainees stand with their hands on their head but there was no evidence that this had been a general practice; yes, heads had been shaved and underwear confiscated but there was no evidence that this was resented as humiliating. On the other hand the report itself admitted that batons were freely used right up to at least 23 April when a warder*

> knocked out a detainee. Warders believed that the detainees were
> 'young hooligans' who needed to be put in their place. In the light
> of these and other admissions the commissioners' conclusions that
> no impropriety took place at Kanjedza were extraordinary.

As I continued, bitterly:

> Mr Micongwe's detailed account it leaves relatively unaffected
> … Mr Micongwe who is a civil servant and was the president of
> a non-Congress youth organization, could hardly be expected to
> realize that he was being regarded as a young hooligan and that
> this explained the baton blows, or that when his head was shaven
> and his underclothes taken and he was made to keep his hands on
> his head, no deliberate assault was being made on his dignity.

As *Dissent* revealed on 12 November, the Nyasaland authorities quietly took action to tidy up Kanjedza. Major Willey was replaced by a Mr Smith, who had experience of prison administration and who at once introduced new amenities and improved welfare provisions.

## *Dissent* after Nyasaland

Both John and Whit Foy were in Britain in 1960, leaving me solely responsible for *Dissent*. But it was agreed that it should carry on. John records me in September as trying to find co-editors. Issue 14 in December 1959 contained an article by me on the Gokwe detainees, 'written several times as things developed', and by Whit on the Monkton Commission which had to be re-written when Labour boycotted and which I told John was 'less than his forceful best'. This was Whit's final contribution. On 18 December 1959 I reported to John developments in the struggle over Whit. 'Old Forshaw, who is at present Superintendent of the Harare Circuit [of the Methodist Church] tried to block a motion by Nathan [Shamuyarira] and Stanlake [Samkange] at the Harare quarterly meeting to invite Whit as Superintendent in 1961. Result of this was a vote of no confidence in his chairmanship by 60 to 7. Rather crushing for the old man but well deserved. Another blow against paternalism.' This was a victory for Whit but the war was lost. At the General Synod of January 1960 it was decided that Whit should be transferred to Britain and he soon left. I remember his final service at which he asked me to read the great text in which the voice of God is heard in the temple asking 'Who shall I send and who will go for me?' and I replied in the reading, 'Send Me'. I felt that Whit's mantle had descended on me. But I also felt over-burdened and over-exposed.

I wrote to John on 5 February 1960 to defend recent issues of *Dissent*. He had written from Edinburgh a critique of *Dissent* 15. 'De Tocqueville is very neat and telling – a good point I think to call a halt to our literary-historical excursions. They give just that hint of the belletristic which goes a little incongruously with Dissent's format and more general tone. I thought [this issue] was perhaps a little overwrought – the word in both senses – that is, the impact would be stronger if the emotional or moral tone were a little flatter and if the writing and argument were a little less literary and a little less indirect and convoluted.' I replied:

> *One knows that it is difficult to keep a moral balance and that a certain stridency is likely to creep into one's writing just because no-one here seems to react to anything which is not shouted at the top of one's voice. The difficulty with* Dissent *is its extraordinarily diverse public. It is not like* Tsopano *[which Peter Mackay now edited in Malawi] which is committed to a particular line and party and which is read by others just to see what line that party takes or likes.* Dissent *is read by local liberals to hearten them – though they are pretty disheartened now – by Africans in increasing numbers; by overseas 'experts' for information and by reluctant conservatives here. The things which do not appeal to all our audience appeal to some. But I agree there is a danger of Mandarin … I feel a bit battered and rueful. The signed editorial in* Dissent *14 has drawn fire on me in a fairly concentrated way including a nice smear piece in the* Sunday Mail *suggesting that I was inspiring the NDP [the newly emerged nationalist party] and inducing students to join it.'*

# CHAPTER FIVE

# 1960

# The National Democratic Party

On 18 December 1959 I wrote to John Reed that 'rumours of new African parties are more persistent than usual and now some interesting and eminent names are associated with them. I know that the detainees themselves are trying to sponsor a Southern Rhodesian 'Malawi' and that approaches have been made to various figureheads. I think so far without success. Certainly if I were a Southern Rhodesian figurehead myself I would not consent to do a caretaker job. The situation is so different from Nyasaland and we have no Bandas in jail. Perhaps, though, one of them may try to take over effective leadership at this point.' By the end of 1959, however, these efforts at last bore fruit. 1960 began with an event which transformed African politics in Southern Rhodesia. On 1 January a new nationalist party was formed. On 6 January I wrote to John Reed:

> The situation here is confused. The Selukwe detainees [the Congress 'hard core'] smuggled out of jail a set of principles for a new party plus a note saying they approved of any party founded on these bases. They wanted to obtain leaders of stature and respectability to attain and re-assure support. They had various people approached through their emissaries – Herbert [Chitepo], Nathan [Shamuyarira], Takawira, Musarurwa – but without success. The Beatrice Cottage group [the elite African settlement] was already itself planning a 'non-party' passive resistance campaign and was in any case not too eager to accept the role offered by the Selukwe men. So the smaller men got together and produced not one

*but two parties – the National Democratic Party and the United People's Party. The principles of both seem identical and it looks like personalities all over again. Meanwhile the Passive Resistance Movement was building up. So all was confusion. However a day or two before its inaugural meeting of January 1ˢᵗ the NDP approached the Beatrice Cottage group. An agreement was reached whereby the cottagers agreed to postpone their campaign and give advice and behind-the-scenes support. Leo Takawira and Dr Pswarayi were the most ready to give support, Herbert the least interested. Accordingly Leopold was invited to address the inaugural meeting of the NDP, not as a member but as an adviser.*

*I went to the meeting. The interim executive are mostly minor trade unionists and ex-detainees. Not good or exciting speakers. Audience about 900. Line: very much Congress principles but no violence. Leopold spoke – very well I thought but too moderately and too tactically shrewdly to be appreciated by the audience. Slight dent in the harmony of the cottagers and the NDP because the meeting's Chairman – who was none other than Tranos Makombe [an ex UCRN student] – was told to stress after Leopold's speech that his views were not the party's. However, the cottagers are now trying to persuade the United People's Party, of which I know nothing, to sink differences and amalgamate with the NDP, the amalgamation to receive tacit cottage support symbolized by Leopold's appearance on the executive.*

I did not note in this letter that Sketchley Samkange, whom Shelagh had met in Khami, was an initiator of the NDP, but in the months that followed we came to know him very well as a close friend. Sketchley was a man of great gentleness and courage, deeply committed to non-violence and without a trace of racial feeling. Shelagh and John and I came to love him. John records in his diary for 8 August 1960 his visit to Sketchley's austere cottage in Highfield:

*Sketchley talks about his arrest last year and what it was like to be in Khami and about the founding of the NDP. Much of the early planning was done very secretly in the house where we are. 'It was in that bedroom that the party was first planned and all swore that nothing we said should go beyond the curtain at the door. It was down here in this corner that we first worked out a constitution.' Sketchley never seems to be touched by dark doubts. He looks forward not to a time when the Africans have won, but to a time when there will be no bitterness or difficulties between Africans and Europeans. And although there is no trace of reluctance or weariness as he faces a return to prison he is all the time wishing for the time when there would be no need for people to keep going to prison. He says he would like to see 2000 Europeans in the NDP – this would be a kind of guarantee of good will between the races.*

At any rate we ourselves were soon associated with the NDP. In April 1960 I told my parents that 'Shelagh with her usual courage has joined the NDP openly and is now more notorious than I am.' I myself remained in Todd's Central Africa Party and in March 1960 told John that, 'I am a member of the CAP executive – power at last but in a rapidly sinking ship.' But I was closely linked to the NDP leaders. It was not surprising that the exiled Joshua Nkomo should write to me from London to ask what the NDP was and whether he should support it. Nkomo was certainly not, as has often been asserted, the founder of the NDP. In the summer of 1960 various leaders of the party testified on oath that Nkomo had had to apply to join the party and was only allowed to do so on condition that he dissolved his Congress support committee in London.

On 19 January 1960 I told John that Herbert Chitepo and Michael Mawema – the former trade unionist president of the NDP – had offered a signed article by an NDP leader to appear every two or three months in *Dissent*. 'In return they will circulate *Dissent* among their members. They want at first another 500 copies produced and say they will help with the work.' On 5 February I wrote that there had been 'a nice smear piece in the *Sunday Mail* suggesting that I was inspiring the NDP and inducing students to join it.' On 20 February I told him that:

*Mawema and Sketchley actually came and worked for several hours on the duplicating and stapling of* Dissent *together with Hasu Patel and his brother Natu. It was quite a sight seeing them all charging around the stapling table and discussing Gandhian non-violence ... Mawema himself is a very different kettle of fish from George and Chikerema. He was in Israel when the emergency came and is primarily a trade unionist. He is a pretty moderate sort of chap and it looks very much as though Leopold [Takawira] will become President and Mawema Vice President. I think the NDP is going to try a fairly long period of caution. They are thinking in terms of passive resistance: not even that really but rather moral suasion by means of hunger strikes and so on.*

In mid-April I described how Shelagh had been 'exhausting herself more over the Detainees, the NDP, etc. than is good for her. The trouble is that she has found a cause and there is really no holding her. By her NDP joining she has neatly trumped me with the Africans and I am now very much Mr Shelagh Ranger. She wields much more influence in NDP councils – at least on certain issues – than a backbencher should and does not know whether to be pleased or cross about it. She even made a speech the other day after which Africans dubbed her 'Mrs Danger'. I am to make a speech myself next week – for the CAP in Mabvuku. I shall probably get stoned unless Shelagh intervenes to protect me.'

In April too Shelagh and I gave shelter to Frene Ginwala. Frene had left South Africa the day after the Sharpeville shootings and flown to Salisbury to try to arrange the escape of Oliver Tambo, who had got as far as Botswana. She had at first turned to the Indian High Commissioner, Korana, but he found her presence a diplomatic embarrassment. So he asked us whether we could accommodate her. I wrote to my parents:

> She was a most intelligent and energetic young Indian and she
> fascinated us with her stories of the situation in the Union. I made
> her give a Political Seminar to the students to pay for her keep
> but she extracted a heavier toll in nervous energy. It was all quite
> above board but also very secret and cloak and daggery since the
> point was to bluff the Union authorities about what was going
> on. Even so they nearly caught up with the refugees at the last
> minute when an extradition order was applied for in Blantyre.

Frene spent much time on the phone, and after she had gone I was visited by the CID. 'You have had a lady staying with you who has made lots of phone calls,' they said. 'Can you tell us what they were about?' I replied that they surely did not expect me to have listened in to a lady's telephone calls. She gave me a letter designed to help out if ever I got deported. It was to Oscar Kambona in Dar es Salaam – though by the time I did arrive in Dar after my deportation in 1963 Kambona was on the verge of dismissal and revolt against Julius Nyerere and I did not present the letter.

Meanwhile the NDP meetings grew in size and enthusiasm. Sketchley Samkange put into practice the principles of Gandhian non-violence, leading detainees' wives in a hunger strike outside the Prime Minister's office. He also continued in his efforts to recruit whites. When John returned in the middle of the year Sketchley met him at the airport with a statement of NDP principle and membership application forms. 'The aims and objects are given very generally,' noted John. 'Some things strike me as strange. For example they want a government established on the principle of One Man, One Vote in which the people and their chiefs shall have the right, etc, etc. The last aim is entirely Pan Africanist – To support the demand for All African Freedom and Pan-Africanism by promoting unity of action among the free people of Africa.' John decided to join.

On 30 June Shelagh and I told John that we were going to an NDP meeting in Highfield 'to celebrate the independence of the Belgian Congo'. The 'large hall surrounded by a barbed wire fence ... is quite full. There is a long platform or stage at the far end and behind a proscenium arch with about fifteen or twenty people on it.' Silundika, who 'is supposed to represent the more extreme wing of the party is speaking in English, quickly, incisively but without animation', being translated into Shona 'with great vigour and feeling'. Silundika said that 'different countries need different forms of government. The Democracy of France is not the Democracy of England. The Congo will find its own form of government ... an African form suitable to the place and the people.' There were shouts of 'Long live Lumumba'. A woman spoke 'with extravagant use of gesture and of her whole body', translated into English by Sketchley. 'She speaks of the hunger of her people, the poverty of the Reserves. The gay flamboyance of her manner keeps her speech from being sombre. The audience is delighted'. An official draped himself in a black and white toga. Everyone raised their hands in prayer. 'The whole evening has a certain ritual about it.'

And John was soon caught up in the continuing programme of welfare visiting. On 1 July 1960 he and Shelagh set off to take Mrs Hamadziripi and Mrs Musarurwa and two children to Lupane restriction area, north of Bulawayo. about ten restrictees gathered from the three hutments. 'Shelagh deals with their complaints; complaints against the inadequacy of their government allowance and complaints that their relatives have not been visited by the detainees' committee; requests that the committee should secure the recognition of more people as dependents; inquiries about the committee. Suggestions that now the number of men detained are much smaller, the committee should be able to deal with matters more promptly – the endless involved grievances of men left with little to do all the while except contemplate their grievances. Resentment that the NDP had not sent anyone down to the Native Purchase Area to form a branch, although they, the restrictees, had surreptitiously interested many of the African farmers in the place in the party. Resentment against the government; against the detainees' committee; against the Africans who are at liberty.' Maurice Nyagumbo 'tells Shelagh that the committee should not use the money for visits to them but put it to other purposes ... he goes on talking while he keeps the flies from the cups by waving *Commonsense in Africa* all over them.' Despite all the complaints, John found that 'the meeting is not wretched, a dry grinding of the spirit. There is plenty of laughter, even if some of it is cynical and some a little bitter. And between the restrictees themselves I don't detect any tensions, rivalries or hostilities. It has been a splendid day. In spite of everything the men in Lupane do not seem to me despondent, destroying themselves and each other with frustration. They seem to have built themselves lives. I was surprised how neatly dressed they were. Nearly all of them wore trousers, neatly pressed. Many of them are studying either by themselves or on courses from Ruskin and other places.' Back in Bulawayo on 3 July Shelagh talked with Joshua Nkomo's brother Stephen about the creation of a committee for the Lupane restrictees.

## Friendships with the Detainees

These visits created warm and genuine friendships. The Nyagumbos were one of the founding families of St Francis Church and two of his sisters were part of the community there. Maurice was first detained at Kentucky prison and then moved to Marandellas in mid-1959. Shelagh visited him in Kentucky after she had been to St Francis at Easter 1959. I visited him in Marandellas on 6 February 1960 when he thanked the Committee very much for having made it possible for him to visit his sick child in Bonda hospital. By now we were deeply involved with him and his family – making sure his wife had her allowance, that his land was tilled, that his brother Edwin's school fees were paid, that Maurice himself had books and examination fees, and visiting him whenever we could. At Maurice's request I wrote on 27 March 1961 a very stern letter to Edwin, who had been misbehaving at Mutambara Training school:

> *I hope you will appreciate that your brother is spending a great deal of money for your schooling and that he now owes the Committee a considerable sum. It would be most unfair to him if you did not make the fullest use of the opportunity of training which his generosity is making possible for you and also if you did not make the most economical use of the money made available to you. I understand also from the Head-Master's letter that he is displeased with your behaviour at school. Given all the considerations in this case – the fact that you seem to need and spend more money than other dependents of restrictees and detainees; the fact that your school authorities have reason to complain of your conduct and work – I must give you a very serious warning that unless all this improves in future the Committee will be unable to give you any sort of financial or other support.*

This was a much sterner letter than I later sent to any of my own daughters! On

1 May 1961 Maurice thanked me for it – 'I am sure that did a lot to discipline him.' Much later we became responsible for Maurice's daughter, Chipo Sheila, in England and I even presided as Maurice's surrogate at her wedding.

Maurice was a passionate and angry man. He was notorious amongst the other detainees for his readiness to assault arrogant officials. But he was also very responsive to friendship. By June 1960 he was already in Lupanda detention camp, Lupane. Shelagh wrote to him on 25 June saying she was bringing Mrs Hamadziripi to visit the camp the following weekend:

> *We will travel to Bulawayo on Friday, 1ˢᵗ July and stay the night*
> *there. Then we will drive out to see you on the Saturday morning.*
> *I hope you will all be at home and I am looking forward very much*
> *to having a long talk … Mr Shamuyarira has just telephoned*
> *to say that he has heard the Minister's decision. ONLY FOUR*
> *MEMBERS OF THIS COMMITTEE ARE ALLOWED TO VISIT*
> *THE PRISONS, namely Mrs Chitepo, Mr and Mrs Haddon and*
> *Mr Shamuyarira and they were allowed to visit only once a month.*
> *This is indeed a blow and we shall have to fight the decision. I*
> *think that this is a declaration of war by Government against our*
> *Committee and I think we should treat it as such. Up to now any*
> *member of the Committee has been able to visit any of the prisons*
> *at any time. And the Prison officials have on occasion asked us*
> *to go there – when there has been some trouble or the detainees*
> *were particularly restless. Only a few weeks ago when the peo-*
> *ple in Gwelo were on hunger strike I understand Cameron asked*
> *our Committee's help. We were in Nyasaland at the time – so*
> *I am not quite sure how it happened. But Victoria Chitepo and*
> *Eileen Haddon went down there and persuaded them to give up*
> *the hunger strike, and as a result the chaps were moved to Ma-*
> *randellas. Anyway we can talk about all this when I see you.*

The result was the visit of Shelagh and John Reed which has already been described. John Reed had then recorded that Maurice advised us not to waste money by visiting him. But we continued to do so. Early in 1961 Shelagh and I went with Basil Nyabadza and some of the Sisters from St Francis to visit Maurice and the other Lupane restrictees. As we sat around the fire at night the restrictees taught us a splendid Methodist hymn, 'Rakanaka', which was to become one of the hymns at St Francis. Maurice was deeply touched. On 22 January 1961 he wrote to Shelagh and me:

> *It was indeed very hard for me to say goodbye to you. I*

*couldn't help dropping tears as you drove off. I sat down
next to the place where you were cooking, and could vis-
ualize the way you were going about serving the people. I shall not forget the wonderful time we had.*

*Basil Nyabadza, John Reed, Terry Ranger, Shelagh Rang-
er and St Francis Sisters visiting Lupane restrictees (incl.
Maurice Nyagumbo, kneeling left), January 1961*

On 13 June 1961 he
wrote to Shelagh: 'I do
believe, Shelagh, that
you are all praying for
me and my poor family
at home. But believe
me, a letter from each
one of you is more real
and a relief to my con-
fused soul.'

This friendship with
us, which comes so
strongly out of Maurice
Nyagumbo's letters, is
well known because of
John Conradie's edition
of Maurice's autobiography, *With the People,* but perhaps the most impressive evidence comes from Robert Chikerema, against whom we had given evidence and
with whom John was so fascinated as a determinedly hard man. In July 1960 Chikerema was in Marandellas prison. Shelagh wrote to him there, with apologies for
addressing him by his first name. He replied to her on 18 August:

> *Please make no apologies concerning the use of my first
> name. After all your family and I have been greatly at-
> tached to each other through thick and thin and our friend-
> ship is deeper than any I have ever experienced.*

## The Assault on the NDP

In Salisbury, meanwhile, pressure had been building on the NDP. In the early morning of 7 July 1960 the NDP offices were raided by the police and everything taken,
including the typewriter. The circulation list of the *Democratic Voice* was seized and
a couple of days later the Indians who received the broadsheet had their houses
searched. John hid all his diaries.

There was still time for simple pleasures. My favourite eating place was the Curry House. It belonged to a former England rugby international, Tug Wilson. No doubt it served very Anglo-Indian curries but the helpings were lavish and we thought delicious. Tug admonished me. 'If you want to bring a friend that's fine. If you demonstrate against me I shall drive you into the ground.' I was in no doubt of his ability to do so. I didn't demonstrate against Tug, even when I launched later on the Citizens Against Colour Bar campaign. But I did take Sketchley to eat there. We all had dinner there on 16 July. John recorded that 'no-one seems to mind Sketchley and we eat extensively. Sketchley tells us about his name and his clan names and his totem names. The African waiters are so fascinated that they cannot help chipping in and explaining all the other words for crocodile. We drive Sketchley back to Highfield and see his two bare rooms by the light of a candle.'

Sketchley dined with us at UCRN the next day, with 11 other people, off a rural chicken we had been given. Erskine Childers, who was out recording for the BBC, was present. So were Angeline Dube and Clyde Sanger. They debated how long the NDP had before a ban and arrests. Sketchley told us that he hoped for six months, by which time the party would be so organized that the arrest of the leaders would not matter. In the event he only had two more days.

In the early hours of 19 July 1960, Sketchley and Mawema were arrested and charged under the Unlawful Organisations Act. Shelagh and I also had a nocturnal visit from the police. At 4 a.m. we were raided by two CID men and a woman accompanied by a uniformed and armed policeman. The police searched methodically, opening every book and shaking out every record sleeve. I noticed that their warrant was made out in Shelagh's name and so was able to prevent them from taking away any of my notes on the formation of the NDP and other dangerous political confidences. In the end they took only a few letters to Shelagh from Molly Clutton-Brock and a copy of my land policy for Congress. After they had gone I at once moved my African political material to my office in the History department and we advised John to conceal or destroy his own papers and correspondence. As John notes, I told him 'with disgust and anguish' about the arrests. 'In the leadership of the NDP Sketchley and Mawema are the two men who stand for moderation; they are the two who have European friends and who have from inside the NDP been criticized for this.'

That night Shelagh and I went to an NDP protest meeting in Highfield. It was addressed by Chitepo and Silundika. A general strike was declared, though teachers were told that they should report to their schools and keep children off the streets. At the end of the meeting the crowd marched, first on the Highfield police station and then on to Harare township, led by Silundika and Peter Mackay with linked arms. I returned to the Old Bricks area of Harare the next morning. Police and white reservists armed with tear gas were keeping the huge crowd at bay. I watched from behind the police lines as the NDP leaders negotiated with the police to try to send a delegation to Whitehead. Back at UCRN I reported the day's events to John:

> *The leaders desperately pled that they be allowed to see the Prime*
> *Minister as the crowd refused to disperse until they had and they*
> *were uncertain how long they would be able to control it. The reply*
> *was a message that the Government had banned all meetings in*
> *Harare for three months and the Prime Minister would not address*
> *an illegal assembly or its delegates. At this announcement some*
> *of the people dispersed. The rest remained; the police announced*
> *that they were about to use tear gas. The crowd sat down. Then*
> *the tear gas was set off and the crowd fled but this broke the*
> *calmness of the mood and the situation is dangerous indeed. There*
> *seems a very real danger that the night will see extensive rioting.*

I watched with bitterness as the police opened fire with tear gas, scattering the crowd into the township. I didn't know whether Whitehead had been seeking to provoke this reaction or had been taken by surprise by it. Among the spectators was a young American who had come to Salisbury with a letter of introduction to Shelagh and myself. He had his introduction as I walked away and he heard one of the police say, 'There goes that bloody bastard Ranger.' More surprising was the reply from his fellow policeman – 'Yes, but we'd be better off if we did what he wants.' Back at UCRN I had a phone call from Peter Mackay who told me that the crowds were growing more hostile to all whites. And I learnt that all the African students had decided to go to the townships the next day to show solidarity. The African revolt was gaining ground. This immediate reaction was very different from the subdued response when the ANC had been banned in 1959.

On 20 July the government closed all the schools in Harare and ejected all the children who turned up for class. The children then roamed the streets and were tear-gassed. Then in the afternoon Eileen Haddon phoned up to report that Stanlake Samkange, Sketchley's elder brother and a leading member of Garfield Todd's Central Africa Party, and his African-American wife, Tommie, had been arrested and charged with incitement to violence. John and I went down to Peter Mackay's office where we found Guy and Molly Clutton-Brock and Erskine Childers. Peter urged that all white sympathizers with the NDP should go into Harare and 'be on the receiving end of anything that is going'. I was not in favour of this idea. 'There is, as

Peter admits, always the danger that we will just get mauled by the Africans and this can serve no sort of purpose.' I had promised Shelagh that I would not go into the township, but John drove with Childers to Highfield beer hall where a large crowd had been gathering. 'At the beer hall there are lorry loads of police and beyond them a loose African crowd [which] keeps melting away, then returning – they have used tear gas but no bullets. Armoured cars painted blue are about and there is a light observation aircraft wheeling and dipping over the township.' John and I had to return to UCRN to teach. Peter and Childers went to the court where Stanlake was appearing. At four o'clock three African women students came to my house. They had been in Harare and had missed their tutorials with me. 'They seemed to have gone through their spell in Harare not only unharmed but very cheerful. They tell of being tear-gassed almost as if were merely an interesting experience.' And they insisted on doing the washing up as my maid, Evelyn, was on strike.

By this time the *Central African Examiner* had changed hands and had a new proprietor, Theodore Bull, and a new editor, Jack Halpern. By contrast with the *Examiner's* attack on *Dissent* over Kanjedza, Halpern wanted me to write an account of the disturbances, and Shelagh to write profiles of the NDP leaders. On the evening of 20 July John and I debated whether we should respond to this request or whether we should produce a special issue of *Dissent*. As John noted, 'the *Examiner* cannot reach the African public which *Dissent* certainly does. On the other hand it is still much more respectable.' So we agreed, although John felt 'a little cheated. A good *Dissent* would at least have been a firm gesture about where we stand. Now it will all be lost in the anonymity of the *Examiner*.' But that very night I began to write what became a four-page supplement on the demonstrations – my first substantial essay in contemporary history.

On 22 July Shelagh decided she would try to get clothes and pyjamas to Sketchley in prison. She was told that he and Mawema and Takawira would appear in court that afternoon. So we went to a 'dim, packed court 2' just in time for bail to be negotiated. Outside the court were Tommie Samkange and Mrs Takawira. We all followed the van to Salisbury prison, where we found Stanlake, also out on bail. 'Stanlake is immediately friendly and the sense of African/European coldness is quickly dissolved in his humorous, gentle personality. He pretends to be indignant that his bail was only £59 while his brother rates £200. But his crime at least he says, Public Violence, is one of much greater dignity.' His wife mocked the very idea that Stanlake had constructed a barricade out of petrol containers – that would be more physical exercise than he had ever taken! Sketchley when released was full of schemes for meetings out in the Reserves and we had to tell him that these too had been banned.

By this time the press had picked up that our house had been searched and I became the subject of violent attacks. The *Sunday Mail* reported the search on 24 July together with an editorial on 'the appalling tendency of the Bantu to resort to violence at the slightest provocation. Atavistic hooliganism, it seems, is a part and parcel of the black man's make-up, as it has been for centuries.' In a speech on 26 July Whitehead alleged that 'some Europeans, who were known to be assisting in the organization of party activities' and whose houses had been searched, were 'at the height of things through the night of the disturbances in Harare and Highfield.' In the Southern Rhodesian parliament on 29 July my deportation was demanded; in the Federal parliament on 2 August Lord Graham, a descendant of the gallant seventeenth-century Montrose, accused me of initiating the march from Highfield and then abandoning my African dupes. There were expressions of hostility from within UCRN. The Zhii riots (about which I have recently written in detail in *Bulawayo Burning*) broke out in Bulawayo and several Africans were killed. An agricultural lecturer at College reported it as a fact that Shelagh 'was seen sitting in front of the NDP Land Rover at the height of the riots in Bulawayo'. On 29 July the students met and some of the whites complained that the 'extremism' of faculty members made life difficult for them. They asked why lecturers were allowed to be involved in politics while they were not. They were answered by the brilliant Zambian student, Dominic Mulaisho, who told them they were entirely free to do so. John recorded that he grew 'wild thinking about the students. Can there be anywhere in the world a duller, more hide-bound, grey-outlooked, tamed and cowed set of young men and women?'

Adams was away and the Vice-Principal, Basil Fletcher, took fright. He had been warned by Lord Malvern of the mood in the Federal Assembly and he told me that he would seek to protect UCRN's reputation by sending round the departments a statement to be signed by all staff to the effect that, 'though of course any University teacher has the right to take part in politics, they themselves, as private individuals, feel that in the initial stages of a new university teachers should take it upon themselves to forgo political activities'. Even Professor Stokes 'cannot believe that there is no truth in these allegations' and feared for the History Honours course if I were deported. John records me as bitter about all this, and fearing being 'subdued by the occasion, becoming a persecution bore, or any sort of bore, or a cause'. I took the view that if I were to be deported it would be 'for activities undertaken in a private capacity and this is no concern of the College and involves no issues of academic freedom'. But I refused to back down. I told Fletcher exactly what I had done and not done but gave him no assurances for the future. And I challenged Lord Graham to repeat his allegations outside parliament. Fletcher did not circulate his document and Graham kept quiet.

These events posed me several questions as a historian as well as an activist. It seemed to me that the protests in Harare had clearly been a manifestation of nationalism. On the other hand the Zhii riots in Bulawayo equally clearly had nothing to do with the leadership of the NDP. After 1980 Edison Zvobgo retrospectively praised Mawema and Sketchley for being the most radical organizers of nationalism, attributing the Zhii violence to their organization of youth gangs. At the time, though, it was apparent to me that Sketchley had in no sense either fomented or controlled Zhii. He was out on bail and in Gwelo when the violence began. He at once drove to Bulawayo in the NDP Land Rover to seek to pacify the situation. In Makokoba the Land Rover was stoned by the crowd with cries of, 'We do not know the NDP'. Sketchley abandoned the vehicle briefly to phone me up, explain these events and ask me what he should do. Sounds of rioting and gunfire could be heard over the phone. I told him to get out as soon as he could, and he did so. I have worked for fifty years to try to understand these events.

All this time, while so many people believed I was a power behind the NDP, I was still an executive member of Todd's Central Africa Party. On 24 July I went to Gwelo for a CAP meeting, where I gave my account of the demonstration and its consequences. The meeting voted full confidence in Stanlake and agreed to meet his legal fees. But then developments took place which freed me from the CAP. In London Garfield Todd issued a statement jointly with Joshua Nkomo calling for Britain to suspend the Southern Rhodesian constitution and to send troops to restore order. This was too much for most members of the CAP to stomach and the party rapidly broke up. On 26 August Todd resigned from the party, and the next day I drove out to Highfield and offered my membership of the NDP to a delighted Sketchley. From then until my deportation in 1963 I was a member of the nationalist parties. John records that, 'Terry does not feel at all relieved or delighted [and] says it will in some ways be awkward for his work on African nationalism … We agree that *Dissent* will remain completely independent and that one our functions in the NDP is to retain individual judgement, not to accept party discipline which is beyond that proper to a democratic party. Terry says he hopes he will be able to remain an ordinary, un-influential party member.'

On 31 August, however, the African press carried a speculative article about office holders in the NDP. It assumed that Ndabaningi Sithole would become the first President of an independent Zimbabwe, Herbert Chitepo would become Minister of

Justice, Michael Mawema Minister of Social Welfare, Leoold Takawira Minister of Education, Joshua Nkomo Minister of External Affairs, and T.G. Silundika Minister of European affairs. 'There are several European members tipped for Ministerial posts but this is one of the closely guarded secrets of the party.'

But what did it really mean to be NDP in a world without meetings and at a moment when the leadership of the party was being hotly contested? Shelagh and I had long been close to Sketchley. Now we began to know Mawema. On 5 August, Shelagh, John and I drove out to his house to deliver copies of *Dissent*, in which was an eyewitness account of the Zhii riots. John recorded Mawema's

> *little box-like rooms, with bare stone floors uncomfortably clean.*
> *There is a table in the middle of the living room filling it. You*
> *would have the same in English working class houses. We meet*
> *Michael's wife and baby son, Tafirenyika – "we die for the coun-*
> *try". We sit at the table and talk about the charges against Michael.*
> *He is charged with saying that one day Africans will rule and*
> *that Africans are tired of eating the scraps. The most interesting*
> *of the citations of Michael's speeches is that on what is now the*
> *Mazoe Orange Estate many thousands of Africans were killed*
> *during the rebellions. And that no African should eat an orange*
> *from Mazoe, for that would be to eat the blood of his ancestors.*

On 7 August, Guy and Molly had a party at Cold Comfort Farm where me met and talked with Mawema again. We took Sarah Chavunduka and met there the Chitepos and their children, the Mawemas, Peter Mackay, Enos Nkala and Willie Musarurwa. John records some of the conversation. 'Terry began a debate on what it means to be African by saying how much he wishes he was black, because for the black man everything is still open, everything is still to do – a new state and new culture to build up. He can become a great vernacular poet and still be a great politician – whereas for the European everything has been done, there is nothing left.' This was clearly a variant on my growing feeling that to be an Africanist historian offered challenges and opportunities which one could not find in European history. But Sarah and Mawema insisted that there was no reason 'why Europeans cannot take part in the reconstruction'. 'They really believe,' noted John, 'once there is no more discrimination against Africans the bitterness of the past will be directly, blankly, forgotten; that the fury of the struggle will vanish the moment the struggle is finished. To be an African, says Sarah, is to accept Africa – its climate, its country-side and its people. There is no other qualification. If only it might be so.'

The trials of Mawema, Sketchley and Stanlake began on 10 August. I went to

Stanlake's trial, John to Mawema's and Sketchley's. Both courtrooms were packed and set for high drama. Crowds of Africans sat on the floor and more and more tried to get in. By the afternoon the police could not control the crowds and asked Leopold Takwaira to address them in Shona. The case was adjourned. 'Mawema is carried out shoulder high from the Court building. The NDP Land Rover is densely surrounded, everyone congratulating Mawema and each other – though nothing of course has happened.' On 12 August Stanlake was acquitted – 'huge crowds outside the Magistrate's court pushing the car all the way back to the Beatrice Road cottages'. His old mother, the remarkable Grace, was overjoyed and tearful. Much later, in *Are We Not Also Men?*, I was to devote a chapter to Grace, but to me on that day she was just old lady. From Marandellas prison Chikerema wrote:

> *We were jubilant to read the outcome of Stanlake Samkange's*
> *case. But much as I tried to picture the scenes that took place in*
> *Harare, I could not for the life of me imagine Stanlake playing*
> *'rock and roll' with drums and dustbins around Stoddart Hall!*
> *And along the roads in Harare. Whoever said he saw him playing*
> *such a game needs the immediate attention of eye specialists.*

Among the Ranger Papers are my longhand notes of Stanlake's trial and Shelagh's shorthand record of Mawema's and Sketchley's. They make interesting reading. The evidence brought against Stanlake was particularly weak. Much of it was given by Reserve Constable Bellingall. He admitted, 'that he had no police experience and was a travelling salesman. He had no contact with Africans and had not seen the accused before.' He failed to pick out in court the officer who had given him the order to arrest. He admitted that he had not made a report immediately the accused was arrested. It was not until 2.30 that afternoon that he made a statement at the charge office. He admitted that, 'in a situation like that one was looking after one's own interests' and that he did not notice any other Reservists. Besides, he knew very few Reservists. The only man he could recognize and remember was Stanlake, because he wore spectacles.

Bellingall revealed the weakness of depending on the general white population to police Africans. But Shelagh's notes of the Inkomo trials reveal how much white civilization was at stake. The Crown contended that 'the government of this country is primarily a European Government, representing the view of the majority of Europeans in this country. Therefore an attack on the Government must be construed as being an attack on the persons whom that Government represents, namely the Europeans.' No nonsense about partnership or multiracialism here! By contrast, Herbert Chitepo argued for the defence that, 'the government cannot be considered synonymous with the Europeans ... The government has never been equivalent in this country to the European community.'

It was striking that the nationalist discourse, as quoted by the prosecution and given in evidence, was so historical. Leopold Takawira, in his statement of 8 August 1960, described a speech about 'the agreement which Lobengula had entered into with Rudd'. He said that if ever there was an agreement giving the Europeans the right to live in this country there was no record of it. He said that the most unfortunate part of the matter was that if there was such an agreement it was an agreement made between a very illiterate man and the well-educated and diplomatic whites. Lobengula, if he signed such an agreement, did not understand it. The person who was employed by Rudd to interpret the wording of the document to Lobengula spoke Tswana and did not know Sindebele. Lobengula, on the other hand, spoke Sindebele and did not understand Tswana. Even today, Africans who were asked to interpret legal language into Tswana found it very hard to do so. How much more would this be the position with an interpreter who did not even understand the language very well?

The government had learned from the reactions to the trials in Salisbury, and moved the rest of the Mawema/Sketchley trial outside the city to Inkomo barracks, which very few Africans reached. On 22 August Sketchley came to say goodbye, expecting a five-year sentence. That night he slept at our house with his key defence witnesses. And now Shelagh came into her own. Herbert Chitepo asked her to take shorthand notes of the trial proceedings so that he might have an immediate record. Her notes, partly transcribed, are among the Ranger Papers in Rhodes House and I have quoted from them above. The trial at Inkomo did not begin until 30 August, three days after I had joined the NDP. The barracks was oddly informal. The courtroom itself was a low, thatched building with no ceiling, and beams of barked branches. Apart from ourselves, Tommie and Stanlake Samkange and Sketchley's girlfriend, Joyce Manguni, there were hardly any spectators, making it a low-key affair very different from the tumultuous scenes in Salisbury. But in its own way the trial was dramatic enough.

Most of the state evidence was derived from the reports of African detectives, but these had been tidied up and 'Englished' by their white superiors. The defence spent hours cross-examining the African witnesses who turned out not to know the meaning of the English words inserted into their testimony. It was a humiliating business, one's delight in the demolition of state evidence balanced by unease at a demonstration of African incompetence. At the end of the day's proceedings the Magistrate reserved judgement until after the weekend. That night Sketchley had an anonymous letter warning that he would be sentenced to ten years and that he should jump bail. John, however, did 'not see how the sentence can possibly be heavy. The two utterances on which he is being tried are really very modest indeed and the evidence that he actually said the only really damaging phrase – a statement that the Government had used petrol bombs against the people – is insecure indeed.' On 5 September, Sketchley was acquitted of sedition and fined £30 on the public order charge.

Despite the absence of an African crowd the trial became legendary while it was still in progress. On 28 August, for instance, Shelagh and John and I went to a large meeting of the NDP in Highfield. Two white CID men sat by the speakers and the large crowd shouted out in derision the name of the most incompetent of the African detectives who had given evidence, Magama. They were rebuked by Enos Nkala, who told them that 'Magama is just doing his job as you are doing your job. You must not hate him but you must hate the system.' Nkala stressed that the NDP was non-violent, but he worked up the crowd by telling them of people driven out of Sinoia by the District Commissioner. 'Why don't they come and kill us first?' cried out an old man near us. Nkala also spoke of employees in Salisbury who had been sacked because they were members of the NDP. 'You,' he tells the crowd, 'will never let anyone harm the NDP.'

This meeting was also the first occasion on which what became a key nationalist slogan was enunciated. John records that Wellington Malianga stressed non-violence and 'the method it stands for is government by the people of the people for the people. The crowd are delighted by the phrase which they seem never to have heard before. And when he attributes it to Abraham Lincoln they laugh hugely though I do not understand why.'

Shelagh wrote to Chikerema on 1 September 1960:

> *I wish more people could go out to Inkomo to see what goes on there. It is very educative. I have been there every day … Some people have been suggesting that I must write a book about all the interesting things that have been happening and generally about the trials. What do you think of the idea? Something ought to be written for the sake of posterity but I do not think I am very well qualified to do it. When Terry will get down to his book I don't know. He says he is still collecting material. Something ought to be written and in a popular style that would sell while people are still interested in these events. The trouble is that we are all too busy. We need to be put away in some remote area of the coun-*

*try where there is no telephone or outside communication and
with nothing else to do but write. May we come and join you?*

Chikerema responded enthusiastically, writing back from Marandellas on 12
September 1960:

> *Today is so-called Occupation Day. Throughout all my life I have
> never felt called upon to celebrate the meaning of that day but in
> the past year or two I have found myself quite eager to celebrate
> Occupation Day but attaching to it a very different meaning. I
> now regard it as an important day of planning a better future
> for us all. Therefore today I have offered a short prayer for you
> all asking God to help you in your struggle against evil forces....
> I think you should write down your experiences including the
> miniature trials taking place at Inkomo. Do not wait for anyone
> to use your good material. You and a very few others have been
> in the struggle right from the very start. You have got all the
> facts … You have seen and experienced the whole drama. So in
> my opinion you are best suited to write this book from your own
> point of view. It will receive a country wide greetings! Please go
> ahead. Yes! You and Terry are welcome here as 'detainees'.*

By this time, as *Dissent* recorded, African intellectuals were moving en masse
into the NDP. Among them was Herbert Chitepo, freed from any commitment to
multiracial politics by the collapse of the CAP. Herbert now planned to capture
for the NDP the more radical of the white CAP members and he told me that he
wanted us to establish a Salisbury North branch which they could join. John and
Shelagh took up this idea. On 11 September they went to Highfield to discuss it with
Mawema and Sketchley. They took with them the Quaker, Margaret Moore. They
found a meeting of the NDP Women's League in progress to which both Mawema
and Sketchley spoke. It was agreed that NDP members should demonstrate against
Occupation Day in Cecil Square and that Duncan Sandys should be met when he
arrived in Salisbury for constitutional negotiations. 'Where he sleeps, we will sleep.'
Afterwards they went to Sketchley's house for a drink and Enos Nkala came in. 'He
is more extreme than the others,' noted John, 'and yet there is about him something
pathetic. He is always saying in his speeches that he doesn't care what they do to
him, they can kill him – as if he was trying to convince himself.'

Within the NDP, Nkala and Sketchley were at odds. Nkala wanted Mawema
replaced by a more radical leader; Sketchley was committed to non-violence as a
principle, Nkala as a tactic. Meanwhile the newly recruited elites coveted the leader-

ship positions. All this came to head on 22 September. Sketchley had invited John to come to lecture the Highfield Youth League on democracy. When he arrived he found the Youth Leaguers planning a violent reception for Edgar Whitehead should he try to visit and speak in Highfield. 'Sketchley is very disapproving. What after all is the point of damaging a Prime Minister's car or throwing things at him? They must maintain their superiority to the methods of the government by a policy of non-violence.' Then Sketchley went off to attend an NDP executive meeting leaving John locked in democratic debate.

This meeting went on till half past four on the morning, and turned out to be a decisive blow to Mawema and Sketchley even though no alternative leadership was elected. Sketchley phoned me up later in the morning and I passed on to John the news of Mawema's ousting from the leadership. 'Herbert Chitepo was to have been there but spent the night at High Table and Adams's house.' John thought that was 'sickening'. He also noted that 'there has been no agreement on a new president, neither Malianga or Takawira, though apparently three votes were taken, getting the necessary votes. Talk of calling in [J.Z] Moyo from Bulawayo or making Nkomo the President.' Robert Mugabe, though now back from teaching in Ghana, and having joined the NDP, did not feature as a candidate. 'What madness,' thought John, 'to overthrow Mawema just at this moment, when he is being tried virtually as leader of the NDP.' I drove out to Mawema's house in Highfield as a gesture of solidarity.

The next month, though, clarified the leadership situation. Joshua Nkomo had compensated for more than a year of inaction and disengagement by his joint statement with Garfield Todd calling for the suspension of the Southern Rhodesian constitution. On 30 October an NDP Congress in Salisbury elected Nkomo as President; on 20 November he at last returned home to a welcome at Salisbury airport by a crowd of 50,000 people. John, who was there to see friends off, noted: 'Nkomo appears, surrounded by the NDP leaders. He is embracing one after the other. I see him hugging Sketchley. They are really excited, moved to see each other and not embarrassed by their feelings as Europeans would be.'

This was in fact almost Sketchley's last appearance in the front ranks of the NDP. Disillusioned by what had happened, he moved to work with Peter Mackay in Malawi. But it was not the end of NDP gestures to its white and Asian supporters. As his farewell contribution, Michael Mawema organized on a Friday in early December a chicken dinner in a township restaurant for top NDP leaders and leading whites and Asians. Shelagh, John and I were there. So was Peter Mackay. Nkomo presided; Mawema waited. Mugabe was there, sitting opposite Leopold Takawira. Mugabe was new to us and lying low in the NDP. We watched him closely to try to pick up some clues. We saw a rare playful moment. Mugabe ate his food quickly and with every evidence of enjoyment. Then he lent over and tapped Leopold Takawira on the shoulder. 'I am surprised at you, Leopold,' he said. 'As a good Catholic you are eating meat on Friday.' Much upset, Leopold protested that Mugabe had done the same. 'Ah', said Mugabe, 'but I am not a *good* Catholic.'

# History

My greater immersion in African politics during the year seemed promising for my research. I wrote to my parents in January 1960 to tell them that, 'my African politics project is coming on splendidly as a result of all the apparently irrelevant stuff that one does'. By the end of the year I was 'spending days in the Archives getting the most fascinating material [though] unless I do nothing but ten hours a day archiving my concentration lapses'. So both contemporary and past material was coming to hand.

But as so often with reports to my parents about research, I was being over-optimistic. As long ago as April 1959 I had even envisaged publishing both a revision of my thesis and a book about African politics by the end of 1960 – 'a good demonstration of versatility'. In November 1959 I wrote that 'I hope to complete my thesis revision before Christmas and then get down to some African research'. In fact the thesis was never revised, and the African research resulted in publication only in 1967, with *Revolt in Southern Rhodesia. The African Voice in Southern Rhodesia* took two further years to appear.

This delay was partly due, of course, to involvement with detainees, *Dissent*, the NDP, etc. I told my parents in January 1960 that, 'we are just off on a 700 miles trip to visit some of the detainees and take them clothes and books. After that I have absolutely refused to do anything charitable or political for the rest of the vacation and have reserved it for some solid work [on] African politics.' But it was also due to conceptual and practical difficulties with the research itself.

In September 1960 a pan-African history conference, funded by Leverhulme, took place at UCRN – a triumph for Eric Stokes and a test of how far we had become an African institution. I wrote to my parents that it went very well. 'The high powered academics who gathered here really seemed to enjoy themselves. Best of all though were the two tours – one of four days to Zimbabwe and Inyanga and the other a day's trip to the Falls.' In Mutare, the African delegates – who could not stay in any of the hotels – were accommodated at Sir Stephen Courtauld's mansion at La Rochelle. Arthur Porter of Sierra Leone gave a wonderfully funny impression next day of a conversation over the port between Courtauld and the historian

Roland Oliver, which consisted entirely of grunts of interrogation, assessment and appreciation. At Great Zimbabwe we stayed at the Catholic Mission at Driefontein, where they put on a play about Fatima. I shared a room with Ndabaningi Sithole who could barely conceal his astonishment at Catholic alcoholic hospitality. At the Falls, where 'we sat down to lunch at a long white-table-clothed table under the trees by the river immediately above the Falls, we might have been a Maupassant picnic party by the Seine on a really glorious summer's day.' Eric Stokes and Ronald Robinson enlivened the bus journeys with competitive Kipling ballads. In Umtali, Jan Vansina enlivened the hotel stay by swopping round all the shoes left outside rooms to be cleaned.

Vansina's impression of the intellectual side of the conference, and particularly of my role in it, has been given in his autobiography. Much to my subsequent students' surprise he found me darkly handsome, always dressed in a suit, not much interested in African history and obsessed with racial discrimination. Later students did not see me as handsome, never saw me in a suit and suffered from my intense interest in African history. But Vansina was right to think that in September 1960 I was obsessed with discrimination and with African politics. It was soon after the arrests of the NDP leaders and the subsequent demonstrations and shootings. Our house had been searched on 19 July. It was only a month before the conference that I had myself joined the NDP. We had Ndabaningi Sithole among us as a delegate. During the conference, Sketchley Samkange and Michael Mawema were on trial at Inkomo barracks. On 4 September John notes in his diary that there was an NDP meeting being held in Stoddart Hall. 'Terry is showing round members of the History Conference so he cannot come. He hopes he will be able to bring his historians into the meeting later on.' John and Shelagh went, Shelagh sitting on the platform. The crowd around John speculated who he might be. Then Eric Stokes 'arrives at the Hall with a group of historians and is allowed to take them up to the balcony. The audience of course takes them to be another reinforcement of plainclothes policemen, and when they leave, which they do after about ten minutes, they are given a tremendous jeer.'

The conference ended with a final dinner on 14 September. I went to that and then on to a party at Richard Brown's flat. But at 10 p.m. Sketchley phoned John to tell him that, 'the meeting in Highfield this evening, which Whitehead was addressing has broken up in disorder without Whitehead being given a hearing. His car has been stoned and the police are still restoring order. As Sketchley talks, tear gas shells go off. Sketchley did not go to the meeting but he thinks Terry was there and that if he is OK he should be home by now.' John and Sketchley discussed what to do if I had been arrested but John then saw my car arriving. 'Historians are getting out and bidding him farewell and thanks.' Sketchley phoned again: was John 'sure that it is really Terry who has come back?' Apart from revealing Sketchley's tender concern for his white friends, this episode ensured that the history conference should end as it began for me, surrounded by the clamour of nationalism. Vansina notes in his autobiography that had he lived and worked in Southern Rhodesia he would have shared my obsessions. At any rate, this context helps explain how impossible it was for me to separate life from art.

Of course, all this meant that it would have been highly desirable for me to present at the conference a fully-crafted and illuminating paper on nationalist history. During the conference George Shepperson gave a public lecture on 'Some External Factors in the Development of African Nationalism'; Ndabaningi Sithole spoke on 'The Interaction of Christianity and African Political Development'; there was passionate debate around H.P. Gale's presentation on 'Freedom – and the Historian in East Africa', which called for resistance to nationalist revisionism and sought to rally historians in defence of the Corfield Report on Mau Mau. There was plenty about African nationalist politics at the conference. But I did not respond to Shepperson's call for detailed studies of the pioneers of African nationalism nor attempt to trace the outlines of African politics in twentieth-century Rhodesia. My paper – 'Some Attitudes to African Nationalism' – was programmatic, refuting Perham's contention that southern African nationalism was a recent, self-created, mushroom growth but still laying out what needed to be done rather than doing it. For my research the conference came two years too early!

I had told my parents in February 1959 that I might get access to 'an imposing collection of papers belonging to one of the first African leaders'. These were the papers of the Reverend Douglas Thompson Samkange, which covered the period from the late 1920s to the early 1950s. His son Stanlake, Sketchley's elder brother, was custodian. Stanlake was himself both an ardent admirer of his father and becoming a professional academic Africanist historian. It was reasonable enough that he should wish to reserve the Samkange Papers for himself. It was only after his death that his widow, Tommie, invited me to examine the papers and to write my study of the family.

Had I gained access to this material in 1959 I should have been able to connect the fumbling protest efforts of the 1920s to that re-emergence of Congress in 1957. Without it, though, there was a huge gap. There were no other papers in African hands that could rival the Samkange collection, which had required the coming together of a man who kept all the letters that he wrote and received, and a family which understood the value of this collection and who had the space in which to house it. Meanwhile I was collecting information on much more recent and much more distant events.

My claim in January 1960 that I was getting 'a whole sheaf of confidences' referred to information about what was going on at that moment. My ten hours a day in the National Archives was on much earlier material. In those days the Archives implemented a 30-year rule, so that in 1960 I could only see material up to 1930, and even then files for the later 1920s were often held back because they also contained material going on into the closed period. The material which I was allowed to see had not been produced by Africans. In those days the Archives Oral History collection was restricted to interviews with leading white Rhodesians. What *was* available was white observation of Africans – in the files of the army, the police, the CID, the Ministry of Justice, the Native Affairs Department – by every Rhodesian institution whose job it was to watch and report on them. The observers may not have understood what they were observing, but they watched any unusual movement like a hawk. They noted anything that seemed like a revival of 'traditional' politics; anything which seemed to link with movements elsewhere in central and southern Africa; anything which seemed to promise – or threaten – 'modern' forms of protest. Rhodesian administrators were even more disposed than I was to define almost every form of African political agency as 'political'. Rhodesian missionaries interpreted every African initiated church as a challenge to colonialism.

This meant that when I came to write *The African Voice in Southern Rhodesia* the material from the Archives sustained the treatment of an extraordinary variety of topics – chiefs and paramountcy movements; spirit mediums; African initiated churches; embryonic trade unions; witchcraft eradication movements. Official reports defined as 'political' material which even I was not prepared to include in the book. One of the ironies of my research career, indeed lay in the very first document I summoned up in the National Archives. It was a file labeled 'Drilling by African Mine Labour', and I called it up hoping it would describe militancy among the African proletariat. To my disgust it was about the uniformed Beni dance associations which had spread from east and central Africa during and after the First World War. It seemed about nothing else than fancy dress and I sent the file back without taking a note. Later I was to write a book about the Beni Societies (*Dance and Society in Eastern Africa*) in which I interpreted them as profoundly if ambiguously political. But I could never find that file in the National Archives again. (On the other hand I have come to see most African initiated churches as much less 'political' than the missionaries and Native Commissioners believed.)

One of the dangers of relying so heavily on the National Archives was that my 'nationalist ' assumptions went unchallenged and were indeed sustained. In the Archives, as in my book, all these various African responses were presented as part of a single anti-colonial response. It has taken me many more books, climaxing with *Voices From the Rocks*, to appreciate the infinite variety and internal contradictions of African responses.

But another danger of focusing on that material available in the National Archives was that it might make the period 1898 to 1930 seem trivial. Later on, Lord Blake, in his history of Southern Rhodesia, dismissed the inter-war years with aristocratic disdain. In the history of nations as in that of individuals, he said, long periods went by without anything very interesting happening. In fact, the two decades 1920 to 1940 were crucial to establishing and defining the Rhodesian system. But it was hard to see that in 1960. There were many moments when I wondered whether I had a significant subject at all, and whether the assorted movements, churches, unions, etc. had not been genuinely marginal. (I have been encouraged since then by the fact that some of the topics to which I devoted half a chapter have become the subjects of entire theses or books.)

Meanwhile, I was gaining that 'whole sheaf of confidences' about African politics in the early 1960s. Sketchley Samkange told me about the in-fighting within the NDP in the first half of 1960; Ndabaningi Sithole sent me copies of the negotiating documents for the 1961 constitutional conference; Joshua Nkomo confided in me his plans to form a government in exile in 1963. I have drawn on these confidences in writing this book. But they were of little use for the history of African politics I was beginning to write in the 1960s.

In the closed 30-year period African politics had changed so much that it seemed difficult to make a connection between 1960 and the 1920s. What I needed was what has come to be called 'personal reminiscence', of the sort I have made so much use of in my later books, especially *Bulawayo Burning*. Some of my reluctance to make use of this can no doubt be traced to my training as an Oxford historian. But in 1960 this sort of open-ended life history was despised by Africanists as well. Indeed, at the Leverhulme History Conference Jan Vansina distinguished between valuable oral tradition and subjective and unreliable personal memory.

So I responded to my dilemma not by making every effort to fill the gap through oral research but by following the documentary trail backwards. By October 1961, for instance, I was 'working on what remains of the material relevant to my work and hope especially to get something solid on the 1896 and 1897 risings here in Southern Rhodesia, how they were organized and so on.' A year later I had almost finished my research on the risings. As it turned out I was equipped to write two books. One – *The African Voice in Southern Rhodesia, 1898-1930* – drew on my earliest archival research. The other, *Revolt in Southern Rhodesia, 1896-7*, drew on the research I did in 1961 and 1962. They were published out of sequence so that the earlier research material supported the second book and the later supported that first book. I was also able to write a stream of commentary on the African politics of the 1960s, which form the subject of this book. But what I could not write was a consecutive narrative of African response from the 1890s to the 1960s. My trilogy on African politics in Southern Rhodesia remained 'frustrated'. Shelagh ought to have written her account of the Inkomo trials instead of waiting for me.

I knew that there were individuals who were still active in Congress in 1959 and who had been active in African politics in the late 1920s. The most conspicuous of these was the veteran Sergeant Masotsha Ndlovu, who had been Bulawayo leader of the Industrial and Commercial Workers' Union (ICU) in the late 1920s and early 1930s. Ndlovu had been active in Benjamin Burombo's African Voice Association, and in 1957 had joined Congress. In 1960 I was reading CID transcripts of his ICU speeches in the Archives and I was visiting Masotsha himself in Khami prison as a Congress detainee. In 1960 he was mainly concerned with getting a new set of false teeth. Neither he nor I talked about the past. Masotsha was a very present-minded man, but it astonishes me now that I did not try to question him about his activities between the early 1930s and his detention in 1959. He was, after all, literally a captive informant. At any rate, unable to get access to the Samkange papers and unready to collect personal reminiscence, there was a gaping hole in the middle of my narrative.

So, as I have said, I went backwards. Even here – in my narrative of the risings of 1896-7 – I could have sought oral evidence. In 1960 I was dealing, after all, with events only just over forty years old and there must have been both surviving personal reminiscence and family memory. Though it is hard for me to realize, we are further away now from the subject of this book than I was in 1960 to the great uprisings. But there was so much documentary material available for the risings in the Archives that my efforts were restricted to collecting it all before I was deported. Yet here at any rate I was never in any doubt that I had a grand theme. The events of 1896-7 offered me a chance to reconstruct a grand narrative in the way that African politics, 1898-1930, did not. Nor for that matter had seventeenth-century Anglo-Irish history offered the same opportunity. All those long-ago battles had been described and no seventeenth-century historian set out any longer to combine military, political and ideological history within a narrative framework. Writing about 1896-7 gave me a marvellous opportunity – however far short I was to fall – to write an epic account of the total encounter of two societies.

Many years later I discovered a cry of despair and hope to which, without my knowing it, *Revolt* had been a response. The *Bantu Mirror* – which in my unregenerate nationalist days I would not read because it was a paper for 'good boys' – had been running a series on Rhodesian history. The African journalist who wrote it had stayed close to the orthodox Rhodesian line until he got to 1896. But then he could not stand it any more. On 3 May 1956 he quoted from a 'well known' Rhodesian history book, debating with it with increasing fury. The book said that the Ndebele chiefs had 'fomented' the Shona rising. 'But they never did any such thing. They had enough on their hands in Matabeleland to worry about Mashonaland.' The book said that the Shona knew all about Ndebele cruelty and feared them much more than they did the whites. And yet the whites had been much more cruel. The book libeled the Shona as 'avaricious, cunning, great cowards, callous … with respect for nothing but brute force'. They had been 'treated for years with great, almost excessive, lenience by the white man'. The journalist could stand it no more. 'This is a good example of how a historian may be totally wrong in his assessment of a situation. The Mashona rebellion was actually caused by white excesses.' He concluded: 'It is high time somebody did rewrite this type of history before it is too late.' *Revolt in Southern Rhodesia* was just such an attempt at a rewriting.

# Discovering the Countryside

1960 had been an exhausting and dangerous year. We needed some escape from the political tension. In October I told my parents that 'the situation in Southern Rhodesia is going from bad to worse. I can see nothing likely to repair it. I am afraid that riots and shootings will continue and probably get worse and that the NDP may well be banned.' Tension had been increased by the emergence of a white terrorist organization, the Rhodesian Republican Army, which phoned our friends and us up and threatened to come and shoot us. In October Shelagh took refuge at the African Church of St Francis in Makoni district and we planned to spend Christmas there.

On 30 December 1960 I wrote to my parents about 'a marvellous Christmas':

> *I should like to describe St Francis but despair of doing so adequately. The first thing you notice is the church itself – one of the smallest and by far the nicest I have seen in Africa. It lies to your left as you come in and in front of you is Basil Nyabadza's white-washed house with its rickety green roof and the row of rooms which serve as kitchen, store houses and living places for the 'Mothers', the old lady members of the community. The whole*

*Mission is surrounded and infiltrated by trees and if you look down from the granite hill nearby you can at once pick out the Mission because of the greenness of the trees around it. If you look at it from this hill you are seeing it from behind and you notice the gardens which run along behind the houses and the duck pond and the cow byre. Seen from this angle the Mission looks like something out of seventeenth century Italy. The church particularly is a splendid creation. It is rather ramshackle but cared for most tenderly and always spotlessly clean. It has a tower which almost leans on the Pisa model and a choir gallery which shows alarming signs of collapse and an altar which is raised up by several steps, with doors which close across it on the Byzantine model.*

*The community began as a breakaway from the Anglican church. Basil Nyabadza's father was a catechist in the Anglican church, based in the area around St Faith's. Francis was a great preacher … He was something of a visionary – he had, Basil tells us, his special places for prayer in the hills around. Gradually he built up a devoted following and gradually built up hostility from others in the church. Eventually he went off to the area where St Francis now is to withdraw from the activity which was causing so much controversy. But he was followed there by many of his disciples and there they remained, having prayers among themselves and seeing visions and going every Sunday to the church at St Faith's for mass. Then they built the church.*

I explained that the young girl followers became an order of nuns. Basil succeeded his father and added hymns and canticles – 'Who is the God of St Francis? He is the God of the awesome and great rock.' Basil was not a great preacher or visionary. 'He has not tried to extend the community. He has concentrated on maintaining it [and] has made it much less poor.' The place was delightfully rustic. 'You see Basil one minute milking the cows and the next taking Evensong in his black cassock. One moment you see the Sisters coming home in a lorry in their blue or grey working clothes covered with mud from brick making – the next in church in their black and white habits singing fit to raise the roof. The whole place sings day and night.'

We had taken with us the great Swedish Lutheran missionary bishop, Bengt Sundkler, who had revolutionized the study of African initiated churches in his book, *Bantu Prophets* – he was 'bowled over' by St Francis. Shelagh and Patricia

Chater, who had moved to live at St Francis after the collapse of the St Faith's co-operative, taught the Sisters to sing a chorus from the Messiah. 'As for me I painted doors and mended window frames and made plasticine animals for the crib and sang the bass part in the Messiah chorus and decorated the Christmas tree and even gave a recital of extracts from operas for the benefit of the Sisters who had never heard opera before.'

> *On Christmas day everything was ready – the Handel chorus was splendidly sung. Church over, the presents were given out to the accompaniment of much singing and dancing. It was a sight to see the Sisters doing a sort of modified tribal dance! Then we had a great Christmas dinner of beef, for Basil had killed an ox. Then after Evensong the whole community sat around a log fire in the courtyard and ate more beef and sadza and Shelagh's Christmas cake and made speeches. The best moment for me was the christening of a bull, born on Christmas day by the noble name of Ranger. Its father was the bull Afrika; its mother astonishingly a cow named History.*

*Anna and Leslie Ranger (r.), with Shelagh Ranger (l.) and Basil Nyabadza, at St Francis, Christmas 1961.*

St Francis became almost as important to me as it was to Shelagh. Basil became one of my closest friends. I took my History Honours students to St Francis to explore the caves in which Chief Chingaira Makoni had been besieged in 1896. Its combination of prophetic Christianity, African peasant life, and sensitivity to landscape was reflected in my writing for decades to come. Basil reluctantly took part in a workshop I organized at UCRN on church and state in Southern Rhodesia. When I returned to Zimbabwe in 1980, and wanted to make a study of rural history and of the liberation war, St Francis was my natural base. It features in my *Peasant Consciousness and Guerrilla War*. It was always in my mind when I was writing about African initiated churches.

# CHAPTER SIX

# 1961

# Citizens Against the Colour Bar

For me personally 1961 was memorable for two things. First, Sketchley Samkange drowned at Mlanje on 20 May. Second, I at last took the attack on segregation to the streets of Salisbury with the formation of the Citizens Against the Colour Bar Association. There was a sort of link between the two events, both involving ordeal by water and both quite distinct from the activities of the NDP. Sketchley was in Malawi to escape from his disillusion with the NDP. His death enabled me to continue to think of him over the years as the pure nationalist knight who would never have become involved in the brutalities and corruptions of later nationalism. Moreover, it was thinking of Sketchley, as well as of Sarah and other people I loved, which brought me to find the colour bar literally intolerable. Very properly, Joshua Nkomo as President of the NDP took the view that a campaign against the colour bar was not a central nationalist concern. Africans wanted, he said, not to swim with whites in pools but in parliament. This was true, but the exposure of how deeply segregated Salisbury was at least called the bluff of a government which had launched the 'Build a Nation Campaign'. I was sufficiently independent of the NDP to be able to create and command a quite separate movement. As CACBA was a release, Sketchley's death was deeply and unmitigatedly tragic. CACBA activities, though often frightening, were also very entertaining. Then there was John and Shelagh's involvement in forming and running the Salisbury North branch of the NDP; their demonstration against Occupation Day in Cecil Square; and a climax to the year in which my father was assaulted in mistake for me. 1961 was the most packed year yet.

# The Death of Sketchley Samkange

On 17 May 1961 John and I joined Sketchley and Peter Mackay for a holiday in Mlanje. Sketchley had rejoiced in and worked for the success of the Malawi Congress Party but he could not see a role for himself in the NDP or in Southern Rhodesia. As for us, as John noted, 'we felt the particular delight that Mlanje has'. We climbed to the Chambe Plateau and had tea in the clean modern house of a forester. Sketchley drove to Blantyre to attend Dr Banda's dinner for the new governor. On Saturday 20 May – a glorious day of sun – John showed me a rock pool with no deeps, which made it 'a suitable place for Terry as a non-swimmer to disport'. Then he waded downstream to the main pool where Sketchley and two young men from the Malawi press were swimming. John went in. He did not see well without his glasses and did not recognize the African swimming near him. But the swimmer was in difficulties. 'I grabbed him by the hand and tried to pull him in. We struggled in the water. We both went right down. I remember looking up through the green water to the light. I fought to the surface and tried to swim. … I let go my grasp and swam to the shallow water to think what to do.' John still did not realize it had been Sketchley. But Peter dived in and brought the body out. 'I see that it is Sketchley – water pours out of his mouth.' I was then called down from my safe pool and Peter and John and I and the foresters took it in turns to give artificial respiration. 'From time to time water and vomit came up. But no real sign of life and no pulse. We work on. The light fades and lamps are brought from the house. It is, I think an hour and twenty minutes before the doctor comes. A middle aged lady, taciturn. I think she sees it is hopeless when she arrives.

'This is the most shattering thing that has ever happened', said Peter. 'There were a dozen things that could have prevented this. Pip had come to a full stop. He was desperately unhappy; he did not know what to do next.' The doctor thought Sketchley had had a heart attack and died in the water. But both John and I felt guilty. John because he felt that he 'could have saved Sketchley had I been more able, had I been braver', I because when the lamps were brought in I allowed myself to think how picturesque the scene was. Arrangements to fly the body to Harare were delayed. John and I resolved to drive straight down to Salisbury to see the family and Joyce Manguni, whom Sketchley had entrusted to my care when he expected a long sentence in 1960. We drove to Blantyre and found Chisiza's house full of women. John noted that one of them was Dorothy Masuka. 'I am nearer to breaking down that at any moment before. When we last saw her – it was our first time of seeing her – it was in the lounge of the Shire Highlands Hotel, five days ago. Peter had brought her and Chisiza and Sketchley. We had not seen Sketchley since he went back to Nyasaland. Then Sketchley, sitting at the back stoep at Mlanje, saying that he didn't really approve of Dorothy Masuka. She was shallow, he said, and wouldn't stay in Nyasaland without a boyfriend'.

We drove on to the ferry and on to Tete. I slept in the back seat. The car spluttered, dried up and came to a halt. We left it all night to cool down. Then next day we came to a wide river but 'found that we had no respectable implement in which to fetch water for the radiator. In the end I use my bush hat.' We limped to the Southern Rhodesian border. It was agreed that I should seek a lift to Mutoko, send a mechanic back for John and then try to hitch on to Salisbury. This worked and in the end we all got to Salisbury before the plane carrying Sketchley's body. Paid for by the Malawi Congress Party, and escorted by Stanlake, this flew in on Tuesday, 23 May. Guy and Molly and a hundred others were there. The funeral took place at 3 p.m. at the Samkange's farm, Tambaram, in Makwiro. 'The coffin was given by Malawi and there was a printed note, "Dr Banda and the Malawi People". We stood around the coffin singing. Michael Mawema hid his face in a handkerchief. The women wailed.'

A Nyasa spoke of 'how Dr Banda loved this young man and how he would have liked to come to this funeral himself … Michael Mawema talked about their work together when they formed the NDP and how they had been arrested together last year and shared the same cell. Sketchley had sung all through the night and said in the morning that if he died before freedom came he knew there would be others after him. He could make friends with people of all races and so we see the white people who are here today.'

The funeral was a deeply moving occasion. After it I drove to Walter Adams's house to report on what had happened, Walter's Russian-born wife, Tania, was there. She remarked that all the wailing was just a peasant custom and meant nothing. There was some truth in what she said but I was mortified and furious. Shelagh, meanwhile, had 'taken it much better than we had expected, partly because she was not there when it happened and partly because she really believes that it is all for the best'.

It was inevitable that within two weeks of Sketchley's death John and I should have taken two major multiracial initiatives, determined as we were not to let his causes die away.

## Legal Action and Divisions over the Constitution

African politics in 1961 was dominated by the issue of the new constitution negotiated between the British and Southern Rhodesian governments with the participation of Nkomo and Sithole. From London, Ndabaningi Sithole sent me copies of some of the key negotiating documents and it became clear that any agreement accepted by the NDP would have to involve a great deal of compromise.

Meanwhile. people impatient of compromise were launching a petrol-bombing campaign under the command of a mysterious 'General Chedu'. Others were shouting independence slogans, like the Nyasa 'Kwacha'.

On 10 January 1961 I wrote to Jane Symonds to comment on Nkomo, back from London:

> *Everything was in his hands ... If the others are to be kept in detention he should be arrested himself. I have heard Joshua speak twice since he returned from London – one at a meeting of 20,000. He seems to me to have gained greatly in stature. At the moment all is waiting for the constitutional talks. I am glad that Joshua came back at once so that he could take a firm grip on the situation here. If he had gone to the West Indies, as was at first announced, there would have been serious disaffection about the 'apology' and so on. But at the moment his authority seems very considerable. At the moment there is a big police hunt on for the petrol bombers. They have pulled in numbers of the Youth Council but so far failed to involve any of the 'mother body'. The Committee is going to provide a defence for them on the grounds that the penalties they face are large and that because of the police eagerness to get convictions there is a danger of injustice. We have been given money to pay for the defence from the collection taken at the meeting of the 20,000. This is a difficult business because any defence must look a little like tolerance if not approval of the bombing which was in fact not only a cowardly but also a futile business.*

On 5 April 1961 I wrote to tell her about the result of the original NDP cases. 'Sketchley Samkange's appeal was upheld in the High Court. Mawema, who was up on a charge under the Law and Order Act was acquitted. A number of prosecutions against people who shouted 'Kwacha' have been dropped. A very important victory was the abandonment of a charge against Nkala as a result of a ruling by the judge. This was a sedition case and the ruling had wide effects as a precedent. Michael Mawema's appeal comes up on May 5. We have decided to brief local men – Goldin and Chitepo – now that Maisels can no longer take the case.'

The Committee had also been following up the detention of 'vagrants'. 'The whole business has been a ridiculous failure. There are no trained social workers to run the camps: the numbers now involved are now very small; no further arrests are being made; it has, of course, no effect whatsoever upon the likelihood of riots; and it looks as if the whole thing will be quietly wound up in six months or so. At long last we are ready to bring suits against the Minister of Justice in the case of the men shot last October which I have been plugging away at in *Dissent*. Our solicitor has given it as his considered opinion that the shootings were in every case "totally unlawful".'

So the SRLAWF committee was riding high. But other news was less good. Nkomo had returned from the constitutional talks and given a press conference explaining why he had accepted the proposed new constitution. There were only to be 15 African seats but he put a great deal of stress on the idea of a Bill of Rights. I attended the press conference and sat there miserably at what seemed a failure by the NDP, unconvincingly defended. Nkomo's acceptance of the proposals was immediately repudiated by Leopold Takawira in London and Michael Mawema in Salisbury. Our detainee friends were very divided. On 15 February 1961 Maurice Nyagumbo wrote to Shelagh from Lupane:

> *The results of the constitutional talks were very disappointing.*
> *Franchise was raised instead of lowering it. Only 15 Africans in*
> *the Assembly House of 65 members. This is ridiculous. It seems*
> *as though the British Government is now believing the theory*
> *of the settler's government that partnership means white man's*
> *rule. Black man's rule means dictatorship. Anyway, we shall*
> *stand firm to our policy of votes for all, so that the people of all*
> *races in Zimbabwe may have a representative government. We*
> *believed that only by such a government can peace be expected.*
> *Yes, I know that some people might think a Bill of Rights might*
> *make our task an easy one. We should all remember that this*
> *Act will not work as it does in Britain and other Commonwealth*
> *countries. Here it is going to work in the sense the settlers will*
> *find necessary. And after the withdrawal of the British pow-*
> *ers from the colony's constitution the situation will be like that*
> *in South Africa. However we believe that nothing shall ever*
> *stop our great march to democracy which we all long for.*

By contrast, Chikerema and Nyandoro were firmly in favour of the constitutional agreement, on the grounds that after years of fruitless struggle it opened the door to pressure from inside the system.

An NDP Congress in Bulawayo in March agreed to accept the constitutional agreement, but only under very rigorous conditions. On 2 April 1961 Maurice wrote to Shelagh:

> *Thank God that the expected split in the NDP was avoid-*
> *ed at the recent Congress. But please approach the people at*
> *Marandellas and stop them from giving stupid statements to*
> *the press. If they won't be careful they are damaging their*
> *reputations outside. I personally am worried with a chap*
> *like [Edson] Sithole, whom the people believe to be an active*
> *younger chap. Now I am afraid he is spoiling himself. In-*
> *deed that is what the government intended to see. I hope you*
> *shall find it in your duty to go and see them on this issue.*

This revealed Maurice's confidence in Shelagh. But as I wrote to Jane Symonds on 3 April, 'unhappily there has been a good deal of tension at Marandellas culminating in a quarrel between the detainees there over the constitutional agreement. They are now divided into irreconcilable groups and since Shelagh and I have once again been totally banned from visiting there is little we can do to help the situation.'

But I did write an impertinent letter to Chikerema on 5 April:

> *My wife's mother has now arrived and would very much have*
> *liked to see you but unhappily as you may know the com-*
> *plete ban on either myself or Shelagh visiting Marandellas has*
> *now been re-imposed so that we cannot bring her there.*
>
> *I agree on the whole with the ideas you express about the con-*
> *stitutional agreement. But I cannot help thinking that it is a great*
> *pity that you in Marandellas who have been so united up to now*
> *and have successfully resisted every pressure put upon you should*
> *quarrel about an issue which has been settled now by the NDP*
> *Congress at Bulawayo. I have written to Mr Mhizha in the same*
> *terms and Mr Musarurwa has been to see him to tell him that the*
> *stand he is taking is no longer relevant now that this matter has*
> *been settled and that Michael Mawema has accepted the Congress*
> *decision. To my mind you ought all now to support the conditional*
> *acceptance which came out of the Bulawayo Congress. Anyone who*
> *knows you all will know how ridiculous it is to suppose that any of*
> *you could betray your principles and it seems a great tragedy that*
> *you should in any way have given your opponents an opportunity*
> *to make capital out of your decisions. I hope you will understand*
> *that I am not at all suggesting that you and George [Nyandoro] are*
> *at fault in this matter but merely that it seems a great pity that you*
> *should be divided, for instance, from Edson [Sithole] with whom*
> *you have worked since the days of the Youth League. Because you*

> *and George are the leaders it is in some ways your responsibility*
> *to try to achieve unity again among yourselves. I do not suggest,*
> *of course, that you should apologise to anyone but if you could*
> *find it possible to make a request to the prison authorities that*
> *Mr Mhizha be allowed to return to Marandellas and to write or*
> *speak to him on the lines that I have suggested – that it is ridicu-*
> *lous for old comrades to fall out in this way and that there should*
> *be unity at this moment – I think that you would then have done*
> *all you could towards effecting a reconciliation and Mhizha would*
> *be a most unreasonable man to refuse such a generous and frank*
> *overture from you and George. It is not my business, I know, to*
> *interfere in matters like this and I do not do so as Secretary of the*
> *Committee but merely as someone who considers himself a friend*
> *of all of you at Marandellas … I hope you will forgive me, there-*
> *fore, for the impertinence of suggesting a course of action to you.*

Alas, this letter did nothing to heal the rift. But on 14 May I reported to Jane the 'remarkably successful' progress of Mawema's appeal. 'The judge's decision makes it virtually impossible to use that section of the Unlawful Organisations Act in that way ever again and frees the NDP from the threat hanging over it. It also, of course, means that the Government's plan of action which was put into such costly effect last July has completely failed because all the appeals have been now been success-ful. There were three men then arrested … No charge was ever brought against Takawira; all charges against Sketchley Samkange were dismissed … and now the Mawema case has been decided in a way disastrous to the Government's hopes.'

On 28 May a number of leading young Indians came to see me. They talked about forming a Salisbury branch of the NDP and about the campaign I was organiz-ing against the colour bar. John and Suman Mehta went next day to see Ndabaningi Sithole who 'was very anxious that it should go ahead. He will let us have a list of all Salisbury European members tomorrow. We will then call a private meeting to which we will invite all the present NDP members in Salisbury and elect a commit-tee. Later on the branch will be inaugurated by a public meeting at which members of the Executive will be present.'

There was a good deal of misapprehension about the City Branch. NDP execu-tive members wanted it because it would display white and Asian support at a time when any support was welcome. In the event, however, the branch was overwhelm-ingly African in membership and John found himself the most democratic chairman of an NDP structure. The branch came to be an instrument of criticism, rather than of support, for the National Executive of the NDP. We wanted it because despite Sketchley's and Michael Mawema's experiences we took it for granted that the NDP was the people's party. But in fact in May the NDP was very weak. The tensions between nationalism and trade unionism had been exacerbated by Nkomo's threat to destroy industry, which the trade unionists could not support. Reuben Jamela and Michael Mawema appealed to trade unionists like Maluleke and there were discussions about a new party. In May, Jamela and Mawema were forced to make public statements repudiating that idea. But behind the scenes it was being planned, and it enjoyed the support of the Malawi Congress party. On 31 May I told John that I had been warned that 'many of the students will probably hesitate to join a Salisbury NDP branch because they are no longer sure that the NDP is the party to belong to'. 'This is very serious', noted John, 'and makes me feel once more that we ought to wait until the NDP leadership has been settled.'

On 31 May also I told Jane Symonds that, 'we learn that the Native Department expects there to be serious trouble at the end of this month as a result of African disillusionment with the outcome of the Constitutional talks and that steps are being taken to prepare against this'. On 8 June Michael Mawema publicly resigned from the NDP, 'and it now looks as if the announcement of a new party is imminent. It is referred to as the Zimbabwe Party.' The African students in Carr Saunders grouped together in sullen factions. On 10 June Michael Mawema and Patrick Matimba tried to announce the formation of a new Zimbabwe Party. They were manhandled and Patrick was beaten unconscious. John noted:

> *In a way it is a good thing that the new party has been so de-*
> *cisively rejected. But it is disgusting that this kind of treatment*
> *should be given to a man who has done so much for the move-*
> *ment as Michael Mawema … Yet even this incident may be*
> *better than two parties, endless retaliation, street fights.*

The next day I visited Mawema and met Matimba, both still confident. I went on to see Herbert Chitepo. 'Both seem very anxious to attract or keep Europeans. Herbert says he feels the NDP has neglected its Europeans and in future will be calling on them more often for ideas.' The City Branch still hung fire. On 13 June John learned from the young Madimutsa that the beatings were organized by the Youth League. 'Madimutsa is concerned to denigrate Mawema and to indicate that in effect great restraint has been observed. Mawema after all used violence to preserve unity when he was at the helm of the NDP … He falsely claimed to have founded the NDP.'

On 14 June, Joshua Nkomo spoke at UCRN to the African Current Affairs Association, John thought 'with fire and good humour'. He insisted that only 'when we have the vote will the time come for the parties to start and to seek votes from the people'. Mawema's new party, meanwhile, violently criticized Nkomo's initial acceptance of the 1961 constitution. Kwame Nkrumah called the NDP and ZNP leaders to Accra. As Nathan Shamuyarira told us later, when Nkrumah 'found out that their main charge was that Nkomo had accepted an agreement and then repudiated it he declared that this was a normal political procedure which he had been through himself several times. The leader often has to make the decisions and then returns to find that his party will not accept them. Provided he follows the will of his party and does not stand out against it he cannot be regarded as untrustworthy. The ZNP must come together with the NDP.' On 24 June John met Jamela in Highfield. He denied 'that the NDP conference was a great triumph for Nkomo and his group, for in fact they were very severely criticized – everything short of actually displacing them … Clearly Jamela has little faith in Nkomo and thinks that the strong differences inside the party may continue. He mentions a split between intellectuals and the people.'

Still the City Branch did not begin. By now the various factions of the NDP were seeking to mobilize support. A referendum on the constitutional proposals had been announced. Nyandoro and Chikerema, still in detention in Marandellas, urged *Dissent* to come out in support of the proposals and to campaign for a Yes vote in the referendum. Mugabe urged us to campaign for a No vote. In the end John and I tossed for it and one wrote the Against and the other the For articles. As I read them now I really cannot remember who wrote which.

On 25 June John and I lunched with Bernard Chidzero – on another of his agonized visits – at the Curry House, where we met with Gabriel Peters of the Christian Action Group and 'two enormous Indians who smiled benignly throughout the meal'. Mugabe came in to pick up Bernard and we took the opportunity to question him about the referendum. 'According to your own conscience', he says, gently closing his eyes and smiling.

On 20 June I had told Jane Symonds that 'the government has been cunning and has recently released all the detainees from prison only to thrust them into "restriction" at Gokwe. It means, of course, that the amenities such as lectures and film shows and so on are no longer available. It also means that visiting is a much more cumbrous business and, of course, Shelagh and I are once more banned from entering the area. However, Monica Brewer from Mukwapasi [the clinic at St Faith's] and Willie Musarurwa, our chairman, went to Gokwe last week end and saw them all. I fear they are divided between NDP and ZNP and it may be difficult to retain the confidence of all sides.'

Chikerema wrote to me from his new home on 16 June 1961:

*I had hoped to see you and Shelagh in Salisbury prison and to convey to you in person my hearty most condolences on the sudden death of our fellow freedom fighter, the late Sketchley Samkange. As we did not meet, may I say how sorry I am that you and some of our friends had to experience the shock and agony as the result of his sudden death. I know what it is to lose a dear friend and a colleague in an accident of that kind. The shock of it is quite unbearable. He was a fearless young man and a genuine friend of us all. The many of us who knew him intimately were terribly shocked …*

*Well, Terry, here we are in Gokwe. This place is not as bad as I had imagined it to be. Our chief complaint is about the climate of this area. I have never experienced this kind of heat! I understand it will be worse in two months time. We found ready made tin huts which are as hot as a furnace during the day. One can hardly stay in them. I suppose the idea on the part of the Native Department is to get us brainwashed with heat until we decide to return back to political 'cooling chambers'. If that is the case I am very sorry we are unable to assist them. Instead we are very busy contacting people in and outside our restriction area and pretty soon we will open branches of the NDP in and around us!! As far as I am concerned we are back to freedom of organization within our limited area.*

*I take this opportunity to thank you very heartily for the work you and the Committee undertook to assist us during our previous detention. This we will always remember. Now that we are virtually free, though in restriction, may I ask you sincerely to stop worrying for us now. George and I have discussed this matter and feel that you have done your best and you now need rest. We feel that you need not worry visiting us as this place is too far away. We will be able to take care of ourselves in most things. Jungle life is not known to all of us here. We will be able to cope with it.… The Lupane boys are here. In our section we live with four strong supporters of the NDP. The rest were sent to Mkumbwi I. We are very happy.*

On 11 August I told Jane that

*the general situation here is depressing at the moment, with the NDP in confusion and the UFP acting like bland dictators – banning public meetings so that we can all have a "rest", threatening to cut off BBC broadcasts and generally showing*

> *that they have been encouraged by the referendum result to feel*
> *very great men indeed. The restrictees are fighting the Native*
> *Department. They refuse to accept their allowances unless the*
> *Native Commissioner comes to pay them without a police es-*
> *cort and the NC refuses to come unless escorted by the police.*
> *Half of the restrictees crossed over the restriction area boundary*
> *and are awaiting trial on that. Few of the members of our Com-*
> *mittee are allowed to visit Gokwe and the last time we sent our*
> *welfare officer, Muchada, he was arrested on a charge of having*
> *stolen the Fund's motor cycle and kept in jail for more than 7*
> *hours! His letters were taken from him and, we suspect, copied.*

On 21 November I was obliged to report that Muchada had had to be laid off and that the Committee was 'in dire straits'. By contrast:

> *John Reed and I have recently been very active in the*
> *NDP. We are on the Executive of the Salisbury City*
> *Branch of which John is Chairman and have found*
> *ourselves giving speeches all over the place.*

# The Salisbury City Branch of the NDP

In this state of confusion the City Branch of the NDP was finally launched. Its opening meeting on 29 August 1961 was addresssed by Ndabaningi Sithole. It consisted of 60 members, a large African majority, the UCRN radicals and Asian supporters of nationalism. John Reed was elected Chair; Shelagh became Secretary. A key figure was the anti-discrimination activist, the much-admired Lovemore Chimonyo, who was the major translator of speeches between English and the vernaculars and hence had a great influence on proceedings. I was not elected to office and remained as a branch member, though I was regularly invited to speak to NDP meetings in the rural areas. Margaret Moore, the Quaker wife of the pacifist bank clerk Stanley, represented the northern suburbs. 'I dreaded this meeting as much as I have dreaded anything', noted John. 'Afterwards a great content'. On 6 September a Council of Women was set up for the branch. Teresa Chirunga made 'a fiery speech in Shona – all about the women going into action with their babies on their backs so that the police cannot fire on the men'. Shelagh was elected as chairwoman; Teresa as Secretary; Margaret Moore as Treasurer.

For several reasons the Branch was surprisingly influential. It operated at the heart of the white city and had the responsibility of confronting Rhodesian rituals of conquest, like Occupation Day. John Reed was an impeccably democratic chairman, so that although the Branch had the reputation of being 'academic', its resolutions faithfully reflected the majority view, which was suspicious of intellectuals. It was courted by national executive members who lobbied for their particular policies. Lovemore Chimonyo told John in early September, 'that we are regarded as a kind of model branch. Everyone is watching us.' John records me as saying to him, after a particularly difficult meeting, that 'with this branch we are attempting something very difficult indeed – much more ambitious than when we first thought when we mooted the idea of a few Europeans and Asians getting together'.

We found that the Harare district branches were planning a challenge to the NDP leadership. The Highfield branch wanted to get rid of all the present executive except Nkomo and Mugabe. 'The rank and file of the party are strongly opposed to participation in the elections. But the executive wants to take part.' Meanwhile, the City Branch itself faced an immediate challenge. The NDP executive declared that Pioneer Day, 12 September, should be a day of fasting and mourning. Nkomo and most of the executive would fast in Highfield. The City branch had to fast in Cecil Square, the ceremonial heart of white Rhodesia. Shelagh and John and Lovemore Chimonyo went down – I was teaching. John describes the event:

> *One of the two lads I am talking with points out Chimonyo approaching. He is greatly admired. 'If all Africans were like Chimonyo,' they say, 'we would have freedom today.' Under his arm Lovemore is carrying a rolled up leopard skin. I wonder with some alarm what this may be for. But he uses it not to wear it but merely to sit on.*
>
> *By now the ladies in their hats are coming for the ceremony, the consul generals and the commissioners. Dube from the branch appears, wearing very ragged clothes and bearing a placard painted with slogans ... Youth Leaguers are walking slowly up and down the aisles holding up placards ... I am surprised that they have not been immediately arrested ... Shelagh and Chimonyo have come and taken up positions on the grass to one side of where the ceremony is taking place. We sit on the grass ... They are playing God Save the Queen. Suddenly we are sitting on the grass not by ourselves but as a group of a hundred or so and the group grows as more and more Africans come to see what is going on, then themselves sit down. The police also surround it and on one side numbers of Europeans. In a moment it seems, without any planning we have a situation, we have a demonstration. It lasts a long while – well over an hour.*

> *It is tense and there seems no way of easing the tension ... There are a number of maidish old ladies. One comes to tell Shelagh to sit with her legs properly. 'You are showing everything.' Another rushes up to dance on the placards. A man throws a handful of peanuts at me ... A young man comes up to shout at Shelagh. I rebuke him for his rudeness. He tells me to go away from his country and says I am a kaffir lover. We are there for a long time.*

The police then brought dogs to break up the demonstration after Shelagh told them that 'she could not dismiss a meeting that had not been called'. John was assailed by a European who refused to believe that he was not Dr Ranger.

They then went to the much more peaceful setting of Highfield Post Office. Joshua Nkomo was dozing in an armchair listening to radio news about the Cecil Square incident. The *African Daily News* arrived with 'very good pictures of myself, Shelagh and Lovemore sitting in Cecil Square'. Then there were songs, climaxing with 'If you believe what Nkomo says Zimbabwe shall be free', which John describes as 'a very tedious song and it has to be repeated a great many times. But it is moving to sit here among so many people, in the cool.' The City Branch had passed its first test with flying colours.

Its next task, on 14 September, was to debate whether the NDP should take part in the parliamentary elections under the 1961 constitution. 'There is a great desire to speak. Very many people make their contributions. At the end we have a show of hands. Those against the NDP trying to get 15 members into parliament 103. Those in favour 3.'

The Cecil Square demonstration drew John into a public discussion of history. On 14 September the *Herald* published a letter from Colonel Hickman, a courteous ex-policeman who sat on one side of a National Archives table researching the early history of the BSAP while I at on the other side researching revolt. 'The last straw,' wrote Hickman now, 'was the conduct of a European woman and white man who sat on the grass and there reclined, chatting among themselves while the Last Post and Reveille were sounded and the National Anthem played – an unutterably sordid breach of decent conduct and therefore contemptible.' On 18 September John's reply was published. It was all a matter of historical interpretation. 'For those who believe that the coming of the Pioneer Column was for the good, it is proper that that they should thank God for it. Those of us who believe that the coming of the Pioneers and the subsequent conquest were an unfortunate foundation on which to build our country and an unhappy way for this part of Africa to make its transition into the modern world, have our right to keep this day as a day of mourning.' When

John next saw Silundika and Mugabe they thanked him for this letter.

This was at a meeting for Coloureds in Arcadia on 19 September. Silundika spoke, and Mugabe more briefly. John spoke 'about City Branch and democracy'. I told them: 'You have no choice except to join us. It may be a risk but it is a risk you have to take.' We were seeing quite a bit of the Mugabes. On 21 September Sally Mugabe spoke to the City women's meeting about Ghana and national dress. By this time the Branch had an office in Railway Avenue, staffed by Lovemore. John was more and more involved in NDP district activity. On 26 September he attended a district meeting which was largely taken up with 'wrangling about the secretariat ... Later on there is some political discussion tho even this has to arise out of complaints from one section of the party against another. I read a resolution I have prepared for Congress calling for the setting up of committees to study topics like Education, Land, Industry. This is acclaimed. But the suspicion that at party level nothing will ever get done leads to a proposal that we establish a committee at the Branch level to begin looking into these problems. I am put on this committee.'

On 5 October the branch met to choose delegates for a party Congress in Bulawayo on 21-22 October. Stanley and Margaret Moore and ten members were brought from Marlborough in the NDP bus. 'A good house, but a difficult meeting. Lovemore uses his position as translator to make my control of the meeting impossible.' Lovemore tried to get the Branch to endorse 'the detailed Highfield scheme for complete reshuffle'. John tried to get the City members' view. 'There is wholehearted support for Nkomo and wholehearted agreement to the idea that Geeorge Nyandoro and Robert Chikerema be brought on to the executive.'

Then John went out to Mondoro Reserve for a meeting at Mbayira. Everyone gathered to shake his hand. 'I feel very isolated and ashamed at not being able to speak the language. A curiosity around which everyone gathers.' By this stage police permission had to be sought for all speakers. John had been approved, along with Moyo from Mufakose. They were tape-recorded. The meeting began with mbira music and invocations of Chaminuka.

> *I have got used to finding in the towns Africa much like*
> *working class life in England. And now to come here re-*
> *vives in me the strangeness I felt as a boy going for the*
> *first time to the country, the people slightly pathet-*
> *ic yet frightening, so many of them just a little mad.*

On the way back Moyo told him 'of the religious element at the meeting. He speaks of Chaminuka and how when all the people are united behind the spirit of Chaminuka the bullets of the European guns will turn to water.'

The forthcoming Bulawayo conference was the first at which resolutions were to be received from branches. John submitted two from the City Branch to Silundika. Meanwhile, the Branch extended itself northwards. On 12 October there was an evening meeting at Margaret Moore's house in Mabelreign. John and I and Lovemore found twenty people gathered – 'party members from round about, the next door neighbour's house-boy, delivery men from the Redman Compound'. John talked about the Branch and there was then discussion of grievances.

> *As always it starts with land and cattle but by the end of the*
> *evening we have got on to the question of what needs to be*
> *done in the towns – wages, unemployment, benefits and old*
> *age pensions. The town worker is left breathtakingly with-*
> *out any security whatsoever. And it seems it is the return*
> *home to the Reserves and the belief that in the end one has*
> *a home and that this home is in the country that has made*
> *it possible for this deep neglect to continue for so long.*

Margaret Moore was elected Chair of a Mabelreign Ward Committee.

On 14 October there was a District meeting to discuss resolutions to the Bulawayo Congress. Apart from the two City Branch resolutions, all were from the Highfield Branch, 'written in a strange incomprehensible English'. John describes the 'meeting in the office in the corner, now used by the Publicity Department, amongst drifts of scrap paper or spoilt sheets. It is desperately hot. The meeting wears on through the afternoon and into the evening. There are uproars and at no time does the chairman seem in control of the meeting or even very anxious to control it. We have to discuss resolutions such as the President should be given full power to dismiss any member of the Executive. (We Africans know about dictatorship, We have always had dictators in the past); that the District should be abolished; that an NDP office should be started in Nyasaland as a retort to Banda's announcement that he will organise the Malawi Congress Party through Southern Rhodesia – usually interpeted as an intention to provide an organisation for the Zimbabwe National Party against the NDP.' Malachia Madimutsa, recently a schoolboy in Chipinge, defended Banda. 'Dr Banda has mainly criticised the party for its handling of the constitutional conference – and that handling was bad – and the party still hadn't said anything to repudiate the new consititution. Nyampaingidza calls him a Tshombe and they threaten each other.'

In these unpropitious circumstances, John, Lovemore and a university librarian, Eunice Herbst, set off for the Bulawayo Congress on 21 October. John booked a room at Jerry Vera's Happy Valley hotel. The Congress discussed whether to participate in elections. 'Speech after speech against participation', notes John. John got up and proposed that since the feeling seeemed to be against participation, the Chairman should call on anyone who wished to defend it –'and if no-one does that the vote be taken and we get on to a detailed discussion of how the constitution can be smashed'. This was agreed, but John notes that the meeting soon degenerated into a discussion of how to keep confidentiality and 'allegations that it is the young men who sell themselves to the government while we old men almost in our graves go on fighting for our freedom'. In the end all that could be decided was that the NDP Executive be left to decide the plan to fight against the new constitution – 'I imagine that this is what the Executive all along intended.' John was unhappy. In his opening speech Nkomo 'called on everyone who has a voting card to send it back to Whitehead. This is I am sure a mistake. I would myself have a powerful campaign to recruit voters – spoilt papers would be much better publicity than a boycott. The UFP would be puzzled and kept guessing … but it would be impossible to get up and explain a scheme like this to a meeting like this.'

That night the Salisbury District Executive planned to move a resolution next day of no confidence in the national leadership. This did not take place until after 9 p.m.

> *Sithole resigns the chairmanship to Takawira (who is suddenly at the meeting from London) and the Executive leave the front and go to sit in the meeting. Then Tekedi rises to launch the attack on the Executive. He is clearly not highly prepared and has little feeling for the mood of the meeting or how it can best be swayed. The speech is the usual stuff garnished with claims of policy failure: insubstantial resentment at behaviour, the failure of the strike, the use of cars on private business, being late in the office, the neglect of Nkala's wife when Nkala was sent to jail. The meeting grows restive and then obstreperous … Herbert Chitepo gets up and speaks in Shona in a low voice as if he were pleading with children. Bvunzahabaya from Highfield – where these people, Silundika, Mugabe all live – gets up and speaks. He says he is going to tell them what he has seen. From what he has seen (by this time he has lapsed into English as all the towns- people do when they get excited) they are all a bag of lazybones. At this, Mugabe, Silundika leap to their feet to protest against this insult. Uproar breaks out. Bvunzahabaya withdraws but by that time he could hardly be heard . It takes a great while to reduce the meeting to speakers one at a time again. The moral-*

> *izers say: "What are we here for? We are here to find ways of*
> *winning our freedom. We are not here to attack one another."*

By now it was nearly midnight. Lovemore's aunt 'receives the Mudzimu and does a few stately gyrations in the aisle – and strikes a pose just in front of Silundika, who is on his feet looking very annoyed. She keeps a fixed, aloof look. Then she makes a speech upbraiding these internal dissensions.' It was decided to adjourn and to return to the no-confidence motion in the morning. Outside they discovered serious rioting but managed to make their way back to the Happy Valley Hotel. 'Lovemore mentions that the hotel is owned by a UFP man, a stooge, and might well be an object of attack by the rioters.' And in fact the hotel was attacked the very next night. The next morning – 23 October – they went for a few hours to the McDonald Hall. Mukono began the attack, but much more skillfully, 'so that instead of rousing his audience with resentment with what he is saying he has them listening to him'. They left to drive back to Salisbury, Lovemore convinced that the no-confidence motion is to be carried, John sure that it would not be. And indeed it was not. The *Daily News* published a press statement issued by Mugabe, as publicity secretary. 'One district tried to move a vote of no confidence ... it was defeated.' Mugabe's statement emphasized that it had been resolved to return voters' cards; that Africans should not vote; that the ban on rural meetings be defied. Congress were 'worried about the conduct of the youth section and would like to have it properly established'. It was a neat tidying up of a chaotic Congress.

Back in Salisbury John and I reviewed our positions. 'I am made to feel deeply and dangerously committed,' noted John. 'I wonder if I was aware where I might find myself when I took the chairmanship of the Salisbury branch. Did I think hard enough?' According to John, I said that I was 'at the moment not anxious to get any more deeply involved with the NDP.' 'He wants to stay here and sooner or later one will be called upon to break the law and then one's career in Rhodesia comes to an end. Terry's fear is that he (or I for that matter) have only one chance to break the law. This is likely to be thrown away by the party on something pointless and not even be effective as a demonstration. This would certainly mean losing one's job at the university, prison, deportation.'

But on 25 October 1960 the Branch met and decided that John should remain chairman while he was out of the country on leave. 'Shelagh, now deeply again in the throes of the religious phase, resigned as Secretary.' Lovemore became Secretary. John attended a District Committee meeting on 28 October, 'a session for licking wounds after the defeat'. It was decided that Nkomo be asked to meet heads of branches, and that a Mashonaland Provincial Council be established. 'The real purpose of the Provincial Council is intended to be the extension of the influence of the Salisbury branches to the whole of Mashonaland, a process of education of the rural branches in the vicinity of Salisbury in the inequities of certain members of the Executive. There is a danger here. The Salisbury branches have obviously been impressed by the support the Executive has in Bulawayo. This could very easily start being formulated in tribal terms. And if a Mashonaland Provincial Council is set up and busies itself with the expulsion of certain leaders popular in Bulawayo then the party may well be split along very useless lines. On the other hand there should be a provincial council … I do not say a word.' At this point John had become frustrated: 'The attack on the NDP is starting … The trouble is that almost anything said about the NDP is likely to be partly true since the NDP is so large, scattered, disparate and undisciplined. The party is looking more and more brutal, unthinking, primitive and obstinate. The NDP is full of very angry young men – thrown out of jobs, beyond reason, beyond even the basic acceptance of tactics.'

John wanted the NDP to issue a blueprint for the new Zimbabwe. On 2 November he dined with Tranos Makombe, our ex-student, now active in the NDP. 'Tranos reveals that moves [towards] policy have been made but that it is impossible on the Executive to get agreement on any principle. Some want socialism, some want high capitalism. Still, some groups have been set up to formulate policies, very small groups made up of Executive members. It was intended to have policies ready for the Congress. Of course they were not ready in time. There is a two man committee on education. One member is Mugabe.' I spoke with Nkomo at much the same time and was given the came answer – any detailed policy would alienate those who did not agree with it. The NDP could only unite around the franchise.

And so John went to England. While he was away the NDP was banned and many of its members, including myself, were banned from public meetings or from entering the Reserves. On 13 December 1961 I wrote to Canon Collins about 'the arrest of women demonstrators'.

> *The situation is that a small emergency committee has been formed to deal with the particular problems of the women, which expected to be in existence for only a few weeks. The new committee is entitled the Women's League, Aid and Welfare Committee. Its chair-woman is Mrs Victoria Chitepo; its Secretary is Mrs Angeline Kamba, a university graduate and wife of the solicitor, Walter Kamba, and there are four other African members of the committee. My wife is also a member. The new committee has already*

*received a donation from SRLAWF committee which is well content to leave the business in the hands of people who so well know the situation and who have already been so active in prison visiting. We will allocate £50 a week …. At the moment the women themselves evidently desire not to be defended or to pay their fines but to serve their jail sentences – which are quite long ones of 10 weeks or so. The new committee is at the moment, therefore, purely welfare in its operation. I think myself that the women's resolution, though thoroughly commendable, may not endure for ever, especially since the banning of the NDP. The welfare need for the women is acute and the new committee have done excellent work on this. For instance one woman is a widow who has 8 children to care for: the new committee has arranged to look after them while she is in jail.'*

*… I should say something about the general situation here. So far very few leaders or members of the NDP have been arrested so there has been no actual call for the Committee to respond to our latest emergency. The Government's intention appears to be to control the leaders by prohibiting them from attending public meetings for three months and from entering Reserves and Tribal Territories for a similar time. This order, which has been applied to scores of people, including myself, is in many cases a real hardship. Take the case of Mr Chimonyo who was working as paid Secretary for the Salisbury City Branch of the NDP. He is now without a job and he is debarred from going to his home in the Reserves … The NDP ex-leaders have not attempted to organize overt demonstrations against the ban. Their policy is rather to make it ridiculous by starting up another party as soon as the general ban on meetings makes it possible to do so. The interim leadership of the new party will be different from old NDP executive … It is in this connection that our famous Mawema case is important because its outcomes prevents the Government from dealing with the situation under section 4 of the Unlawful Organisations Act.*

*My own house was searched and my file of correspondence with you seized by the CID, in whose hands it now is. I surmise that they took that particular file because they were interested in the question of supply of money from outside, though if they expected to find you issuing instructions on behalf of a foreign power they must be rather disappointed.*

John, in England meanwhile, allowed himself a little complaint. Although he was Chair of a branch he was not restricted, nor was his house searched. Yet I, a mere party member, had experienced these fates. On reflection, John concluded that I had been acted against not because of my significance in the NDP, 'but because he is Ranger'.

# Being Ranger in 1961

There was no doubt that in 1961 the name Ranger attracted wide opprobrium among Rhodesian whites. Shelagh took some clothes into the second-hand shop and was told they would not sell anything that had been worn by me. She went with Clive Wake's mother to stay in the Black Mountain Inn, Cashel, one of the unpretentious hotels which have been swept away by the guerrilla war, white outmigration and the rise of international tourism. When she signed the register the pleasant manageress commiserated with her – 'You poor dear, having the same name as that awful man.' 'It is often an embarrassment,' said Shelagh treacherously.

Undoubtedly it was the colour bar campaign which gave rise to most of this hatred. But during 1961 I was also active in nationalism in ways which showed that negative white responses to the name Ranger were balanced by positive African ones. The most dramatic example of this came in June 1961. At this time Dr Banda was denouncing UCRN, withdrawing Nyasa students, and proclaiming his intention to have his own national university. All contact between him and the College seemed to have broken down. But on 22 June I received a telegram: 'Kamuzu needs you. Come at once.' Walter Adams agreed that I must go, even though it was term time. So I flew to Blantyre on 23 June and the next day was ushered into Banda's study, with its carvings representing the Chiradzulu protest tradition, from John Chilembwe's revolt in 1915 to the present. 'You are the only man from that place I would talk to,' said Banda. And then he asked me exactly how much, to the penny, had been spent on UCRN so that he could ask American donors for the same amount. Of course I did not know and was irritated to have been brought so far on a wild-goose chase. My irritation showed, and to placate me Banda promised that I could go out to a political rally at Mlanje the next day. I would travel with Rose Chibambo, chair of the Women's League.

When the moment came, however, this was deemed too grand, and so I travelled in the Land Rover designated to take back the presents which would be given to Dr Banda. I witnessed the remarkable rally. Gowns were bestowed on prison graduates. Banda spoke at length. 'The stupid Federalists ask what will happen if Dr Banda dies. I am never going to die.' (And in the decades that followed I almost came to think that he was right.) Many presents were given including livestock. But I did not have to travel back with them; Peter Mackay came from Mlanje Hotel and took me there for the night. I told John when I returned that I had 'been able to feel that Mlanje was a place of peace and delight and not a place of doom'.

On 1 July 1961 I wrote to tell Chikerema in Gokwe about the visit:

> *Going to see Kamuzu is a complicated business. First I had to get leave from College. Then I had to go to the NDP office so that they would not think I was sneaking off to conspire behind their backs. Then off I flew wondering what he wanted to see me about. I was met at Chileka by Aleke Banda and taken to Ryall's at Malawi expense. No-one could tell me what it was about. Then at 4.30 I was driven to Dr Banda's castellated house with its guards and waited in the 'Kenyatta Room' for the great man to appear. There is a huge picture of Kenyatta on the wall: on the mantel-piece there is a wooden hut with the legend 'CHIRADZULU: THE DAWN COMES: 1915: 1953: 1959', and a carving of Dr Banda about to spear Sir Roy Welensky, though you would not recognize either figure. Then Banda came in, and to my astonishment – and I must admit to my indignation at first – it transpired that what he wanted me so urgently for was merely that I should tell him how much the University College cost in capital grants. And I did not even know! Still, I was honoured to be the only one of that 'so-called university' that he would talk to and interested to hear of his plans to start a College in 18 months time. It looks as if he has the money and the men promised from America so we may see the Livingstonia College flourishing before long. I was also interested to talk to him about Southern Rhodesia. He is bitterly against the Constitution and said he hoped it would be rejected at the Referendum. He was bitterly critical of Nkomo, but he was shaken when I told him – I hope rightly – that you and George were still NDP supporters. He admitted that he respected your judgement and integrity highly and obviously began to wonder about whether his previous assessment of the situation was sound. Next day I went out to Mlanje in his election convoy and saw crowds cheer him all along the road, throwing flowers – and flour – as he went by. There were 30,000 people at the Mlanje meeting and it was somehow the best possible way to come back to the place where Sketchley died. I had not thought I would easily be able to go back to the Mlanje Mountains*

*Hotel where we were when it happened, but that night I stayed
there with Peter and we talked for hours and everything was all
right. So my urgent visit to Nyasaland was worth while after all.*

I ended by telling Chikerema that 'I am now looking at some fascinating files on
the Portuguese rebellion of 1917. Do you know anything about it? I want to find out
if I can what has happened in the region today and whether there is a paramount
chief Makombe any longer. I will send it to you when I have written it up. I am sorry
that we shall not be able to meet until you are either out or I am in but until then
my best regards.'

Chikerema replied on 31 August 1961, apologizing for the delay and explaining
he had been in prison. He went on:

> *Your visit to Nyasaland interested me and now that the Ma-
> lawi people are in full control of the territorial government
> it will be easy for Dr Banda to raise the necessary funds for
> a University College in Malawi. Furthermore it was good to
> know that Dr Banda considers you a good advisor on mat-
> ters of such great importance. I hope you have now managed
> to obtain for him the necessary information. Who knows he
> may one day ask you to be the first Principal of the Malawi
> University College. And if I were you I would take the job.*
>
> *You were quite right to inform Kamuzu that George and I were
> solidly behind the NDP. And we intend to remain so. It would be
> disastrous in my opinion to the solidarity of our nationalist forces in
> 'Zimbabwe' were we to allow emotions to run wild with the winds
> of disappointment and frustration brought about by the new Consti-
> tution. Some of us conditioned our minds long before the constitu-
> tional conference to strenuous struggle against the continuous exist-
> ence of a rule by minority in this part of Africa. Thus the outcome
> of the constitutional conference was not a great shock to us. What
> is of importance now is to keep our nationalist forces intact, avoid
> any divisions and continue the struggle. And for this we require
> the moral support of the peoples of Malawi at all times. I would
> humbly ask you whenever you can to impress this on Dr Banda.
> His statement of support for ZNP (sometime back) served no other
> purposes but caused disunity between the Malawi Congress Party
> and the NDP to the great pleasure of Sir Edgar and Sir Roy.*
>
> *I hope you will be able to influence the course of events in*

*the NDP. I have written at length to Shelagh about my feel-*
*ings regarding the difficulties facing the party. I am person-*
*ally prepared to see the party continuing the struggle outside*
*the constitution until such time as we are able continue our*
*short term and long term policies without alienating the sup-*
*port of our pan-African friends. I may be wrong but I would*
*like to know your assessment of our present predicament.*

The NDP rural meetings to which I was invited to speak were also evidence of the prestige of the name. The one I best remember was in Mrewa where the popular chief Mangwende had been deposed for his opposition to the Land Husbandry Act. I was asked to speak for fifteen minutes. But when I arrived I found that I was the only speaker cleared by the police to have turned up. All the others had gone to other meetings. As I began my oration the chairman passed me a note – 'Please speak for three hours.' As a university lecturer I was able to manage an hour, which was doubled by enthusiastic simultaneous translation. Songs and dances and spirit possessions filled up the rest of the time. I have no notes of what I said, though my next banning order quoted from the tape-recorded text some not very revolutionary stuff comparing Sir Edgar Whitehead to the headmaster of a bad primary school. At any rate the audience was delighted, and when the meeting was over my car was bodily lifted and it was announced that it would be carried back all the way to Salisbury where we would all demand the reinstatement of the chief. It proved much too far and the porters dropped my car off after a mile.

## The Campaign Against the Colour Bar

In 1961 I at last took the fight against segregation on to the streets of Salisbury. On 14 May 1961 I wrote to Jane Symonds of the Africa Bureau:

*I have somehow got myself into the position of planner in chief*
*of an anti-colour-bar demonstration in Salisbury. The idea is*
*to have a small and despotic controlling committee which briefs*
*lawyers to give then an opinion about the legality of a particular*
*course of action and on the basis of that opinion devise a pro-*
*gramme. This committee controls at least 200 disciplined dem-*
*onstrators who are briefed by it and report back to it. The first*
*plan is to attack the segregated bus system and we are awaiting*
*our lawyer's report now. If he finds –as I expect – that there*
*is no legal basis for the segregation and if he finds that a test*
*case could be brought if an African is denied access to a bus, we*

*shall plan on assault on the bus services over one week-end.*

When I discussed this with Chikerema and Nyandoro in prison they urged that I get myself and the other demonstrators arrested. But this was not my idea. The penalties for refusing to obey a legal instruction in Southern Rhodesia were so severe that I did not feel one could ask students and other volunteers to risk them. My aim was to protest against the colour bar within the law but in ways which put effective pressure on hotels and restaurants and cinemas. CACBA had devised ingenious ways of doing this. We would use white members to make block bookings in theatres and cinemas, or to order sumptuous banquets in hotels, so that when our mixed-race teams turned up and were turned away there were embarrassing gaps and wasted meals. We would send small groups into a hotel every half hour so that the manager would have to come regularly to ask us to leave. All this was within the law, and in the end the law turned out to be our best ally as a series of court judgements declared discriminatory practices illegal.

I had many allies. The radical Asians, and especially Sulman Mehta, were keen to volunteer and to take test cases to court. Many of the UCRN African students and a few of the whites took part in the demonstrations. And a great source of legitimacy among nationalists was the participation of the 'freedom sitter', Lovemore Chimonyo. As we have seen, Lovemore was active in the NDP. He was also famous for his actions against the colour bar. *Drum* magazine in November 1961 carried a story about him captioned 'The Man who fights Racialism with his Bottom', fully illustrating and describing his sit-in campaigns. 'Chimonyo's All-Conquering Bottom' narrated his exploits in the countryside as well as in the towns. So his participation in our urban campaign was a great advantage.

On 23 May I wrote to Jane that 'my colour bar campaign is more or less ready. We have our legal opinions and our volunteers and early next week there will be a final briefing meeting. It has the support of organizations as various as the NDP, Capricorn, the Asian Association, the Christian Action Group (of course) ... I hope it is going to develop into something quite formidable.' Citizens Against the Colour Bar Association – an ironic name since I had just been denied citizenship – was inaugurated on 8 June 1961. John Reed describes the meeting:

> It begins with a speech by Trevor Wheeldon who has asked Terry for permission to address the audience because he feels strongly that the time is very inappropriate for a campaign of this sort. And Terry with due liberal principle has given him the opportunity. His argument is that the publicity and upheaval of such a campaign is likely to prejudice the chances of an acceptance of the

*constitutional proposals at the referendum. And that whatever
one thinks of these proposals they are at least a step in the right
direction and if the referendum goes against the proposals and a
Dominion Party government is returned to power we face a future
of bloodshed. He speaks well. Terry replies, saying that he does
not believe that a campaign of this sort is likely to influence the
result of the referendum or not to influence it unfavourably …
The government has already risked deeply offending right wing
opinion by publishing at the pressure of the CAP its proposals
for modifying the Land Apportionment Act. Furthermore there is
always an excuse for postponement. After the referendum it will
be the election. After that the Federal elections. The movement
now has its momentum, it has had its publicity, to draw back
now would be to waste all this and to convince even more firmly those who believe that a multi-racial project like this simply
cannot work. Whatever we do the protests against the colour bar
will go on – they have been going on in Bulawayo and the NDP
will no doubt continue them in Salisbury. An African rises and
makes an impassioned plea that the time can never be wrong for
acting in a just, peaceable, Christian manner … 'There is little
point in voting. Those who feel they cannot take part can leave.'*

So I was elected as Chair, Reverend Henry Kachidza as Vice-Chair, and Laloo,
one of the Asian radicals, as Treasurer. There was discussion of targets and the action to be taken against them.

Maurice Nyagumbo wrote to Shelagh from Lupane on 3 June. 'I hope Dr won't
get himself in jail with his new activities. It seems very dangerous to me. Is it the
same thing, or the same group, where Lovemore Chimonyo and others are said to
be operating? I wish them all a success.' He added that 'Nkomo was here some two
weeks ago and promised us to come and address the local branch soon. We didn't
say anything against him or show any sign of discontent of his leadership. But the
other group booed at him and called him a sell-out … Oh, Shelagh, the news of S.
Samkange's death was a blow to us all here. We shall always miss him in our freedom struggle.'

On 20 June I wrote to Jane:

*It does seem as if the Colour Bar campaign has begun well. We
have planned operations with a military thoroughness and so far
there have been no mistakes. I have more than 200 really very
enthusiastic and splendid volunteers and a fair bit of cash in hand.*

*And there are definite signs of cracking. The Ambassador Hotel
announced that it was going multi-racial last week end, eight days
after we demonstrated against it, though we do not count that as
one of our gains since negotiations must have been in progress for
some time. The cinemas have taken a decision in the last week,
though it has not yet been announced, to integrate at the end of
July, and we think that our two large-scale demonstrations, the last
one on Saturday, involving 100 volunteers, have had an effect. We
demonstrated just over a week ago with 50 volunteers and were
told that it was against the policy of the company and against the
law and so on: but last Saturday the manager went out of his way
to indicate that there would be a change soon. We have met some
of the smaller proprietors and, I think, persuaded them to negotiate
with government for legislation outlawing segregation, with compensation clauses. It is the compensation they are interested in but
I think we persuaded them that integration was coming and that
they should protect themselves ... Add to all this the collapse of the
buses before the NDP demonstrators and it is not too bad ... The
Dominion Party have made a great fuss, demanding my deportation and the banning of the organization, and I have had a number
of threats and so on, but the general public reaction has been one
of indifference ... No Alabama style riots here, though our Teddy
Boys rabbled the last group of demonstrators on Saturday night.*

On June 22 Shelagh wrote to George Nyandoro in Gokwe, telling him about her
busy life and the high morale of the CACBA volunteers.

*Now that I am working in Hermes Books with Jenny Frost (the shop
is in Cameron Street between Manica Road and Speke Avenue)
everyone comes in to see me and tell me all their troubles. It is
jolly nice really and I don't mind a bit and of course I am terribly
lucky to have a boss like Jenny who never says a word. So the shop
is full of Lovemore Chimonyo and his followers telling me about
their latest exploits or some of the delegates to the NDP Congress telling me about their plans, or a member of the Christian
Action Group wanting to know about the proposed expedition to
Mukwapasi Clinic over Rhodes and Founders weekend (we are
forming a work party to paint the clinic). It is a job that might
have been designed for me really: an educational bookshop for
Africans run by the right sort of people in the right sort of way*

*and serving a useful purpose. I can make use of my small talents – typing and bookkeeping. The Citizens Against the Colour Bar march on. Terry has been spending far too much time on it when he ought to be teaching and looking after his students, but of course he loves it and doesn't mind a bit when MPs suggested he should be deported. One of the best things about the campaign is the sort of spirit of cooperation which it has engendered amongst those taking part. I suppose it is like soldiers going into battle. They have a real feeling of comradeship which is quite inspiring.*

John, over-generously, remarks in his diary that he did not believe I was frightened by anything. But he also records my joking that there were two forms of courage – the courage of the subaltern leading his men over the top, and the courage of the staff officer who had to plan the whole operation. Mine was the courage of the staff officer. In fact I did lead 'platoons' on the ground – my particular target being a Chinese restaurant which admitted Japanese but not Chinese. But it was true that every operation needed detailed planning, the allocation of tasks, and a system of report back and response. We would meet at the Capitol Club, select mixed race groups of volunteers, and either Shelagh or I would stand by the phone for reports of developments. And that was scary. There seemed all too much likelihood of white violence. A shadowy organization called the Rhodesian Vigilance Association emerged in mid-June, calling upon whites to defend civilization and accusing CACBA of breaking the law. The Vigilance Association said that it would 'deal with CACBA behind the scenes'. As John noted, 'there may be trouble on Saturday' at the second wave of demonstrations. His diary records his own fears of hordes of 'hairy Afrikaners' ready to defend Meikles Hotel with violence. In the event, fortunately, when John took a multiracial group of volunteers to the cinema on 17 June they encountered 'a crowd of youths in leather jackets who are clearly not friendly. But they look a wretched and dispirited lot, hardly dangerous.' Throughout the campaign, although there were many death threats no action followed.

Amidst the crowded events of those weeks some impressions stand out. One is my negotiations with hotel managers. We were targeting Meikles in particular, sending in as many as eight teams in an afternoon. Meikles was the bastion of Rhodesian tradition, situated at its ritual heart. It was also the hotel at which international journalists stayed. Regular sit-ins were reported and photographed and Meikles was embarrassed. I was called in to a meeting with managers and asked whether I would be reasonable enough to accept a screened-off part of the dining room where Africans could eat without being seen. With all the self-confidence of a 30-year-old I dismissed such an idea with scorn The same pattern followed in theatres and cinemas. It was not long before I was able to report to my parents, and John to confide to his diary, that hotels and cinemas intended to go multiracial.

But the spectacular event took place at the Les Brown Swimming Pool. The Salisbury Council rigorously segregated pools. Sociologists at UCRN, doing research on race attitudes, reported that prejudice was greatest on occasions when people were lying down and least when they were standing up. Sir Edgar Whitehead was reported to be basing his very slow desegregation on this basis. Lying down in water seemed to be worse than all. So I took a mixed group to swim at the Les Brown pool. On 19 August I described to my parents what happened:

> *Yesterday a group of about 20 of us, black, brown and white, went to the Baths on their opening day. I was not in swimming trunks – too cold, can't swim, no longer have the figure. I ordered my troops to be very careful and those who were dressed and did not intend to swim were to stand away from the pool. Everything went well. The Europeans jeered but our demonstrators took no notice and dived and swam happily enough. Then at the very end the local TV people asked me and our chief African demonstrator (Lovemore Chimonyo) to appear before the camera – with one's back to the pool near the edge. Before you could say 'Sir Edgar Whitehead' a small racist dashed out of the crowd, gave me a sharp push and I was in – the shallow end fortunately. As I clambered out all the press photographers were snapping away – I managed to climb out with a cheerful smile and conduct myself with what degree of non-violent dignity was possible under the circumstances and this display of gentility earned me the caption - 'well bred – and dripping'. This lark caused a bit of a fracas during which one of our less non-violent demonstrators [Jaap van Velsen] became involved with a by-stander who turned out to be reactionary champion all-in wrestler.*
>
> *People say we should not tackle the baths first. I disagree. Time is short. Only with shock to their prejudices can we move the whites to integration as they have in Kenya. Generally pressure is on. The cinemas will soon go multi-racial. The baths cannot resist if we go on fighting them. This swimming fight is crucial. If the whites lose it they have lost all round. If we lose it will certainly put things back. But I think we shall win.*

These dramatic events pleased Chikerema and Nyandoro. 'Let me observe,' Chikerema wrote on 31 August 1961, 'that the campaign against the colour bar has been doing a fine job, but must ask you to be very, very careful and never stand near a swimming pool while fully clothed and without a swimming suit! This country is full of savages who will never hesitate pushing a fully clothed leader of the "Freedom Swimmers" into a swimming pool. We were disgusted by the manner in which they treated Dr van Velsen.' I was soon proved right about the success of the campaign but not before a great deal of mockery. 'Attacks on Terry of a more sickening sort continue,' noted John. 'I wonder if I could stand up to it as well as he does.' Even Trevor-Roper in Oxford wrote to me to exclaim how dynamic my life was. But on the baths we won totally.

On 18 October I wrote to my parents:

> *The colour bar campaign has suddenly broken through. The test case we brought against the Salisbury City Council has trium-phantly succeeded – to a degree beyond our wildest expectations. It introduces for the first time in Southern Africa the American ruling that separate facilities necessarily involve injurious dis-crimination; it means that no public facility can be segregated; and it undercuts most of the excuses offered by restaurants and hotel owners. Branches of CACBA have sprung up in other towns in Southern Rhodesia and pressure is now really on. I think that by next year most if not all of the public colour bar will have been dismantled. So I feel an almost awed delight in the success of the campaign, even if we were kicking at a half-open door.*

On 25 October I wrote to George Nyandoro to say that I was 'going ahead with the Colour Bar thing although Joshua has made it plain that it is not of political significance. I am sure he is right on this. When we began I spoke to Sithole and Mugabe and said that this was something which the NDP could not do because it would lay emphasis upon something which was not a political essential and I was sorry that the Highfield branch did go into action so that the party came to be asso-ciated with the attack. On the other hand I still feel that it is important to continue the attack so that the present confusion in the European mind is maintained. The colour bar and swimming may not be important to Africans but it is important to Europeans and may well create so much despair among the reactionaries that it will be difficult for them to make a last ditch stand. They want political power to keep the schools and baths white and if this fails they will be that much less interested in holding on to political power. So you will see a series of court actions in the future.'

And I ended by telling George, whose ancestor had taken part in the 1896 rebellion, that my paper on the Makombe rising was being duplicated and that I would send it to him for comment.

On 21 November I wrote to Jane Symonds:

> *The echoes of the great swimming pool controversy have never entirely died away. Leaving aside the broad farce of the affair the situation is now roughly as follows. When the Salisbury City Council yielded to pressure and shut the baths again to non-Europeans, a member of the CACBA executive and also of the Salisbury Asian Association, Mr S.N. Mehta, brought an action against them for refusing his admission to the baths. The case was heard before the Chief Justice of Southern Rhodesia whose judgement was a real landmark in the legal and political history of southern Africa. He found that the Council had acted illegally in refusing admission to Mr Mehta and to other non-Europeans. He found that although there was no tangible discrimination involved, because Asians were able to swim in pools of roughly equal excellence, there was discrimination to a substantial degree of an intangible character and that Mr Mehta had suffered grave injury to his 'dignitas'. By so finding he accepted some of the American precedents for the first time in Southern Africa.*

I told her that the campaign was coming off the streets and into the courts – 'more dignified and less dangerous [but] also very much more expensive'. And our next target would be the core of the system of white privilege – segregated education.

## History

By 1961 I knew what I wanted to research and was busy researching it. Slowly the papers were coming. In October I sent an article to the St Antony's collected papers on Africa – 'Revolt in Portuguese East Africa. The Makombe Rising of 1917'. John recorded that 'the triumphant rumble' of my typewriter could be heard throughout Carr Saunders Hall. He also recorded my Faculty Lecture later in the year on the early history of African independent churches, somewhat apologetically introduced by Professor Mackenzie who implied that I might be a pain in the neck but I was a very good historian. These were both over-enthusiastically received.

Both really illustrated the dangers of partial knowledge. I wrote the paper about an African revolt in Mozambique without using any documentation in Portuguese and without interviewing any of the African survivors. This was only possible because

Rhodesian administrators were so unsympathetic to the Portuguese and so ready to record the grievances of their colonial subjects. As for the African churches, the 30-year access rule made it impossible to realize how important the apostolic movements of the 1930s had been. The Manicaland churches of the mid-1930s had given rise to million-strong churches throughout southern Africa but my problematic was to explain how insignificant African churches had been before 1930 in Rhodesia in comparison with Kenya and South Africa! One ought not to write until one has the full picture, but the only way to get the full picture was to write. Even when *Revolt in Southern Rhodesia* was published in 1967, I was still inadequately informed.

## The banning of the NDP and after

On November 29 1961 I wrote to John Reed, who was in West Africa. I told him there was 'a horror meeting' of the NDP due for the following Sunday, beginning at 8.30 and going on to 2.30 with two speakers from each branch. Lovemore Chimonyo and I were to be the speakers for the Salisbury City Branch. On 11 December I wrote to describe the meeting. Before I arrived, Joshua Nkomo had asked everyone to take off their shoes as a symbol that we were prepared to destroy industry if industrial interests blocked political change. I arrived to find everyone shoeless and after about two hours I whispered to Herbert Chitepo that I felt conspicuous wearing shoes and that perhaps I had better take them off. 'Oh, no, you don't need to,' he replied. But the moral pressure of all those bare feet got to me and I took my own shoes off:

> *The shoe business was something of a farce, I agree, and your*
> *fear that by the time you return we shall be stark naked has been*
> *echoed in a number of derisive European comments here … The*
> *meeting itself was something of an anxiety. As you know I had*
> *consistently avoided speaking in Harare or Highfield before and*
> *had reluctantly decided to do so this time as one could not go on*
> *avoiding it for ever. I was in a whole variety of anxieties about it:*
> *would the press blow it up into a big thing: would my audience let*
> *me get away with what I had to say: and when I finally arrived*
> *at the meeting would it end without a riot. I do not know how*
> *many people there were – estimates vary from 20,000 to 10,000.*
> *Anyway, the whole area outside the Cyril Jennings Hall was packed*
> *so tight that it was hardly possible to move. As you know there is*
> *a wire fence around the area which enclosed this great mass: and*
> *in a circle round the wire fence were ranged police trucks with*

*armed police on top of them – armed with tear gas and riot guns*
*which they held very obviously throughout the proceedings, every*
*now and then taking aim at one of the speakers. Had there been*
*any kind of trouble there could have been an awful catastrophe. If*
*the police had fired shots there would have been nowhere for the*
*crowd to escape since to leave the area would have meant running*
*straight into the police. Fortunately there was no trouble. It was*
*one of those interminable meetings: a speaker from every branch*
*in the district, intermingled with tribal dances and whatnot. The*
*speaker before me was a fiery young man who made the audience*
*chant 'Violence Pays'. That decided me to give them a little sermon.*
*So I told them that the enemies of the party were hoping to divide*
*it by playing on tribe, race and class: that we must not be divided:*
*that we must live as a nation while the UFP were talking about*
*building one: but that national unity had to be democratic unity:*
*that we were not interested in the sort of unity that was imposed*
*by intimidation or suppression of the other man's views or the sort*
*of unity that was achieved by following leaders blindly. I went on*
*to say that democratic unity, in which we could think and discuss*
*and differ together, was needed especially to frame the shape of*
*the new society we wanted: that we should begin to think about*
*that new society: that we must be confident in our own strength*
*and not use the methods of desperation: that the methods of in-*
*timidation and careless use of violence would damage our vision*
*of the future more than they would damage the establishment.*
*All this, to my great surprise, was well received by the crowd.*

That evening my parents flew in for a month's holiday during which I had promised no further political activities. But it was too late. During the night the NDP was
banned. At 6 a.m. three male and one female CID arrived to search the house and
to serve an order banning me from attending any public meeting for three months.
They took away all the CACBA files, and correspondence with Christian Action in
London. Like a good English mother, mine at once made a pot of tea. She was deeply affronted when the CID refused to drink it, thereby confirming her belief that they
were not real English police. As they were searching, the phone rang and an angry
Rhodesia voice shouted: 'Ranger, if one African is killed today, you die tomorrow.'
The phone rang again and it was Victoria Chitepo to ask, 'Do you have them too?'
Shelagh wrote to John on 19 December. 'They did not seem to be at all interested in
me this time.' 'Every day', she added, 'somebody or other demands our deportation,

imprisonment or assassination.'

But at least with no party meetings, I thought I could keep my promise to my parents to withdraw from politics while they were there. So we went to Malawi and 'received the full VIP treatment'; we went to the Victoria Falls and to the races. Then we prepared for spending Christmas at St Francis. Shelagh went on ahead. My parents and I spent some days at Troutbeck. Then on Christmas Eve we booked into the Crocodile Motel, Rusape. The proprietor foolishly showed the visitors' book to a couple of drunken young white Rhodesians – 'Look, that bastard Ranger is here tonight.' At 11.30 p.m., I heard distant shouts – 'Come out Ranger and take your punishment!' I went to look outside and saw some way away four white louts pushing my father; he was magnificently defying them – 'Old as I am, I can deal with you lot with one hand tied behind my back.' My little mother was under his arm, hissing 'My son may have black friends but you have black hearts.' To complete their confusion I then arrived. 'You should be ashamed of yourselves, assaulting that old man.' My father was furious with me; the Rhodesians were dumbfounded, the proprietor urging them to go away. 'I suppose this is the fabled Rhodesian hospitality,' said my father.

At least the year ended peacefully. My parents loved St Francis and were loved in return. Someone had found a fawn in the bush and I treasure photographs of my mother cradling it in her arms. By the time they left, my father had become really enamoured of Rhodesia. He didn't like the strip roads, or the loutish Rhodesian culture, but he loved the scenery and our African friends. He was tired by his long career of selling and he looked forward to retiring in two or three years time and coming to Rhodesia to be a full-time grandfather. Alas, I had only one more year there myself.

# CHAPTER SEVEN

# 1962

# The Zimbabwe African People's Union

I now knew what I wanted to do for research. Throughout 1962 I sought to do it. On 11 January I told my parents, now back in England after their eventful holiday, that 'the Archives are proving fruitful again. I knew it would be difficult to get down to work again after my holiday so I forced myself to cycle to the Archives the very afternoon you left.' On 3 February I described my daily routine: '8 until 1 and 2 to 4 in the Archives.' On 4 March I told them that, 'I worked in the Archives until the last possible moment. My research is going very well indeed, fascinating material just on the lines I had hoped for.'

I began to write and circulate papers. Indeed, the UCRN History department was building up a public reputation. On 18 June Richard Brown lectured on European nationalism to a huge audience, including 'a full bus load from the townships'. And I was vigilant in the press. In late July Joshua Nkomo returned and there was a ceremonial reception at the airport. He was greeted by a wizened veteran of the 1896 risings who gave him an axe. The *Daily News* carried a government advertisement attacking this nationalist 'reversion to tribalism'. Great Zimbabwe was just a ruin, it read – 'a silent reminder of a dead and unhappy past'. I wrote to the paper: 'The nationalist movement realizes perfectly well that there can be no return to the past. Its desire is to build the future. But it also realizes that a sound future can only be built when people have confidence in themselves and a reasonable pride in their culture and history. There are dangers of course that a false history may be written and false pride created. But this has not happened yet.' The government was arrogant: 'Once we were told that Zimbabwe was too "civilised" to have been built by Africans. Now when scholars have proved that it was built by Africans we are told it is only a ruin anyway. How blinkered and narrow can the Government get, when it expects everyone to celebrate Pioneer Day and to be proud to call themselves "Rhodesians" but regards it as an insult to ask you to call yourself a Zimbabwean.'

I corresponded with the restrictees in Gokwe, about the past, about more recent politics and about future reforms. On 14 March, George Nyandoro wrote to me:

> *The History papers you sent me last time were very interesting.*
> *If you give similar lectures may you send me a copy. It appears*
> *from a number of articles written on African political organiza-*
> *tions that the [Southern Rhodesia] African National Congress is*
> *relegated to the position of being an agrarian movement. This is a*
> *gross misconception of the aims and objects of this moribund body.*
> *The fact that stress and vigilance were laid on land and this aspect*
> *did not mean that we were not fighting for the overall political*
> *concept of self-determination. Agrarian reformation was one of the*
> *phases exploited to achieve this. That there was political apathy*
> *is indisputable and one who intended to inject political awakening*
> *had to exploit all the immediate injustices pertaining to bread and*
> *butter. At the same time followers were given a political education*
> *laying stress on self determination and the concept of majority rule.*

I replied on 3 April. I told George that I had not spoken at a nationalist rally 'since my ban on speaking expired a week ago'. I was concentrating instead on,

> *pushing through some changes here at College which will enable us*
> *to make a bigger contribution to the education of Southern Rho-*
> *desia – a lower entry for a pass degree and so on, which we have*
> *a chance to get, I think. You will have seen that Dr Banda thinks*
> *we are 'colonizing' the minds of our African students and that he*
> *will not send any more to us. I am not surprised at this though it*
> *hurts a little to be regarded as an intellectual colonist; anyway it*
> *looks as if we are to become a Southern Rhodesian university and I*
> *would welcome your views on what we should do. I think since we*
> *have some degrees of really good standard we should keep them*
> *but also introduce some perfectly reasonable degrees at an easier*
> *entry standard – shall we say a pass degree in three years from*
> *Matriculation or four years from School Certificate. Would this be*
> *good? Or do you feel that it would hurt the schools? What about the*
> *medical school – should we go ahead with this expensive project at*

*the moment? Should we be doing more in adult education? And so
on. These are all things I have been turning over in my mind for
some time but now it looks as if we shall be able to get a lot more
support more generally … But this is, of course, very confidential
until any announcement is made. I cannot afford another press
leakage like that last one which will frighten my colleagues away.*

I added:

*I am also working hard at teaching and research. My work
on the rebellion is proving very fascinating. I am learning
a good deal about your ancestor Kunzi-Nyandoro both before, during and after the revolt. I have a lot of questions to
ask you about it when we meet; I have not yet written anything else to send to you but will when I have done.*

## The Colour Bar

The CACBA campaign continued in 1962, though it had moved from the streets to
the courts. There was still resistance over the swimming pools. In February, Lovemore Chimonyo, posing as 'an earnest student of Fort Hare', went to Mabelreign,
where he was shown instructions that the baths were to be closed to Africans, and
to Dr Ranger and Jaap van Velsen! But segregated baths were a losing cause. CACBA
turned its interest on to education. On 3 February I told my parents: 'Recently most
hotels in Salisbury have opened their doors to Africans … We are concentrating
on a test case in the field of education. Here things are going well. Several Asian
and Coloured families have put their children into European secondary schools
throughout the country: one European, Mr Samson, has put his two children into
a Coloured primary school. In most case the children were at first accepted by the
schools concerned and then turned out on the instructions of the Minister of Education. He wrote to the parents saying the schools had been gazetted as European; in
the majority of cases it was found that he was wrong and that no-one had bothered
to gazette the schools in question. So he has now written again saying he is going to
gazette them. He is in a very weak position. The case we take on will probably be
that of Mr Thompson, a coloured man who lives in Sinoia. He lives two miles from
the secondary school but has to send his son more than 200 miles to Bulawayo.' On
4 March I told them that 'everything is ready for the education test case'.

On 24 April 1962 I wrote to Canon Collins:

*Public transport, cinemas, swimming baths, most hotels and restau-*

*rants have all been desegregated since we began the campaign,
and often, if not always, the campaign had something to do with
this. There are, of course, still some hotels and restaurants which
refuse to admit Africans but our attitude is that these are bound to
follow suit as time goes on. Moreover obviously hotels are not the
most important objective. So we are largely turning our attention
to different sorts of activity now: particularly cases at law. We
have two on the go now. One is a key action against the Minister of
Federal Education on behalf of a coloured child refused admittance
to a European secondary school in Sinoia. This is being managed by
a new body – the Central African Education Trust – which consists
of representatives of the Coloured and Asian communities as well
as of CACBA. Everything is ready for this action and we are now
collecting the £1000 which is needed to finance it. The other case
is in the name of an African cook who lives in one of the suburbs
outside the city, to which the court decission in the swimming bath
case does not apply. So although we can only act for a coloured
child over education because of the constitutional division of functions, we hope that by taking a test case in the name of an African
we shall keep it clear that this is a fight against the colour bar as a
whole. There is a real danger that the fight against the colour bar
will seem to be an Asian-Coloured interest and that Africans will
follow their leaders in their correct attitude that politics come first.*

Meanwhile I followed up a wide range of issues. In February the Sinoia Caves Motel 'fined' two Africans 15d each for being 'impertinent' enough to ask to stay there. Yet the hotel was on National Parks territory, and so I at once wrote to the Chairman of the Federal National Parks Board.

## Two Northern Expeditions

In May 1962 I flew to Nyasaland to show support for Sarah. 'She got back from a holiday at the lake to find an attack on her in the Malawi News,' I told my parents. 'Hurt and bewildered she came straight south to seek the advice of family and friends.' Guy took her to see Nkomo so that she could explain her innocence of the charges. Then, 'armed with our support and words of wisdom she went straight back to Nyasaland for her school term'. Sarah had been attacked for Rhodesian contempt towards Malawi, it being alleged that she had called her dog Banda. It seemed a clear case. This young woman who had been the victim of discrimination in Southern Rhodesia was now falsely attacked in a nationalist state. I had no hesitation in backing her, rather than showing blind loyalty to the nationalist movement. This displeased Peter Mackay. But as I told my parents on 21 May, I found that 'the school authorities had refused to dismiss her and had told her that they would not accept her resignation; the staff had stood by her and the children gone out of their way to show their support.'

On 4 May, I wrote on Sarah's behalf to the *Malawi News*, which Aleke Banda was now editing on behalf of the Malawi Congress Party:

> *I realize that a letter from one of Miss Chavunduka's former teachers at the University College in Salisbury is hardly likely to count in her favour with you at the moment. Nevertheless, I feel I must write to urge you to abandon your demand for her dismissal from Blantyre Secondary School or alternatively a student boycott of her. Miss Chavunduka is becoming almost a test case of the effects of intolerance. While at the University College she suffered from the intolerance of some of the white students and later from the intolerance of the white community of Salisbury as a whole. Now, having sought the freer air of an African independent state, it looks as if she will be the victim of a yet more tragic intolerance. It is more tragic because it is quite unnecessary. Europeans in Southern Rhodesia are on the defensive and fear free expression; but no-one in Malawi has any need to be on the defensive or afraid of the expression of individual opinions.*
>
> *To those of us who know Miss Chavunduka it appears frankly incredible that she could have shown herself in favour of Federation, or boasted that she was as good as M.L.C.s or abused Dr Banda. We know her to be entirely a supporter of the national movements: we had hoped that through her stay in Malawi she would learn how to work and take responsibility in an African state so that she could serve her own people better later on. But I am not only concerned with Miss Chavunduka herself – who should at least be given a chance to defend herself against anonymous and second hand allegations arising out of her private conversation – but also with education in Malawi. My own view is that Mr Chiume is a fine minister of education doing a splendid job of re-invigorating the educational system of Malawi. But it would be tragic if at this stage the same sort of fetters and restrictions were to be placed on education there as have hampered it here. There must surely be*

*place in Malawi education for someone of the ability and independence of thought of Miss Chavunduka. It will certainly deeply sadden those of us who support both the claims of the national movements and the claims of the freedom of the individual if there is not.*

In June, I told my parents that Shelagh 'after much travail has finally decided to become a Catholic'. She had been deeply impressed by the sacramental life of the St Francis community, but realized that she could not join something so localized. Influenced by Catholic friends like Clive Wake, and steered by the Jesuits, she professed Catholicism. 'The only trouble is,' I told my parents on 30 June, 'that in our Barotseland trip we shall be stopping exclusively at Protestant missions.'

This Barotseland expedition in July 1962 was an extraordinary experience. We were ushered by my honours student Mutumba Mainga, daughter of an induna at Nalolo, the court of the Queen of the South. We went by Land Rover from the Rhodes-Livingstone Institute and found ourselves bogged down in swamps, and driving along railway tracks. On the Zambezi we travelled in a mission motor boat, the river so full around us that it seemed as if a coin dropped into it would precipitate a flood. I was bowled over by the landscape with the great trees which marked royal grave sites rising out of the plain. Mutumba took me to an audience with the *Litunga* in his capital at Lealui and then down river to Nalolo, where we saw the Queen of the South going to church on Sunday in her Victorian carriage. Mutumba's dignified father presented me with a bull calf which was sacrificed and divided among the people. I loved it all. Here was the closest I had come to Vansina's Africa, with elaborate traditions reflected in music and dance. Thereafter I worked on Barotseland whenever I could and wrote several papers about its inventions of tradition and its religious history.

On 23 September I wrote to Nyandoro, Chikerema and Nyagumbo to tell them about my adventures:

> *Our trip to Barotseland was fascinating. We went with one of my History Honour students, a Lozi girl who spent three months in England last year and met my parents there. She arranged a most elaborate tour for us, fixing up accommodation for and interviews with the Litunga, etc, and everywhere we went she had uncles and cousins to tell us what they thought about things. So we had a marvellous opportunity to discover something of what was going on as well as a good deal about the history of Barotseland which interests me, of course, particularly. I found the setup fascinating: a combination of old-style tribal politics with new-style nationalist*

ones. I found that UNIP will very probably win the two Lozi seats and have written an article for the next issue of the Examiner explaining how Lozi politics strike me. I enclose a copy of it for your amusement. The country itself is quite different from anything else I have seen – very flat but very beautiful and on the whole wretchedly poor. As for the roads, words fail: the road to Gokwe would be an unprecentedly fine road in Barotseland. Fortunately we were able to borrow a Land Rover from Lusaka and so we did not do too badly. We were cut off almost completely from news while we were there and so we did not hear of Dr Pari's death and all the other things until we were back in Lusaka. But we took the opportunity to speak to people all over Barotseland about the struggle in Southern Rhodesia and about how necessary it was for people to throw in their support with the Pan-Africanist movement. We were even invited by the District Commissioner, Mongu, to speak to a group of government officials at his house, where I told them that Whitehead was bound to fail and Miss Mainga, my pupil, told them how Barotseland must be transformed. I enjoyed it all very much. It was really the first time I had seen an old-style African society functioning and as well as its obvious faults the Lozi system seemed to me to have all sorts of interesting and valuable advantages.

# Nationalism

My trip to Nyasaland to support Sarah showed my readiness to criticise a nationalist movement. My running of the Colour Bar campaign was independent of ZAPU; nevertheless, I was much involved with the new party. On 3 February, I wrote to John telling him that there was a general demand that he become chairman of a ZAPU city branch. 'Trapped again,' he wrote in his diary. 'I can't pull out now. On the other hand I can hardly bear going back to to it all again – the meetings and telephoning and waiting about in offices.' When John returned from leave on 1 March he and I talked about ZAPU. I suggested that we call a meeting of the old NDP executive and decide how to proceed. 'Terry does not seem so anxious to keep his involvement in the party as slight as possible,' noted John. John undertook to visit the ZAPU office to discuss how best a new branch should be set up. First, however, he visited the TUC office to talk with Jamela about the the tension between the nationalist and trade union movements. John went on to see Maluleke, who was now leading a split from Jamela, and then went on to ZAPU and agreed to form a branch.

The anniversary of Sketchley's death fell on 20 May, and a memorial service was held by the graveside. 'There was a speech in Shona saying that Sketchley's spirit is still there, is everywhere. There are songs yearning and sad – yet in content entirely political. The local ZAPU leader makes a sharp angry speech and gives the ZAPU cries. Leopold Takawira speaks in Shona of being arrested with Sketchley. Lastly Terry speaks on Sketchley saying what a great inspiration there is for the struggle – his cheerfulness and his refusal to grow tired and disillusioned, his ability to do without the comforts of life or be distracted by them. His gentleness and how he could fight without hating.'

Then on 15 June I was elected to party office. A District meeting of ZAPU was held to elect a new executive. I was proposed as Chairman and as Secretary. John notes that he and Margaret Moore voted against me for both. My lack of the vernacular would indeed have disqualified me. In the end I was elected as District Vice-Chair. 'So Europeans begin to move up the party,' noted John. 'In the concrete situation it is astonishing how there are no prejudices against the European.' From that time on I was Vice-Chair of the District. The Chair was often absent, especially when it came to disciplining the Highfield youth league for offending against the mother body. Even when he was present, District committee meetings were often chaotic. John describes one on 21 July, which he attended with Margaret Moore:

> *Usual discussion about intruders. One man is found who does*
> *not belong to any executive and is suddenly attacked by one of*
> *the near demented youths of the Youth League. Uproar. Dozens*
> *of people are in the scrum, aged women dragging off the youths,*
> *men trying to separate the fighters. The man goes down and they*
> *seem to be kicking him on the floor. He is intoxicated, not looking*
> *as damaged as ought to have been expected. He is set up in the*
> *front and it is decided what to do. Apparently he cannot produce a*
> *card. He is taken outside and it is decided to keep him under arrest*
> *somewhere until they can drive with him to Highfield and go to his*
> *house to see if he can produce a card. Sickening. Yet the violence is*
> *the system here and one can work against it but not clear it away.*
> *Accept the violence of ZAPU or accept the violence of the police.*

The day after I was elected, I carried my new dignity to report to the still restricted founders of nationalism in the remote Gokwe area. Shelagh and John and I spent the night at the Haddons. We rose at 2 a.m. and were joined by Nathan Shamuyarira, Moses Makoni and Jonathan Malambo. We set off an hour later and met up with the Clutton-Brocks in Que Que. Arriving at Gokwe, we camped out by the road at the border of the restriction area while Michael Haddon and Nathan went in to round up the restrictees. They were divided into a ZAPU group – Nyandoro, Chikerema, Nyagumbo, Hamadziripi – and a ZNP group – Edson Sithole, Madzimbamuto, Matimba and Foya. Sithole was the intellectual behind the ZNP, and asserted a full pan-Africanist position, although, as John noted, 'the real objection to ZAPU is not really politics but Nkomo'. We spent the day moving between the two groups, who were 'excited and pleased to see us'.

Back in Salisbury, I was busy with District administration. I was sent to collect information and statistics on the City branch and also employed to set up a UCRN branch under Steve Lombard and a Marlborough branch under Margaret Moore. At the end of July I found myself mainly responsible for organizing the great reception at the airport for Nkomo's return. A huge convoy of battered trucks and cars set off to the airport, the police stopping many of them as not roadworthy. But still a huge crowd assembled to watch Nkomo receive the 1896 axe from a veteran of the risings with Mugabe crouching at his side.

In early September, rumours spread of an imminent ban on ZAPU. It was reported that Nkomo had gone to Dar es Salaam to set up a government in exile in readiness for UDI. John noted that, 'people are scared to join ZAPU because of all the violence, and the party will be banned any moment. It may be too late for a drive to get non-African members. But it certainly isn't too early.' John was worried about Margaret Moore, as violence increased. But even in these perilous times the City branch sought to recruit, trying to set up a meeting with Robert Mugabe in the Coloured stronghold of Arcadia. On 6 September, John noted that, 'Terry returns from the country today. The police are still after him and have called at his house while he has been away this time.' On 8 September the ZAPU head office was searched and a duplicating machine seized. On 14 September there was a meeting of the Mount Pleasant section in my house which John addressed about party policy. 'There is the usual weekend rumour that the party is to be banned tonight … It strikes me with very great force that if the party is banned then the struggle is irretrievably committed to violence and desperate bitterness.' On 15 September there was a District meeting – 'the usual uncontrolled meeting' – to discuss the planned Congress and branch resolutions. On 19 September the resolution were collected together. 'There is a strong rumour that the party is to be banned tonight', wrote John. 'Head Office is getting in touch with the outlying parts. Terry says there has been a call up of territorials during the afternoon.' And indeed in the early morning of 20 September both John and I were visited by the CID to tell us that ZAPU had been banned and that we were restricted to within three miles of our houses for three months. My prohibition asserted that, 'you were a member of the Zimbabwe African People's Union which has been declared an unlawful organisation', and added that, 'information has been placed before me which I am unable to divulge because of the confidential nature of the contents and sources of such information'.

At 7.20 a.m. on 20 September, Whitehead broadcast to the nation. He announced the ban on ZAPU and added that, 'those who have, in turn, led the ZAPU, and the NDP into ways of violence will not be permitted in the future to become the leaders of any new political party, without it being immediately banned'. That same day a White Paper, *Report on the Zimbabwe African People's Union*, was issued. My copy has written on its back my notes on who had been restricted and where. 'Takawira, Mugabe restricted. Mugabe's house being looked after by a young girl.'

I wrote to Canon Collins on that same day:

> *It is still difficult to discover what has happened to the leaders of the Party. Many of them have been taken by the police – Mugabe, Takawira, Silundika, etc. – but it is not yet plain whether they have been arrested with the intention of bringing criminal charges against them, with the intention of detaining them or with the intention of serving upon them restriction orders similar to those served on me. My latest information is that in most cases they will be restricted not to their urban home area but to an area around their place of origin in the country. So far there has been little public reaction though I understand that a crowd has gone out to the airport to meet Nkomo who is due back at 10 am. The police reserve and sections of the territorial army have been called out … The general situation is depressing … [New legislation] makes it unlawful for a new party to come into existence with substantially the same leadership or membership as the banned organization and Whitehead gave an assurance this morning that he intended to see that this was enforced. On their part ZAPU leaders have been saying that the party cannot be banned and that it will operate irrespective of any ban. All this presumably means that African opposition will now go completely underground with a government in exile in Dar es Salaam and no other party able to emerge without risking the charge of treachery to that government. Thus a dreadful stalemate is threatened … The situation which produced the ban was this. After ZAPU's success at the UN there was nowhere else obvious for the party to go. It called for another constitutional conference with Britain in the chair but this seemed improbable … The situation caused a good deal of discontent among party rank*

> *and file and appears to have led to the rise of a semi-organised 'ter-*
> *rorist' movement, the Zimbabwe Liberation Army, which has been*
> *critical of ZAPU and claimed to be behind recent terrorist attacks*
> *on Africans and Europeans … Very recently there has been a wave*
> *of petrol bombing and so on. I will predict with gloomy confidence*
> *an increase in the rate of cases of sabotage. There are many dan-*
> *gers therefore. One is that the situation will so embitter black and*
> *white that a real head-on clash cannot be avoided. Another is that*
> *'General Chedu' will gain the status of a hero in comparison with*
> *the leaders of ZAPU and that control will slip from their hands.*

Nkomo did not come back immediately and John's diary records the frustration and despair of ZAPU members. 'People in Highfield and Harare are really frightened by Nkomo's failure to return … He is faithfully promised tomorrow but there have been so many switches and changes that a sense of almost paralytic fear has been given.' John and other members of the ZAPU City branch met weekly in the Jameson Hotel to discuss developments. He met with Peter Mackay who was furious with the leadership, and especially Nkomo, still out of the country. On 25 September Peter threatened to run a cartoon, headed 'They left their country', pairing Lobengula in 1893 with Nkomo in 1962. John noted:

> *Talking with Peter does not always do one good. There is a kind*
> *of extremity in all he says and he seems to embrace a ruthless*
> *cynicism and a warm hearted belief in Africans and a hatred of Eu-*
> *ropeans here … Yet Peter is at the same time more sickened by the*
> *way many Africans behave than I am. By the timidity and coward-*
> *ice of the older generation like Stanlake, who have havered for too*
> *long and are still havering. Even Nathan, who apparently neglected*
> *all sorts of things when he got back from the United Nations and*
> *went straight by the first plane to Lusaka, afraid that he would be*
> *restricted if he stayed a day or two in Salisbury. Sir Edgar White-*
> *head has won this round hands down says Peter. And it is indeed*
> *remarkable how undefiantly the leadership has behaved. When*
> *Peter views the future gloomily it is always a future in which racial*
> *bitterness has eaten into every fibre of this country's being. He sees*
> *a future of this sort – this country as a boil on the face of Africa.*

John recorded his own motivation: 'I have to believe that my participation in nationalism will do some positive good – make it more likely that some Europeans will be trusted after African government and so less likely that the country will be ruined by premature and complete Africanisation.'

On September 23 I wrote to the Gokwe detainees apologizing for a long silence:

*The fact of the matter is that during the last vacation I was out of Salisbury the whole time – first in Barotseland and then in Matabeleland – running around hunting down history in a Land Rover. And when I did return to Salisbury the pace of events which led to this week's ban was so rapid that I found no time to answer your letters. Now that I am also a restrictee it is perhaps just as well that I was able to spend so much time out of Salisbury during the vacation. I must confess, though, that my restriction order ties me to the most comfortable area in Southern Rhodesia! Margaret Moore has also been restricted – to a 7 mile limit. Nearly everybody who held office at Branch, District or Regional level has been restricted. This morning Arthur Adaareba came out to see me. He has a twelve mile restriction limit. We decided that the Committee should try to collect information about the arrests and discover whose families were in need so that we can do some welfare work. I have cabled and written in full to Christian Action and Africa Bureau in London and hope that we shall get some funds to help. John and I are appealing against our restriction on the grounds that the ban on ZAPU is unjust and I enclose a copy of our appeal.*

*It is difficult for me to tell how the ban has been taken in the townships since I cannot go there. I am sure the apparent calm is superficial and will not last but at the moment there are so many troops and police around that probably things will remain quiet. I am told that on the road to Umtali there are road-blocks every few miles and that people coming in by bus are stopped and searched at every one.*

John and I appealed against our restrictions on 23 September. We pointed out several inaccuracies in the White Paper and its lumping together all violence as committed by ZAPU even when it was the work of, for instance, the ZNP restrictees in Gokwe, who were fiercely opposed to ZAPU. We wrote:

*We know by personal experience that the normal party machinery of the Zimbabwe People's Union in the Salisbury area was not involved in or directed towards any conspiracy or plan to endanger the peace of the Colony. We have at various times been ordinary members of the Party; members of the Executive of the Salisbury City Branch, of which John Reed was Chairman; and*

> *Terence Ranger was a member of the Harare District Executive*
> *which had the responsibility of supervising the nine branches*
> *in the Salisbury area which totaled between them some 70,000*
> *members. In these capacities we have attended public meetings,*
> *private Branch meetings, Branch executive meetings, District*
> *executive meetings, and meetings between the District Executive*
> *and representatives of the branches at which instructions and*
> *information were handed down from the National Secretariat. In*
> *other words we participated over a period of months in the day to*
> *day running of the machinery of the Party in the Salisbury area,*
> *which may reasonably be held to have been the key area of the*
> *Party. We did not once hear any discussion upon, or the issue of or-*
> *ders for, violent or non-violent breach of the law. On the contrary,*
> *we frequently heard and participated in discussions designed to*
> *eliminate breach of law or clash with the police, as in the case,*
> *for instance, of the reception recently arranged to greet Joshua*
> *Nkomo on his return from the United Nations when most elaborate*
> *arrangements were made by the District Council to ensure that*
> *there was no disorder. The minute books of the Branches and of*
> *the District and Regional Councils are now in Government hands*
> *and these will be found amply to corroborate our statement.*

We also dealt with the Government's assertion that the branches of ZAPU were 'really cells … so familiar in certain other countries where freedom is a word little understood by the masses'. We pointed out that branches 'were characteristically very large indeed (in Harare and Highfield certainly containing some 25,000 or 30,000 people) and conducted their business mostly through public meetings'.

On 26 September, I wrote to Collins:

> *The security forces are still mobilized; there are still heavy patrols*
> *in the townships and spotter planes dropping pamphlets; there*
> *are still road-blocks on the roads, and houses and people in the*
> *townships are still being searched. As always in such operations*
> *all sorts of rudeness and petty violence are being done to respecta-*
> *ble people who are complaining about it … Isolated acts of arson*
> *and sabotage appear to be continuing much as they were before*
> *the Party was banned. It is hard to tell if the apparent calm will*
> *break as soon as the forces are moved out of the townships.*

I shared Peter's fury and John's motive. But I was also anxious about UCRN: 'Terry very depressed about the future of the College,' noted John, 'not only the failure to expand secondary schools but with the disturbances in schools and the expulsions something approaching a breakdown of secondary education in Southern Rhodesia. With UCRN losing Northern Rhodesian students and becoming a Southern Rhodesian institution it will have to get all its money from the SR government. They are not going to be able to have it standing half empty. So they will fill it up with Europeans.'

I was eager to combat those at UCRN who sought to censure John and myself. The scientists did not wish to join in an appeal to government not to renew our prohibitions and went so far as to question the integrity and value of our research. On 23 October I wrote to Walter Adams, the Principal:

> In this morning's Rhodesia Herald *there is a report of a meet-*
> *ing you are alleged to have had with the Gwelo Town Council.*
> *In this report you are alleged to have said that 'the university felt*
> *as strongly as the municipality and the general public about the*
> *matter of the participation in politics of certain lecturers.' You*
> *are also reported to have said that 'internal pressures' would be*
> *more likely to have the desired results, with the implication that*
> *such pressures had been, were being or were to be applied. Finally*
> *you are alleged to have said that 'we don't think that dismissal*
> *is the appropriate instrument of registering our personal disap-*
> *proval.' Although no names are mentioned in the report it would*
> *be absurd of me not to realize that I am one of those concerned*
> *in the discussion. I have every reason to know how distorted such*
> *reports can be and I very much hope that there has been some*
> *serious misreporting of your meeting with the Town Council. You*
> *will appreciate that as the report stands at the moment my position*
> *and the position of Mr Reed, and I would suppose of Mr Shamu-*
> *yarira also, has been made very difficult indeed vis a vis both our*
> *colleagues and our students. Unless some correction is issued to the*
> *report we shall be publicly marked as men of whom the College*
> *disapproves, upon whom it is applying 'internal pressures' and*
> *whose dismissal has presumably been at least considered. I am well*
> *aware that in fact there has been no expression of your personal*
> *disapproval and no 'internal pressure' exercised but this not at*
> *the moment the point. These things will now be believed to be so.*
>
> *Perhaps I may make another point. No doubt it is impor-*
> *tant to placate the sort of opinion that Gwelo represents. But*
> *it cannot, of course, be equated, as in the report, with 'the gen-*
> *eral public', even in Southern Rhodesia. As I am sure you will*

> *realize 'the general public' in Southern Rhodesia, in the sense*
> *of the greater number of adult residents, will certainly resent*
> *the impression that lecturers who legally support an African*
> *party are subject to internal pressures and have provoked the*
> *displeasure of yourself and the College authorities. … I should*
> *be very glad indeed of an assurance that you have been mis-re-*
> *ported and still more glad of a public statement to that effect.*

Meanwhile the SRLAWF committee tried to cope with the new situation. On 16 October I wrote to Freda Nuell at Christian Action giving an example of the hardships involved in restriction. The regional organizing secretary of ZAPU, William Mukarate, was restricted to a rural area where, as he wrote, 'My grandfather lived some short time in 1880-1890. I have not a single house nor do I have anything to help myself'. He had no relatives in the area and his wife was restricted to within 12 miles of Salisbury. She had been sentenced to nine months for sedition. On 23 October I wrote to Collins about the difficulties of dealing with all the cases that had arisen – some 1,500 in all. Paul Mushonga, leader of the Pan African Socialist Unnion, had written to Collins, arguing that my restriction made it impossible for me to carry out the work of the SRLAWF and asking that all aid be channeled through him. I responded:

> *I should be very surprised if he has been in contact with many of*
> *the restrictees. As you will realize Mr Mushonga is leader of a*
> *small party which is a rival to the banned ZAPU and to what it*
> *stood for. His party certainly does not enjoy the confidence of the*
> *restrictees, detainees and ZAPU prisoners and it would appear*
> *extremely unlikely that they would be prepared to accept relief*
> *from it. In any case Mr Edson Sithole, who is Secretary General*
> *of Mr Mushonga's party has stated in the press that the party feels*
> *no obligation to come to the relief of the restrictees or their fam-*
> *ilies. Under these circumstances it would be fatal to give money*
> *or any other assistance to Mr Mushonga and I do not scruple*
> *to assert that such aid if given would go to strengthen the party*
> *rather then assist the restrictees. On the other hand, it is of course*
> *true that we cannot cope with the scale of the problems which*
> *face us. Our efforts have had to be restricted to the families of the*
> *men sent to the rural areas and even there we are mainly limited*
> *to the Salisbury area for any effective activity. In the Salisbury*
> *area certainly we now have a very effective apparatus and I can*
> *guarantee that there is no family of either the Gokwe restrictees*

or the ZAPU restrictees in Salisbury and its environs in distress
or in danger of eviction for non-payment of rent or which is in
danger of loss of property through failure to pay hire purchase.

... In the old days we had a rather ineffective Bulawayo
committee to watch the interests of detainees and restrictees
which has now fallen away. But a new organization has come
into existence in Bulawayo under Mr Grey Bango, which from
press reports aspires to being a national relief fund. I am in
touch with Mr Bango and have suggested that his new organisation take the Bulawayo area in the same way as we have now
organized the Salisbury area and that any funds held by the
two groups be distributed to the areas on the basis of need.

In this way I sought to prepare for renewed activity when my own restriction ended.

## Some Representative Letters

My restriction, and later my deportation, generated a huge flow of letters of lamen-
tation, support and occasionally criticism. My students expressed dismay. My old
friends in Britain were baffled by press reports there which depicted me either as a
communist or a fascist. The restrictees in Gokwe wrote to express solidarity. Of the
very many letters in the Ranger Papers I will quote from three.

A letter of 24 September 1962 from Sarah Chavunduka, still at Blantyre Secondary School in Nyasaland, is the most interesting of those from students or ex-students. She reported her reactions to news of the still very recent ZAPU ban:

... and the arrests, restrictions and I do not know what else that
stupid Govt. is not doing. Stupid, as you know, is a Malawi term
to cover all shades of silly and cruel thoughts and deeds! I am
keen to know what exactly is happening. I am very worried over
this. I read such sketchy bits of news as Silundika and Malianga are under arrest – what for? Who else is arrested and what
has happened to others like Rev. Sithole, Mr M'gabe etc. I feel
very ill at ease when my keen pupils here ask me what a 'Government in Exile' is and how it will fight the battle – and am of
course ignorant of how such a system works. Please Terry could
you give me not only the plan as ZAPU envisages it but also what
you think. Mr Silundika was at my house when he came over for
Du's funeral and we talked at length about the task ZAPU was
facing. I did not ask for more than he felt obliged to tell me lest
I should have seemed too forward and curious concerning the

Party's 'secrets'. *I feel enraged to hear about all these arrests and restrictions. It doesn't require much thinking to conclude that you must be one of the very first persons on whom a restriction, if not an arrest warrant, would be served! … Each day I wonder exactly what I ought to do as just one of those in the struggle. I cannot help feeling too far away to be of any use in the struggle, not that I would envisage anything of benefit I could do, but to share even the irritating fumes of their tear gas is good enough. .*

She then told me what her pupils had done:

*Students from this school were so enraged by it all that when I went to take a Macbeth reading lesson with Lower Sixth they would not start on the lesson but asked if they could say something about the banning of ZAPU. In the heat of their fury they said that they would wish to come to Rhodesia to assist in 'fighting'. Of their own accord they organized a peaceful demonstration in the form of a procession with placards through the streets of Blantyre on Saturday morning. There were about 60 placards with all the stock slogans – 'Long Live Nkomo', 'To Hell with Whitehead', 'Southern Rhodesia is a Police State', 'Dr Pari and ZAPU will not die in vain'. I saw the students as they were leaving and without stopping to think whether I was in line with the regulations of my job I picked up one paper and joined the procession hoping to pass as one of the school girls. My slogan happened to say 'To Hell with Federation – it is DEAD'. So I carried it. My hopes of passing as a school girl were shattered when a press photographer said 'Come on Sarah, we must see your face as well!' That much for the demonstration. We have now a ZAPU branch here, just started.*

Students from Northern Rhodesia wrote in similar indignation. It was a moment of Central African pan-Africanism, although like Sarah no one understood a government in exile. Sarah herself soon resigned from Blantyre and headed south to be ready for her whiff of tear gas. So she was in Salisbury for the last days of my Rhodesian career.

My friends in Britain also wrote anxiously. The most challenging of these letters came from my old friend from school and Oxford, Peter Dyson. He wrote provocatively:

*I see that you are circumscribed. It cannot have been a surprise to you. I share with Whitehead the wish that you would not*

*give your support to general movements within which you can-*
*not pick and choose your associates in a situation which has got*
*beyond political right and wrong and become an issue of force.*
*The decision to use force, however courageous, seems to me to*
*be purely personal – one cares enough about something to risk*
*poisoning other people's lives. The nasty thing is that the sins of*
*the fathers ... You are a historian. Can you honestly say that you*
*can think of a civil war in which you would have taken it upon*
*yourself to back the leaders of either side? Damned if I can –*
*whenever I read of such things I think what perfect sweeps both*
*lots of bosses were and I don't see how it can ever be otherwise.*
*I can imagine myself throwing bombs but only for purely selfish*
*reasons. S.R has not got to open civil war yet but it is a couple of*
*years since it became clear that the country could not hope for a*
*unified society without revolutionary change – and under Afri-*
*can conditions that means violence ... and wherever there are*
*whites, in or out of nominal control, it is sheer bloody murder.*

*No doubt in your cheerful way you will laugh at me – but there*
*are a few things which really matter. By all means agitate and risk*
*being slung in the coop if that is what you want to do, but would it*
*not be better to do it on your own or in company you can wholly*
*trust? I know it is supposed to be contemptible to stand apart from*
*the collective will and remain simon-pure. I think, you know, the*
*only chance of avoiding worse violence in SR is if enough people*
*stop giving effective support to one party or another and very firm-*
*ly sit on the fence. And I think all your instincts are that away....*
*Why not try it: at least you would have more time for students!*

As I said in my reply on 5 October 'if the same objections were made to me by
someone here and with less cogency and urgency I should know how to deal with
them, with a mixture of argument and mockery of the "positive fence sitting" principle. But this will not do for your letter and I am grateful to you for making me take
at their full worth arguments which do not get put to me by my friends here.' So I
set out to answer Peter point by point:

*Let me dispose of the incidentals first. I do, you know, spend a*
*very great deal of time on my students already. I doubt wheth-*
*er it would be good either for me or them if I spent very much*
*more. Knowing my English lethargy you would be surprised at*
*the amount of energy that a warm climate has released in me*

*and at the number of things I can combine. As a matter of fact
the almost wholly satisfactory character of my relationships with
the students and ex-students is one of the few sources of strength
which exist for me in the present situation. I admit frankly that
my closest relationships have been with the African students and
it is partly through them, indeed, that I have come to be identified with what you call 'the collective will'. Of course I no more
worship the collective will than I ever did: of course it is individuals that count, as you say, and for me there is no doubt at all
which individuals I am with. You suggested that one should choose
one's company carefully. Well, primarily I am in politics here
because I have chosen the company of Simpson Mtambanengwe
and Sarah Chavunduka, of Cornelius Sanyanga and Mutumba
Mainga, and many others, whose names will mean nothing to
you but who are to me the best elements in a nasty situation.*

I went on to argue that the situation was not yet one in which one had to choose
between throwing bombs, participating in a civil war or sitting on the fence:

*As a member of ZAPU I was not expected to use or support
violence. Nor do I believe that by being a member of ZAPU
one automatically lent moral support to people who had been
asked to throw petrol bombs. It is possible, I do not deny, that
some leaders of the ZAPU were using the Youth Wing in what
was supposed to be carefully planned violence which got out of
hand … In my view the Party was not committed to violence
and there was a possibility of preventing it from being so committed – and after that, of course, a possibility of preventing it
from being committed to total racial hatred. I am aware that
it does not answer the question to say that at public meetings I
spoke against the use of violence though that is certainly true.*

But then I turned to the main question – what would I do if it became clear that
the 'matter is not one of right and wrong but of force against force'. My answer to
Peter was one which gained relevance after my deportation, when John and others
had to choose whether or not to support sabotage and bomb-throwing. For myself,
I told Peter:

*I am much afraid that I will do what you want me to do – retire to
the fence. This will not be logical. I cannot find it in myself to tell
Africans that violence is always wrong and should never be used*

*because I can think of many situations in a European context where
its use has been almost universally admired – say the Resistance.
Moreover I cannot feel as you do that both sides in a struggle or
force against force are equally to be abominated. In the last war,
for instance, I should have known that I was, all things considered,
on the side of the Allies against Germany. Thus I would certainly
know that I was on the side of the Africans. Logically, therefore,
I should be prepared to fight as in a war. But I do not think that I
am. I would hardly have been prepared to fight in the real war anyway for sheer disgust at the lies one's own side told and the atrocities one's own side committed. And if it comes to the underground
or the barricades here I have little doubt that I shall find myself
temperamentally unfitted. I do not regard this as at all admirable.*

*But up to that point I am determined to be in it. You must
accept my judgement that little though one can do to avert it
by any means one can certainly do more by using one's limited
influence within a movement than by sitting on the fence outside it. Another sort of answer is that although I will not be able
to take having to use violence myself I find that I can take being
the object of violence. If it does any good, as I think it marginal-
ly does, for whites to suffer some inconvenience alongside blacks
then I can take a good many further inconveniences yet without
ratting. One does not know how much of this sort of courage
one has – it has to be learnt as it goes along. I discover that I
am quite one of the Public School breed as far as taking punishment goes. But the main point really is that while I can be on a
side I intend to be on it. If you were here you might understand
that the most wretched sweeps of all are our fence sitters.*

Meanwhile the leaders in Gokwe, whom Peter expected to be 'sweeps' and with
whom Sarah in her letter expressed some irritation because they had sent her a message 'not to do it again' when she had done nothing in the first place, were still writing fondly to me and Shelagh. Maurice Nyagumbo wrote to Shelagh on 12 October:

*Personally, I am not at all worried with what is taking place
now because I feel time is on our side and that victory is just
about although we can still expect heavy losses on our side.
But what worries me is how to protect those Settlers when we
take over. Although most of our people do not believe in killing there seem to be a number who may seek to retaliate. I am*

*finding it hard to avoid this situation without a risk to peace.*

On 16 October I wrote to Maurice to say that my own attitude was to wait until a new mass party was formed, 'and then to offer to join it as before':

> *I do not know whether it will be possible for me to do so. It seems quite likely that any new party will now take an exclusively African line and no longer find it possible to have European members. Indeed, the Herald phoned me up yesterday to report that Joshua is supposed to have said just that in an interview from restriction – that the time had come when it was impossible and embarrassing to have whites as members of the nationalist movement …*
> *I have been expecting a development of this kind for a long time … I shall offer up my services as humbly as I know how and it will be up to the leaders of any new party to decide whether they want them or not. I am quite confident that whatever happens in this sort of way one's friendship with all the people who have been working together will not change and it is this that I value most.*

Maurice replied on 20 November:

> *After reading your letter I took it to Chik and George to discuss what appeared to be the new attitude of our Nkomo. We did not reach any decision until we got further information from our new comrade here, Mr Marondera, and also from Mr [Simpson] Mtambanengwe who recently visited us. But we have made our own interpretation on the statement which however is quite contrasted to yours. And we believe our interpretation to be correct.*
>
> *In the last five years Joshua has experienced the terrible hardships which you people have undergone after having joined the nationalist organisation … Joshua was not happy with these waves of threats after threats of deportation orders against you. He realizes how much it will damage our cause if you were to be deported. Thus Joshua decided to make that statement in order to disarm our enemies …*
>
> *I don't want to tell you how much we value your ability in the struggle. But I want to tell you this secret. The first Nkomo parliament will not do without the following people – Guy Clutton-Brock, the already deported Faber, T. Ranger, John Reed and Mackay. I know that you may not believe me but this is the fact.*

This generous letter contrasted, of course, with the situation in 1980 when independence was at last achieved. The Mugabe regime only made use of whites who could command some support from the settler community. But Maurice was constant in his views. By that time Minister of Mines and party Secretary for Administration, he still wanted to reward those who had contributed in the past. So he urged upon a very reluctant Mugabe that some significant role be found for me in the new order. By that time I was Professor of Modern History in Manchester, and was happy when no such role was found.

# Restriction and Expulsion

But as well as an inconvenience and a challenge, my restriction was an opportunity. I wrote to my parents: 'I cannot even reach the Salisbury Public Library, but the archives are within the restriction area … I am damned if I will let them scare me off in this way.' And as I told them on 6 November I hoped to turn this restriction to research advantage. 'Both lectures and examinations are over until March next year and I may be able to get down to some really solid research work. Shelagh is going to Basutoland. Sarah is returning to Southern Rhodesia, home-sick for our revolting colony'. Shelagh, still in the first flush of Catholic enthusiasm, was going on a trip to Cape Town and Lesotho with Hilary and Rosemary Jenkins. I was free to spend all day at the Archives.

On 16 October I wrote to Maurice Nyagumbo:

> At the moment there is not a very great deal that can be done politically. I am concentrating upon writing … Give my regard to Chik and George and Dan. Tell them that my history of the rebellion will benefit from the enforced inactivity as the Archives are within the three mile limit. In June next year we hope to have a conference in Lusaka on African history and I am going to write several papers for it – on the rebellions, on early African political movements and so on. I will send them through as they are produced.

On 30 November, George Nyandoro offered a different perspective:

> If Edgar extends your restriction he will have registered a severe blow to you and more in particular to our country. The research which you are undertaking will have been sabotaged by such an extension. Though I am aware that the History of our country will be put in its perspective by one of our lot, who will not be accused of prejudice when certain facts are in question, it is also vitally important that a person like yourself should go the whole hog in pioneering the insights of Zimbabwe's history – and who knows whether posterity will not find

> *your book the best and more informative than later writers.*

At any rate I made good use of my restriction, spending nine hours a day working on the files. But this industry was interrupted in early December. One day I received a particularly violent death threat. That night I heard footsteps outside the house. I rose, armed myself with my Shona spirit axe, and went outside. I found no one there except the night watchman sheltering in my porch and terrified to see a lecturer in his pyjamas and with a raised axe. Then and there I resolved to disregard death threats. But the damage had been done. Next day in the Archives I found that I could not see and developed a blinding headache. I had contracted tick-bite fever from being bitten by a tick on my lawn. 'It makes me feel very rugged indeed,' I told my parents, 'and really incapacitates one from reading, writing, sleeping, thinking etc.' So, as the Rhodesia Front was being returned in the election, I was on my sickbed. The radical book-seller, Jenny Frost, came in and perched on my bed, greeting the election result with enthusiasm. The feeble liberals had been swept away. 'Now we know where we are!' Since where we were was so horrible, I did not share her enthusiasm.

But my restriction came to an end and I recovered from the fever. I spent the New Year holiday in Barotseland. I was free to travel to supervise honours students in their research work. Two Lozi students were involved, Leshoma Muuka, working on a twentieth-century topic and Mutumba Mainga, beginning her oral history fieldwork. I was supposedly directing them, though I learnt a great deal from observing Mutumba in the field. She carried a state-of-the-art Uher tape recorder, almost as heavy as herself. I watched as she interviewed eager informants from the Lozi subject peoples, and much more reserved royal shrine priests. Up a creek of the Zambezi one day we talked with the keeper of a major shrine. He would tell us nothing. Eventually Mutumba said, 'Let's go, Dr Ranger.' 'Wait!' he exclaimed. 'I have heard of Dr Ranger on my radio.' We embraced on his island in the river – but he still wouldn't tell us any of the traditions. It was a magical time. We picnicked in fields of scarlet mushrooms. On New Year's Eve we heard at midnight a vast cacophony from the plain as every pot and pan was beaten. I was fascinated by observing an ancient kingdom both resolutely traditional and determinately modernizing. To be at the heart of the invention of tradition with my favorite pupil – life could get no better than this. It didn't. As soon as I returned to Salisbury I received a notice of prohibited immigration with instructions to leave the Federation in two weeks.

Shelagh, who had just returned from her South African Catholic safari, was outraged by this notice. So was I. When the three-month restriction order had been served I had been relieved because it was not a deportation. Now I had done my time in restriction it seemed as though the government were having their cake and eating it. But the fact was that it was a different government. The restriction had been imposed by the territorial Southern Rhodesia government; the declaration of prohibited immigrant status was by the Federal Government. The old refusal to grant me citizenship now enabled the Federal Government to use the prohibited immigrant legislation against me. My colleague Claire Palley told me that she had been shown the 'secret' information on which the Federal Government was acting. I replied that there could be no 'secret' information. Everything I had done was legal and open. In fact, as emerged from the court appeal hearings, the Federal Government were using prohibition in a way which had been renounced by the minister when the bill was first introduced. As fully recorded in *Hansard* he had undertaken not to use his powers against people who had been resident in the country for years but only against undesirables wishing to enter. The court was well aware of this, but it had to construct from the language of the Act whether it could be used in this way. In the end the judges found that it could, though they made sharp verbal criticism of government's action.

The process of the appeal gave us more than two weeks to prepare. Much of the time was spent in a frantic rush to finish off my research. I told my parents that, 'I needed another two months in the Archives, but there you are!' I also told them on 16 January that 'my dear history honours students have more or less volunteered to complete my archival transcribing for me', though on 29 January I was writing to them about 'the frantic rush to finish in the Archives'. I was spending eight hours a day working on the files.

There was also the question of what was to happen next. As I told my parents, 'I am determined to get back to Africa. I think I am eminently employable and should be able to get something in the next six months.' In December 1962 Victoria Chitepo had written to urge me to apply for the new Chair of History at the University College of Dar es Salaam, and I had decided to do so as an insurance. Now I also applied for the Chair in Nairobi. I flew to Lusaka to meet Kenneth Kaunda who urged me to wait until the University of Zambia got under way. Walter Adams had the idea that I should become director of the Institute of Social Research in Lusaka, which was still connected to UCRN. I was offered, but refused, a post at Berkeley. Both Lawrence Stone in Oxford and Roland Oliver in London offered me temporary posts. So I had many irons in the fire. Peter Mackay, who had not forgiven me for going to Nyasaland to support Sarah – 'a silly girl' – against criticism in the nationalist journal , told John that he was surprised that there should be protests against my prohibition, when I was planning to leave to better myself anyway. But in fact all these alternatives were safeguards. Had I won my appeal I would undoubtedly have stayed at UCNR and in Southern Rhodesia. As I told my parents on 8 January: 'I love this bloody country and lots of people in it.'

But I lost the appeal, and had to leave. Ironically, as Shelagh and I prepared to go, the Gokwe restrictees were released. I wrote to Canon Collins on 15 January:

> This is hard to reconcile with my prohibition, unless one is a
> Quid pro quo for the other. It may be clever politics. Field has
> certainly pleased the Europeans by acting against me and the
> Africans by releasing the restrictees. In fact none of the Afri-
> can leaders have yet joined issue with the Government on my
> case though protests have come in from all sides. The fact is, I
> think, that this Government is actually more concerned with
> the Colour Bar than with political questions proper. It was per-
> haps significant that on the day I got my order they also an-
> nounced that they would legislate to segregate swimming baths.

I told Collins on 26 January that 'the released restrictees are in great form and received a tremendous welcome back last Sunday. Shelagh and I were privileged to be present at the welcoming dinner for them in Highfield that night …You will find George Nyandoro [who was going to Britain for medical treatment] an irrepressible and ebullient person.' On 13 February, still a week away from the court decision on my case, I wrote to Freda Nuell to tell her of new legislation that threatened the work of SRLAWF. 'This provides that a policeman with or without warrant may search premises and seize any funds collected for the legal aid for anyone who is or has been a member of an unlawful organization. Our legal advice is that if this amendment passes the whole funds of the Committee will be liable to seizure. Another amendment allows the confiscation by the police of all property and funds used for any purpose by anyone who is or has been a member of an unlawful organization, so that our own personal property and money will be vulnerable at any time. Under these circumstances the Committee will obviously face grave difficulties of operation.' Nevertheless, we were determined not only to continue but to extend our work. Now there were no more detainees we intended to work with sentenced prisoners. 'There is no doubt that the Committee should continue to exist. One finds that there are few organizations prepared to take an initiative in a real situation of crisis. The Christian Action Group is one of them: our Committee another.'

ZAPU realized my commitment to the cause, and there were massive African protests against the prohibition. John Reed, who had been in French Africa with Clive Wake, records in his diaries his own response. The news reached him in Mad-

145

agascar on 22 January. 'I am trembling with a kind of shocked excitement.' On 18 January, John and Clive received a letter from me in which I said that, 'In some ways of course it resolves many of one's doubts, but basically I feel awful. I do not want to leave this bloody country. As for the cause I would take it that it now becomes more important than ever for John to stay here and agitate. His citizenship is a great boon. I suppose there will be a lot of talk about people resigning from College now. I hope you two will stay at any rate so that Clive can look after the interests of the dwindling number of African students and John continue to save the College from complete damnation in the eyes of the north. I would like anyway, in very un-British style to say how much your friendship has meant to me.' John records that 'we are both pleased and flattered that Terry wrote so promptly. And I am pleased he sees what I should do myself in the same way as I do. Stay in Salisbury both to agitate and for the College.'

On 4 February Clive and John returned to Salisbury. He attended the appeal hearing, noting that the court was very small. He talked with Peter Mackay who 'objects to the fuss being made over a European who won't suffer in being deported and thinks that discreet persons would have avoided being deported and attracting so much attention'. On 11 February Peter told John 'how remarkable it is with all Terry's enemies no one has come forward to say that all the fuss about him being deported is unreal because he was intending to leave the country anyway. I say that Terry's application for the chair in Dar was entirely as a precaution … Peter seems to imply that Malawi might have denounced him.' On 13 February John dined with Shelagh and me and Sarah Chavunduka. We listened to a 'tape of ZAPU songs which was made for them when their going away seemed imminent.'

On 24 February there was a farewell party at my house. With the release of the Gokwe men, and the return of ex-students and students like Sarah and Mutumba, the party was a great representative gathering. John described the scene: 'Cars line the road in front of the house. On the lawn is a large crowd. Shelagh has invited all the College waiters who stand around. At one end of the room sits Joshua Nkomo under the nodding tufts and tails of his immense fur hat, with his audience squatting around him. At the other end on a sofa sit the Moores and other families looking something like a Victorian photograph. There are several Moore daughters stacked up against the wall. I meet Maurice Nyagumbo. Everybody is at the party … George Nyandoro, Chikerema, Robert Mugabe, the Haddons, Herbert. Even Peter is at the party though sulking in the kitchen. Such an occasion is one of the things that make the misery of the Southern Rhodesian situation tolerable. In spite of everything this can happen.'

146

Finally the time came to leave. I left defiantly. 'Whitehead has gone. Welensky is going. But as for me I shall return', I told the local press. (And I was right, though it took me 18 years.) Then on Wednesday 27 February John drove Shelagh and me to the airport. 'Inside the hall of the airport there are already many people from the University and a few ZAPU people like Robert Mugabe. Upstairs on the terrace the crowd begins to gather. Joshua arrives and with him Chikerema, Moyo. George Nyandoro a little later. I think every member of staff in Arts with wives. And many students. A group of African nuns from St Francis. Several Roman Catholic priests.

*Shelagh and Terry Ranger outside Salisbury Airport on the day of their deportation.*

The crowd is dense and everyone is seeing and greeting people thay have not seen for months. Suman is there and Natu. Davis Mugabe ... Stanlake, Willie Musarurwa, Matete, Moores, Haddons. Shelagh, whose hand luggage is already extensive, is loaded with gifts including a fair-sized pot made I think by George Nyandoro's mother.' The Women's League sang for us – 'Nkomo is a bull, Ranger is a bull,

*Terry Ranger with Mutumba Mainga outside Salisbury Airport on the day of his deportation.*

Shelagh is a militant women'. 'At last the flight comes and Terry and Shelagh go downstrairs. Through the drizzle, they walk out to the plane, Herbert Chitepo, who is going back to Dar, with them. The crowd claps in unison, then sings Ishe Komborerera Africa, while they stand to attention below. Then when they are inside the aircraft – a song about Terry: whatever you do Terry Ranger is still *mwana wepasi*, a son of the soil.' The event, noted John, was hard to see as melancholy: 'Terry and Shelagh certainly seemed to be in heart rather than sad.'

We emerged into the sultry heat of Dar es Salaam to be greeted by the ZAPU choir, led by Victoria Chitepo, singing 'If you believe what Nkomo says Zimbabwe shall be free.' That evening we 'recuperated in the most paradisial surroundings. We have a sort of self-contained flat at the top of the Attorney General's house' in Oyster Bay. Fom there next day, after a leisurely breakfast, I was carried off to be interviewed for the Chair of History by the Principal, Cranford Pratt, and the Professor of Politics, David Kimble. The event was not tense and I began to see good auguries when Kimble asked me how I had managed to do so much research and publication as well as political activity. To this I could only reply that I was a very energetic man. An hour later I was offered the Chair. I replied that I was honoured, but that I had commitments to Zambia. 'Never mind,' said Pratt. 'Let us go to see your house.' So we all drove out to the main campus on its hill above the Indian Ocean. We were ushered to No 10 Simba Road, a gleaming, shuttered bungalow, with its cashew nut tree full of birds and as it turned out also full of snakes. The Indian Ocean gleamed below. Shelagh and I looked at each other and said, 'We'll take it.' The house was our home for the next six years.

Dar es Salaam was in many ways the obvious retreat from Salisbury. Joshua Nkomo was aleady planning to extablish a government in exile there. When I reached London in April 1963 he told me he was pleased I was returning to Dar so that I could play some part in this enterprise. Already in Dar were a confusing jumble of nationalist factions, loosely grouped around the various parties. The Zimbabweans were a disparate group already breaking up into the fragments which emerged from the 1963 split. I gave a press conference to them and other African exiles and got my first taste of the greater difficulties of being a white nationalist in the outside world. The general tenor of the meeting was that the people of Zimbabwe were cowardly and unprepared to fight for their freedom. I felt a populist indignation at this libel and said that the leadership were to blame rather than the people. This did not please the Zimbabwean political exiles who complained to London. Chikerema defended me. 'This is just Terry speaking. If you want him as a member you have to accept that he will speak his mind.'

And so Shelagh and I left Africa, booked to return to Dar in October.

# CHAPTER EIGHT

## 1963 and AFTERWARDS

# Deportation, the Nationalist Split, Dar es Salaam and Writing Revolt

I was soon back in Central Africa. As the Federation broke up I was able to return to Northern Rhodesia to attend the history conference at the Rhodes-Livingstone Institute in Lusaka at the end of May 1963. The conference was a shop window for the Salisbury History department, showing how far it had come since the first speculative debates about how to tackle African history. All the resources of the department were on display. Donald Abraham spoke on the role of Chaminuka and the mhondoro cults in Shona political history; Richard Brown presented on 'Aspects of the Scramble for Matabeleland'; Eric Stokes spoke on 'Barotseland: the survival of an African state' and on 'Malawi political systems and the introduction of Indirect Rule'. Three presentations were made by honours students. Mutumba Mainga and Leshoma Muuka gave papers on the research they had done in Barotseland over the New Year and Keith Rennie spoke on the Ngoni states and European intruders. As for me, I took the opportunity to present the fruits of my archival research. One paper was a trailer for *Revolt in Southern Rhodesia*, the other for *The African Voice in Southern Rhodesia*. The former was entitled 'The role of Ndebele and Shona Religious Authorities in the Rebellions of 1896 and 1897'; the latter was 'Traditional Authorities and the Rise of Modern Politics in Southern Rhodesia, 1808-1930'. Those long hours in the archives were paying off. I don't suppose mine were the best presentations but my sessions were certainly the liveliest. Eric Stokes's friend, Ronald Robinson, who was filling in for me and carrying the honours students to their final exams, expressed scepticism. Jaap van Velsen made a violent attack on my historian's abuse of anthropological material. On 2 June, Richard Brown, back from Lusaka, told John Reed 'how it all went and about Jaap's great assault on Terry's papers. In all something of an occasion. As Richard says, they have built a school of historians here in Salisbury.'

And this was indeed true. When *The Zambesian Past* was published in 1965, with an authoritative survey introduction by Eric Stokes and Richard Brown, it marked a definitive statement of the achievements of the Salisbury department. By that time Stokes was in Cambridge and Brown in Sussex and I was in Dar es Salaam. But the seeds had been sown. The majority of that first honours group went on to do research. Mutumba Mainga worked in Cambridge and London for her doctorate on Barotseland; Keith Rennie obtained a Northwestern doctorate on the Ndau of eastern Zimbabwe; Robin Palmer carried out his important work on land discrimination; Tony Dachs worked on the history of Catholicism; Rachel Thompson obtained an Oxford doctorate on the Aborigines Protection Society. It was a great breakthrough.

# Nationalism

I went on from the history conference to Dar es Salaam, carrying with me a letter from Kaunda and Kapepwe to Joshua Nkomo. To understand the context one needs to go back some months. When I arrived in London after my deportation I saw Nkomo who told me that he had summoned the ZAPU executive to Dar es Salaam in order to set up a government in exile. If the executive could not leave Rhodesia then he would ask me to take part in creating a government structure in Dar es Salaam. Fortunately for me the executive did manage to reach Dar. Nkomo himself went back to Southern Rhodesia to prepare for the exodus. In London I dealt with Ndabaningi Sithole, who was extremely cordial, writing to Shelagh on 7 April that seeing us in London was 'like seeing Zimbabwe in Britain. I am glad you are getting settled but don't get too settled. We need you and Terry in Zimbabwe.'

In letters to John I described the situation in London. On 26 March 1963 I wrote:

> *I am very disturbed to hear of Peter's prosecution [for refusing to register for military service]. They are all wandering about all over the place. Ndabaningi is now in Cairo: Joshua and Chikerema are just coming back from New York: never was there such great whizzing about.'*

On 3 April I wrote about the break-up of Federation and the political consequences:

*Patrick Wall has mobilized vast numbers of Tories to call for the independence [of Southern Rhodesia]; that gallant authoritarian Catholic, Humphry Berkeley, has managed to raise a little group of 20 or so to oppose. Theoretically his 20 may be significant if they really mean to refuse the party whip on this issue as Berkeley himself promised at my London public meeting. On the other hand the opposition is divided. The Voice and Vision boys have come out with a Welensky supporting motion but the Front Bench is solidly on the right lines. Then the United Nations mission is due to arrive in London to put pressure on while old Dupont is still here putting pressure on from the other side. Butler [UK First Secretary of State] is squirming between two fires, Winston Field's possession of all the force and Joshua's threat of an exiled Government. I suppose that what happens depends to some extent upon what happens in Rhodesia itself. Field says that there will not be internal trouble and that he can deal with any attempt to create it. The United Nations say that there is a critical situation. One or the other is presumably right – or so it seems from here. As we know, neither is right. So I am agog for news from your end.*

I continued:

*I did not see Kenneth [Kaunda] again after the decision [on Federation] but I did lunch with Ndabaningi and then talked with him and Enoch [Dumbutshena] last Saturday night after speaking to Simpson's group in Golders Green. The general mood was one of pleasure that at last Federation would break up and that there would then be a very rapid development of the Southern Rhodesian situation ... Ndabaningi says he will probably call me up to town to talk to the UN delegates when they arrive ... Almost my last meeting in London was a meeting with Simpson and his students. I assumed a very pompous air and laid down the law, saying that at this moment of crisis, when the leaders were in any case taking the line they had been urging, there should be a rallying around and closing of the ranks. It transpired that they were all suspicious of the government in exile idea on the grounds that it meant the leadership deserting the front-line. Anyway we had a vigorous and frank discussion which Simpson apparently wanted. Afterwards he told Ndabaningi that it was the first time that anyone had put the issues to them, whereupon Ndabaningi, with engaging candour, replied that*

151

> that was because I did not represent anything and could say just
> what I liked, while he was always taken as speaking for the party.

On 5 April 1963 Eileen Haddon wrote to me to report difficulties over legal aid
and welfare:

> The prison education scheme ran into snags when Patch was
> transferred to Broken Hill (to stand in for the local man who is
> up on a charge of embezzling government funds) and his under-
> study [at Marandellas] became suspicious at the number of Law
> and Order prisoners who are taking courses. Eleanor hopes she
> has now sorted it out with O'Donovan who expressed himself
> delighted with the idea of correspondence courses in the gaols, but
> we have yet to see if the prison resumes the previous cooperation.
> Altogether the situation is grim. My own feeling is that the Exam-
> iner is doomed. Costs are so great and with the end of Federation
> one paper cannot possibly appeal to three large territories.

Moreover, she reported, the nationalist leaders all faced prison:

> Leo [Takawira] has collected 122 days in jail against which he
> is appealing. Joshua and Robert Mugabe are each appealing
> against 6 months. Morton Malianga lost his appeal and has five
> years. Robert Chikerema and Maurice Nyagumbo are on ap-
> peal against 6 months and three years respectively. There have
> been lots of recent prosecutions for possession of explosives,
> subversive literature, etc. Enos Nkala is implacably against
> Joshua because they have not managed to pay his fine and it
> looks as if he will have to serve the full 15 months. The pris-
> on [Marandellas] is divided between for and against Joshua.

Within a few days of this letter the whole executive had jumped bail and made
their way to Tanganyika. Chikerema was left behind to hold things together and to
begin recruiting young men for guerrilla training.

On 16 April I pointed out to John that the reported rumour of withdrawal to Dar
had turned out to be correct:

> George [Nyandoro] is now in London and the rest in Dar. Joshua's
> instructions to me to go to Dar in the event of their all being arrest-
> ed in Southern Rhodesia, now – thank heavens – falls away. The
> whole thing is a gamble which may result in the collapse of Joshua's
> leadership. The idea is, I have come to believe, a good one provided
> (a) that events move as fast as Joshua assumed they would, (b) that

152

*Tanganyika will allow a Government in Exile to be set up, (c) that effective leadership remains in Southern Rhodesia [which] largely depends on Chikerema, the best man for the job. Ndabaningi tells me that to his knowledge Tanganyika had not given approval of a Government in Exile a month ago. I assume that Joshua has since negotiated on this. But I also assume that Nyerere cannot possibly allow a G in E until such time as Southern Rhodesia has either been granted or has seized independence and this now looks like a procedure of months rather than days or weeks. Joshua's trouble is that he reasoned that the new legislation gave him only a matter of weeks inside Southern Rhodesia before Field moved to destroy nationalism there: hence his time-table ultimatum to Butler, etc. In purely internal terms some vigorous response was certainly called for, but externally, as a result of Butler's equivocation and Field's apparent decision not to proclaim unilateral independence, the whole pace has slowed. This may mean that Joshua can do nothing in Dar for months and that will undoubtedly demoralize the movement. The idea of a G in E is an excellent one and a formidable threat … But Simpson and his fellows will not wait long.*

I told John that Ndabaningi 'is not on friendly terms with Joshua. He is a splendid person not only in human and moral terms but because he is more sensible and practical than the others.'

Meanwhile John in Salisbury was picking up rumours that 'Robert Mugabe and Leopold Takawira were very reluctant to leave the country and had to be driven to do so by the rest. Unless they left, they were told, they would be expelled and discredited. This may be true. If either had stayed they could easily have taken over the movement.'

My Zimbabwean friends both in the country and out of it were thoroughly confused. On 23 April Stanlake Samkange wrote to me: 'Everybody who is anybody is running away and only stooges and political fools like ourselves remain. I cannot say I understand the trend of thought which inspires it all. I cannot attempt to guess. I had thought that suffering was one way of advancing the cause. I had always thought that a fighting speech was a means of courting arrest. Maybe that's because I am a political fool. I do not think anybody here knows what to do next.' Stanlake congratulated me on Dar. 'If anybody deserved being a professor of history it is you – who have not only tried to unearth a great deal of it but have also lived it and contributed to it.' Stanlake added that he and his mother would be delighted if I dedicated *Revolt* to Sketchley.

It soon became clear that some of those who had gone out to Tanganyika were just as confused. On 14 May 1963 Maurice Nyagumbo wrote to Shelagh from Mbeya in south-western Tanganyika:

> *Believe me Shelagh I hardly spend a day at one place which*
> *indeed makes it impossible to write. I was asked by the National*
> *Executive to be here at Mbeya and I have already been here for*
> *the last six days. I don't want to stay here too long because I feel*
> *there is a lot of work to do at home than in Tanganyika. I know I*
> *am going to meet a stiff opposition within the executive members*
> *on this subject but I definitely must go back home. I know that I*
> *am facing a prison sentence at home but I feel it is much better to*
> *serve the sentence than to run away from it. I saw John Reed the*
> *other day who appeared to be very much confused with what is*
> *going on in our political circles. In fact I am also confused at the*
> *moment. I don't know what is going on now. I am being pushed*
> *from one place to another. That is why I feel I must say no to stay*
> *here in Tanganyika even if it means expulsion from the party. This*
> *is because I definitely feel no purpose will be served by our staying*
> *here. But, as I say, I don't know the plans ahead yet, which I hope*
> *I shall be informed about, and I must be convinced with the plans*
> *before I agree with them. There is of course a lot of discontentment*
> *amongst our people at home to the present move which was taken*
> *by the National Executive. But it has been our efforts all along to*
> *stop them from denouncing our leaders as it will spoil our case …*
> *Some of us must remain at home to be with the people even if it*
> *means to be in jail with them. How is Terry? Is he through with*
> *his book yet? Tell him I am looking forward to a copy of his book.*

This, then, was the situation at the end of May 1963 when I attended the history conference in Lusaka. At the end of it I was I was summoned by Kaunda and his foreign affairs minister, Kapepwe. Kaunda reasonably and Kapepwe extravagantly denounced the idea of a government in exile, accusing Nkomo of cowardice. They gave me letters to deliver to him and Nyerere in Dar es Salaam, demanding that he return to Southern Rhodesia at once. I wrote to John on 4 June:

> *A very hectic week in Lusaka has just come to an end …*
> *I have seen Kenneth and Kapepwe and been given a letter for*
> *Joshua. This says he must return. One gathers that Nyerere*
> *has been saying the same. Kenneth says he is sure Southern*
> *Rhodesia will neither be given nor take independence and he*

*may be right. He seems pretty well informed but says that it
is a drawback not being able to consult Joshua or a representative of ZAPU over ZAPU attitudes to developments. In short
Northern Rhodesian policy to SR is difficult to evolve and UNIP
obviously feels the need of a lead from ZAPU. As do we all.*

*I had a session with Nathan [Shamuyarira], Willie
[Musuruwa] and Ariston [Chambati] – futile and despair-
ing but interesting. One gathers that a new party is now
really a possibility – a new party which continues rather
than rivals ZAPU. UNIP apparently advises this.*

I concluded: 'I shall of course know more in Dar.'

And soon I did. I found a demoralized executive. Maurice Nyagumbo, who had
arrived in Dar from Mbeya, was bitter against Nkomo. I have a photo of him on the
beaches of Dar, holding a dead shark that had been washed up on the beach. Maurice
prised its mouth open. 'As I do to this shark so I shall do to Nkomo,' he declared. I
stayed with the Chitepos and found Victoria also very hostile towards Joshua and
demanding action against him. I had never been close to Mugabe but this was the
moment when I was closest. He was disconsolate. I delivered the letter to Joshua.

I wrote to John that TANU was thinking of inviting Southern Rhodesia to join
the East African Federation, offering Field access to the northern markets in exchange for liberalization. 'Generally neither Nyerere nor Kenneth appear to feel that
the situation in Rhodesia is as desperate as ZAPU feels. Meeting them gives one
confidence, I hope not falsely based. They are certain that Field will neither be given
nor take independence and that this is not a real issue. And Joshua will certainly <u>not</u>
be allowed to establish a Government in Exile'. At this moment Nkomo was planning
to visit Yugoslavia. The disaffected executive members planned to wait for him to do
so and then intended to summon an executive meeting which would depose him and
elect Ndabaningi Sithole. They had no intention of forming a new party. But their
plans leaked out.

On 12 June I wrote to Shelagh from Berlin, where I was visiting my friend Ger-
hard Ritter:

*I hope you have by now received my two letters from Dar es Sa-
laam. There still remains some Dar news to tell despite two letters.
On the Sunday I saw Maurice again. He had decided not to go to
China [for military training] much to my relief. He had also decided to go back to Southern Rhodesia and wanted my advice and also
my help to get something definite out of Herbert. While talking to*

*Maurice we met Mugabe who told us the sensational news that the letter I had carried from Kenneth to Nkomo and Nyerere had had a drastic effect. Nyerere had summoned Nkomo and told him that he must leave Tanganyika at once; that TANU was fed up with his inactivity and that he should go back and lead his people. In any event he was to get out of Tanganyika. Joshua almost collapsed at this, poor fellow, and panic was reigning. Joshua had been booked to fly to Yugoslavia but he now cancelled the booking and said he would fly to Southern Rhodesia before Nyerere could deport him!*

*Of course, these events did not suit Herbert and the conspiracy since they formed a sort of compulsory saving of Joshua from himself. Joshua's flight back could make their plan hard to carry through. But the incident had clearly brought matters to a head and Herbert sent off cables calling Ndabaningi and Leopold [Takawira] to Dar as soon as he heard of it. Herbert and Maurice came out with Mugabe to see me off at the airport and there planned a scheme of action. So I suppose things should be decided one way or another in a few days or weeks. Maurice promised to keep in touch with us or have others let us know where he was. He was to set off for Lusaka on June 10 carrying letters telling Kenneth and then to return home. I know that this exposes him to danger but I am sure he will be happier this way than any other.*

*I flew off in the middle of this with affectionate farewells from the rebel band. Herbert was cross that I was not going to Cairo or London or somewhere useful: even he could think of nothing to be done in Berlin. He has, as you know, grown up and developed a lot; I find him quite impressive now and certainly much more flexible and imaginative than Nkomo. He and Victoria were exceedingly kind to me once again and Herbert and I had several philosophical cum political conversations which he seemed to enjoy. I am on his side and on the side of Ndabaningi and Maurice and Nathan but I wish it was not a question of sides.*

A week later I told John that I had reported to George Nyandoro, ill with TB in hospital in Ascot.

*I found George ready enough to criticize Joshua, against whom indeed he feels bitter. But he says, reasonably enough, that Joshua is being made a scapegoat for the rest of the executive and that there is such competition for leadership amongst them that he does not think a single candidate will emerge. Moreover, now that Joshua is back in SR he feels that it would be better to retain him as leader, but within the framework of a new mass party in which his powers would be curtailed and be subject to democratic supervision.*

*George says that Joshua has been allowed too much power by an executive which attacks him in private but will not object at executive meetings and that it should be easy enough to restrain him.*

Meanwhile John had been confiding to his diary. On 9 May he had predicted that 'a move against Nkomo's leadership is now only a matter of time. As a European there is nothing I can do and it is essential not to get involved in this ... But I am worried that the younger nationalists, like our students, may move too soon or ineptly and get themselves discredited, perhaps permanently.' On 10 June he received a letter from me from Dar which he immediately destroyed. On 6 July he recorded Nkomo's speech in Chaminuka Square. 'He named the men he claims to have turned against him and are forming a new party. These include Nathan Shamuyarira, Parirewa, Hamadziripi, Nyagumbo, Davis Mugabe and Nkala. Nkomo says he has heard some of his old executive have turned against him but he does not believe this. So Nkomo has decided to provoke a split himself. Peter says he is fairly sure that there was no such plan to form a new party – and I was under the impression that it was the Nkomo faction that were moving towards a new party. Certainly it seems the only chance for Nkomo's continued leadership.' John told Nathan that 'the City branch will have to keep strictly out of this, accepting the leadership that emerges but taking no part in the quarrels about who should lead.' John noted that that weekend the *Daily News* blamed the split on the old district committee and Parirewa and Ranger, its chair and vice-chair!

On 13 July Suman Mehta told John that the City branch had been summoned to send delegates 'to the conference which Joshua is calling in three weeks time to settle the leadership'. John felt that 'the City branch ought to be represented but I am convinced not by any non-Africans. There is Lovemore and the students at the College [though] since the students have publicly denounced Nkomo possibly sending one of them might be construed as a deliberate partisan act on the part of a branch executive controlled by non-Africans.' John despaired of the rancour already apparent between the factions. 'Things are so undirected – and though bitter so un-ideological and hardened – that a patched up peace might be an outcome and the party even more helpless and useless than before – if that could possibly be.' On 30 July he noted that the rebels would not attend the meeting 'so we have to refuse if we are invited. I don't think we would be able to find any member of the branch who would be willing to go.' Lovemore had told him that 'those who walk at night in Highfield are likely to be challenged and asked their allegiance'.

On 24 July Nathan Shamuyarira wrote to give me his version of the split:

> *The political difficulties you ran into in Dar es Salaam have now*
> *developed into an open split here. The nationalist movement has*
> *never been split so sharply in known SR history. By and large*
> *Umtali is solidly behind Sithole, Fort Victoria is behind Takawira*
> *and Bulawayo behind Nkomo. Gwelo, Salisbury, Marandellas,*
> *Sinoia and others are all split in roughly equal halves. Generally*
> *opinion among the educated people – teachers, orderlies, second-*
> *ary school students, etc., – is behind Sithole. And mass opinion*
> *behind Joshua. Joshua and Chikerema thought it would be a clean*
> *sweep after denouncing ten of us here and the 4 in Dar es Salaam*
> *but they are running into a lot of our support in the countryside.*
> *They have had to cancel meetings in Fort Victoria and Umtali*
> *and we have booked some there for this weekend. In Salisbury,*
> *Highfield and Mabvuku are behind us. Harare and Mufakose*
> *are totally against. The bulk of the people have been influenced*
> *by the reaction of the Youth Council whose members are able*
> *to shout down people as stooges in beerhalls and the streets. In*
> *Highfield our youth shout down Joshua as Tshombe every day of*
> *the week. At the University the students (who are taking part in*
> *politics for the first time) are solidly behind us but the staff and*
> *waiters are with Nkomo. Your letter was stolen from my desk.*

Nathan was over-optimistic in his assessment. Before the end of the year both he and Stanlake had left for universities in the United States. Nkomo had won the first round. His conference took place at the Haddon's Cold Comfort Farm. His leadership was confirmed and a People's Consultative Council was set up as a thin disguise for ZAPU. The absence of the City branch was noted. Ruth Chinamano berated Margaret Moore for not attending. But John's policy of neutrality paid off. The branch waited until it became clear who had majority support and then rallied to his leadership. In the end this turned out to be Nkomo. But in the meantime John and the branch were courted by the other side. On 1 August John noted that Nathan Shamuyarira had assured him that any new party would want Europeans to join it 'whatever capital the other side tries to make of this. Then he says a curious thing. "In fact we may welcome a little neutralization by Europeans. What we are frightened of is that people will see these people as more extreme than Nkomo, what are they going to ask us to do? Nkomo didn't make many demands, he didn't expect much.'" On 8 August, the day ZANU was formed, Nathan again assured John that 'non-Africans will be welcome in the party and not just tolerated as they were in ZAPU'.

Meanwhile I had been laid low with fever, brought on by my absurdly demanding Africa Bureau lecture schedule. On 25 July I wrote to John to say that I had seen no one and relied for my impressions of the struggle on letters from Maluleke, Nyandoro, Basil Nyabadza, Stanlake Samkange and various students. From these I had the impression that,

> *Joshua has much more support than one might have supposed. It means that several things have gone wrong with the revolt. The first, no doubt, was that Joshua was allowed to start the attack rather than the initiative being held in rebel hands; the second, which all my correspondents speak of, is the failure so far of the rebels to gain a platform from which to state their case against Joshua as contrasted with the public meetings he has been holding. I take it that they were not allowed to use Radio Tanganyika for broadcasts. It looks as if the TANU/UNIP support, on which the rebels were counting for immediate and impressive support if the coup came off, is waiting for the outcome of the revolt. In short, a misfire. George Nyandoro comments: 'At home ZAPU executives are throwing bricks at each other. If this mud-slinging goes on for some time as the trend seems to be, my fear of bringing in tribalism in our politics may develop with disastrous consequences. This Congo episode of individuals dismissing and suspending one another will be the order of the Zimbabwean struggle for the next six months. How the two sides will be able to keep the nation together appears to be a mystery.'*

Maurice Nyagumbo suffered directly from the split, his store in Makoni Reserve being burnt down. However, he continued to be active. In early August he wrote to me and Guy Clutton-Brock asking us in Sithole's name to try to raise funds. But as I told John on 6 August, 'we do not know what is really going on at the other end and whether, for instance, the policy is still to capture ZAPU or to form a new party … It was hard enough to raise money for ZAPU united but to raise money for a group of people with no formal statement and no formal organization, etc., etc., will probably be impossible.' On 9 August John commented on this. The formation of ZANU had clarified the situation but 'obviously if there are two parties it will be difficult to raise money for either'. John noted that 'if I were an African I would be with Sithole. But as a white man I am not so sure.' On 13 August he and Margaret Moore decided to meet with Sithole.

I wrote to John on 18 August: 'Today I hear on the radio that thousands of Nkomo supporters marched on Salisbury from Mabvuku and were tear-gassed by the police. So it looks at the moment as if Joshua has the local initiative.' But the overall impression was one of chaos. 'George says he has had desperate letters from the Cairo office which is quite out of funds and has no idea what to do next. He also says that Nyerere has closed down the Dar office and refused to allow any ZANU office to operate, and that he has cleared out all the old ZAPU representatives on threat of deportation. There seems to be a danger that the whole structure of overseas representation will collapse … The Dar collapse is a particular disaster. As for London the position is fairly absurd. Mukono, who is an executive officer of ZANU, is struggling to keep an office going which is still a ZAPU office and he has no idea of the attitude of ZANU to the whole business.'

In Zimbabwe, Nathan Shamuyarira hoped that George Nyandoro would consent to act as ZANU representative in London. But I told John that there was no chance of this:

> I saw George a week ago and the development of his thinking is clear. He says the split is proving disastrous, with overseas offices collapsing, financial support drying up and a dangerous division between the masses and the intellectuals. His position in any case is a middle one. He shares the feeling that Joshua's leadership has been faulty, but he says his own career began with an attack on the caution and sterility of intellectual leadership and he cannot easily find himself now on the side of the intellectuals against the masses – especially since some of them are the same men who used to enjoy leadership because of their qualifications but did nothing with it. George is distressed by the letters he says he has received from ordinary members saying they resent the open claim of some of the rebels to represent an elitist group. Anyway George feels that there is a need for someone outside the two factions, first of all to try and clear up the financial problems in England and secondly to operate at some stage to try to achieve re-unification. His thoughts at the moment are moving in the direction of trying to get control of the American money promised to ZAPU, some 10,000 dollars, and with this to clear all the debts of the party in England and then place the rest in a trust account until such time

*as the situation is clear. George feels that whether he comes out*
*for one side or another will make very little difference now to the*
*fact of division and he prefers to operate as if above the contest.*

On 30 August I wrote to John: 'You are quite right, of course. History is made in this chaotic way and it is no use applying Marxist or any other analysis to it.' I saw Mukono in London and George in Ascot. On 17 September I told John that 'I have received a royal summons from Mugabe and Mukono so I am going to London.' And gradually George Nyandoro's position hardened. I told John on 20 September that Chikerema had publicly claimed George for ZAPU and that George would not disavow it and 'desert the masses'. 'So George is now solidly with the Chikerema movement though he insists that he will always be ready to meet Herbert or Mugabe or any true nationalist.'

John Reed then came to England. On 23 October he lunched with Shelagh and me at my parents' home in Kingston and then we drove out to Ascot to see George. We were leaving for Dar on the coming Friday so it was our last opportunity to see George and to introduce him to our newly adopted baby daughter, Franny. George greeted her warmly and gave her the Shona name of Chipo. John recorded that:

> *George is still unsubdued. He reckons to be up in November*
> *and perhaps back in Zimbabwe by the middle of January. He*
> *is now quite resolutely a supporter of ZAPU and Nkomo. He*
> *says Mugabe has visited him and made it clear that there was*
> *no possibility of compromise until Nkomo went and George says*
> *Nkomo has his faults as a leader but he is clearly the choice of*
> *the people and he cannot be thrown over to satisfy a clique of*
> *the leadership who are anyway as much to blame for what has*
> *gone wrong in the past as he is. ZANU, then, since there is no*
> *possibility of compromise will have to be crushed … George is*
> *harsh but listening to him accepting the people's verdict with a*
> *shrug is not so disheartening as listening to Mugabe saying that*
> *the masses don't understand and will accept anyone as leader.*

We then all drove back 'through splendid autumnal scenes at Virginia Water'.

# Dar es Salaam

A week later Shelagh and I drove our new Austin Mini Countryman with Franny Chipo in the back through France to Marseilles where were due to board the *Pierre Loti*. The boat was full of French soldiers bound for Madagascar. I found the relentless frivolity of shipboard life tedious and gave the French a splendid example of 'mad dogs and Englishmen', setting myself up on deck as we passed through the Red Sea and writing 'The Last Word on Rhodes?', a critical review of an uncritical biography, which was later published in *Past and Present*. We were the only passengers to disembark at Dar amidst many expressions of concern from the French that we were risking life in a socialist country. We spent that sticky night in the New Africa Hotel close to the waterfront. There was a moment when we heard the ship's bell calling passengers to another excellent meal when we almost wished that we were still on board. But this weakness passed and we settled down to live in 10 Simba Road and to assess life in Dar es Salaam.

Dar was very different from my earlier expectations. Neither ZAPU nor ZANU could operate freely, being limited to four representatives in the capital and with many of their activists sent down to Mbeya in the south-west. There was nothing structured for me to do about Zimbabwe and I merely collected what news I could. On 28 November I wrote to John about a conversation with Victoria Chitepo.

> *She says she longs to get back to see for herself; that of course mistakes were made but the only thing now is to press on. She admits that ZANU has some strange supporters and has acted as a way back for all those stranded. Stanlake is chairman of the Highfield branch; Savanhu is "working hard"; Mbofana of the Daily News is a member, and so on. She says that the Liberation Committee in Dar es Salaam have invited Nkomo and Sithole to appear jointly before it and will attempt to create a united front. Nkomo is apparently due next week for this session. The Liberation Committee will not finance any splinter party but this total financial pressure is no doubt undercut by the fact that Ghana, at any rate, and no doubt others as well, are hostile to the committee and apparently supporting groups which it has decided not to recognize. There is a real coldness towards Ghana here.*

On 10 December 1963 – the day on which I had gone to Zanzibar for its illusory independence – I wrote to John:

> *Meanwhile ZAPU versus ZANU continues before the Committee of Nine. Tranos Makombe and Enos Nkala represented ZANU, J.Z. Moyo and Silunduka represented ZAPU. Reports, needless to say, vary. Tranos says that ZAPU were humiliated and compelled to withdraw the document presented to the Committee because of its slanders and inaccuracies. Victoria was chortling with glee. Silundika says the Committee will be sensible enough*

*to take the right decision. (You see I can still talk to both sides.)*

But this did not last for long. John writes in his diary for 16 March 1964, after he had seen George Nyandoro in London: 'I get the impression that Terry is now completely identified with ZANU though not Shelagh. ZANU correspondence files at Dar have fallen into ZAPU hands and possibly there may be some letters of Terry's. On the ZAPU side I am regarded as having remained neutral.'

I was always likely to be seen as ZANU even though I was now trying to be neutral. After all, I had delivered the Zambian letter in June 1963; my friends were among the rebels; I admired Sithole. But the last straw for Chikerema and Nyandoro was one of my quixotic gestures. Nathan Shamuyarira had been teaching at UCRN. He came under attack through a repetition of the scandals which had been raised against him by white Rhodesians in the past. This struck me as caddish. In July 1963 I wrote to Nathan to say that I hoped these slanders would not deter him from serving his people. Nathan opened the letter and left it on his office desk, as he confessed in his letter to me of 24 July 1963. At this point the faculty and students at UCRN were all ZANU; the staff were all ZAPU. The office cleaner pocketed my letter and took it to Chikerema who subsequently carried it about in his breast pocket to demonstrate my treachery. I remember driving down one day in early 1964 to visit Joy and Jimmy Skinner, who had moved to Dar and were living in a house on the beach. As my car entered the drive another car sped out of it. It was driven by Chikerema and Nyandoro, desperate not to have to meet me. Given our earlier closeness when they were in Gokwe the breach was very painful. (Chikerema made it clear, however, that he still regarded Shelagh as loyal.) So I was cut off from ZAPU/PCC.

But even if I had wished to be so there was no way of being active in ZANU. Despite the assurances given by Nathan to John in June 1963 there rapidly developed within ZANU a chauvinistic reaction. In March 1965 I told John of ZANU statements, 'some really distasteful stuff', reviving the old canard about Garfield Todd beating 'naked African girls' and alleging that the PCC was run by the Haddons, Palley, Leo Baron and 'other imperialists', who took bribes down to Joshua in Gonakudzingwa. It wrote of ZAPU/PCC as 'recanting, revisionist, recoiling and infested with white settlers – a multi-racial mixed grill'. From 1964 my contacts with nationalism were limited to letters and visits from Zimbabwean friends and my regular interactions with Herbert Chitepo.

These interactions gave rise to some interesting notes, particularly about Manicaland. On 13 June 1964 I wrote to John that 'from what one hears the eastern districts are back in the days of 1962 only more so'. On 12 September 1964 I reported that I had seen Herbert. 'He attacked the efficacy of isolated acts of sabotage while at the same time proudly telling us of the evidence the prosecutor wanted to lead and didn't in Sithole's trial which shows that the eastern districts were a hive of sabotage and subversive activity.' On 29 July 1966 I reported to John from Lusaka that 'I have seen something of Herbert Chitepo who is extremely elated at what he regards as the success of ZANU's new policy. He claims that they now have overwhelming mass support in Rhodesia. I have never seen him so confident.' And I remember that when news came of the killing of the Afrikaner farmer, Oberholzer, in Melsetter by the Crocodile Gang, Herbert came to my house on the Dar campus. He felt emancipated, after all the doubts and hesitations, now that blood had been spilt.

After 1966 there were few references to Zimbabwe in my letters to John. But this did not mean that Shelagh and I were cut off from individual Zimbabweans. Our house in Dar was a refuge for old friends, many of them fleeing north. Eileen Haddon had written to tell me of the difficulties of the Defence and Welfare Fund. I had deposited secretarial files in the National Archives in Harare but the police raided them there and removed many of them in an attempt to prove Michael Haddon guilty of defrauding the Fund by paying money intended for it into his own personal account. He had, of course, been asked to do this by the Committee in order to avoid seizure of its assets. His trial took place in July 1966. As Committee Secretary I could testify to the facts. I was asked by Michael's defence lawyer, Tony Jaffey, to come to Salisbury to give evidence. I was told by Rhodesian Immigration that I must arrive at Salisbury airport on 26 July 1966; be met by Tony Jaffey; stay at his house and not communicate with any other person. I must leave as soon as possible after I had given evidence. In the event the charge was dropped and I did not have to go. Michael, however, was sent to Umtali prison for technical fraud of the sort being resorted to by many Rhodesian businessmen under sanctions. Ironically, Eileen and Michael had earlier been recruited on a visit to Lusaka by a British intelligence officer, Daphne Park, and asked to report on sanctions evasion. Maybe his trial was a punishment for this. On his release, he and Eileen caught a slow boat up the coast to Dar es Salaam, where they stayed with us, lounged on the beach at Bagamoyo, ate large quantities of giant prawns, and revolutionized Dar cooking as Michael worked with various restaurants to produce wonderful meals.

John Reed stayed with us many times. After his appointment as Professor of English at the University of Zambia I made many return visits to his house in the bush in Lusaka, surrounded by bright lights to protect against Rhodesian raids. Early in 1967 John was nearly arrested on a return visit to Southern Rhodesia on a charge of sabotage, which carried the mandatory death sentence. He, the young historian, John Conradie, and Giovanni Arrighi had been working with Chikerema and Nyandoro to smuggle in grenades from Lusaka and distribute them to African activists so that effective protests against the declaration of UDI could be made. When their African contact man was arrested and it was clear that he would soon disclose under interrogation the details of the plot, John courageously flew down from Lusaka to Salisbury to warn Conradie and to give him a message from Chikerema that he must get out. John himself was able to fly out again but Conradie was arrested later that same day at Salisbury airport. He was on his way to South Africa to be best man at his mother's second wedding. Conradie, to whom I had earlier offered a job in the History department when he visited us in Dar, was sentenced in February 1967 to 20 years in prison. He had told me that he could not take the job in Dar because the Tanzanian sun was too hot for his thin skin but had not revealed his commitment to the sabotage plot. Later in Salisbury prison he became great friends with Maurice Nyagumbo. Giovanni Arrighi, who had been the moving force in the sabotage plot but who had been deported from Rhodesia just before his involvement was known, came to teach in Dar. All this dramatized the transformation of white radical activism in Rhodesia. I have often wondered whether I too, had I been able to stay, would have smuggled grenades and distributed them to sabotage groups. I think that the answer I gave to Peter Dyson's letter would have prevailed and I would have sat on that particular fence. I hope so, because it was a futile as well as a dangerous and random activity.

John's diaries for the period between 1963 and 1966 reveal a fascinating interaction among the surviving white radicals. Arrighi was a convinced Marxist revolutionary. He despised the Haddons as capitalists, revered Guy as a sort of Tolstoy figure, and clashed violently with Peter Mackay, whom he regarded as a mere romantic adventurer. For his part Peter denounced Arrighi, telling him to go back and make his revolution in Sardinia and not import irrelevant Marxist ideas into Africa. Peter's own memoir, *We Have Tomorrow,* describes his own much more effective assistance to ZAPU in the 1960s when he helped build training camps in Zambia and shuttled guerrilla recruits up the road from Botswana in his Land Rover or drove them across Lake Kariba in his motor boat By the late 1960s, however, Peter had moved to Dar es Salaam where he made close friends with Nyerere's personal assistant, Joan Wicken, and was involved in the project to build a new capital. Peter was in Dar when Jenny and Albert Macadam and their three daughters, in flight from Dr Banda after his clash with his ministers, came to stay with us. Peter took us all out in his motor boat for an overnight stay on an island off the coast. Our quarrel was long forgotten. Meanwhile I continued to receive letters from old friends. I quote from some of them here because they carry on the stories of characters who have appeared in this book.

On 28 August 1963 Sarah Chavunduka wrote to me from her rural home in Dowa:

> *Yes, I reject Nkomo's 'leadership' for so many reasons which all*
> *boil down to the fact that he has been a thoroughly bad leader.*
> *There was no serious intelligent thinking, planning and deter-*
> *mination during his long term of office. We have gone from one*
> *blunder to another and our opponents have had all the chances*
> *in the world to push ahead their plans. All this dissatisfaction was*
> *present deep down in us, but while there was no alternative there*
> *was very little one could do. Our wrath came to boiling point when*
> *the question of independence cropped up. The whole world was*
> *up in opposition to independence being granted to S.R. The only*
> *country where there was no noise and protest was right here in*
> *S.R. There was no political party to voice the opinion of the people.*
> *The so-called leaders were all out of the country and nobody ever*
> *heard what they said even from wherever they were. We knew*
> *of no further plans in the offing. We did not see the effectiveness*
> *of a 'banned party'. Everything seemed to have come to a tragic*
> *standstill. In the meantime the forces of white supremacy were*
> *working feverishly to entrench themselves. It is in this mood that*
> *rumours of the sacking of Nkomo caught us. We had no idea who*
> *would succeed him but one thing we agreed upon was that NKO-*
> *MO MUST GO! What we wanted was a leader and not Nkomo*
> *for Nkomo's sake. He has nothing to lose for he has not put that*
> *much in the struggle. We are not going to offer him even honorary*
> *leadership for he has done nothing to deserve such an honour.*
>
> *Coming to Rev. Sithole I had no hand in choosing him as a*
> *replacement to Nkomo ... I do not have reason to question his*
> *ability as a leader as yet since he has still to prove himself. But*
> *I cannot help to ask these questions. Although we put the blame*
> *on Nkomo for the past failures, I am tempted to blame the entire*
> *executive because it was their business to see that Nkomo worked*
> *with them and took action which the entire executive was to*
> *account for ... I also do not forget that Sithole was present at the*
> *fatal acceptance of the present constitution. If he was all that wise*
> *he could have given our land the services it desperately needed*
> *then. I am not also impressed by the present Sithole executive which*
> *is all the same old types. I cannot see that they have suddenly become*
> *wiser than they were when chasing around with Nkomo ... As it is*

> now they were outwitted by Nkomo – *the first victory of his political
> career* ... *But since they are now the alternative to Nkomo I have
> no choice but them. So I am a registered member of ZANU.*

Sarah turned to historiography with equal trenchancy:

> *One evening I spent all night defending you when by chance
> sociable Theo asked me to the same dinner as a certain Dr Rob-
> inson whom I gathered had come all the way from Cambridge to
> help the history department as a result of your departure. As the
> evening wore on we started discussing the history department.
> He discovered that I had done history with you and Professor
> Stokes. He then confessed that he found it very difficult to teach
> African history to African students and he wondered how Ranger
> did it so successfully as it appeared. He soon came to the point
> that he thought you approached not from the historian's point
> of view but from the African point of view ... he said it was an
> assumption he had made from how well Ranger and his Afri-
> can students had fared. We argued for a long time till Theo ...
> came to join us. On hearing his argument Theo said if it were
> so how is it so that Ranger commanded an equally high respect
> academically and otherwise from his European students?*
>
> *I hope that [Robinson] had not managed to establish a connec-
> tion between himself and the students. Stokes, Ranger and Rob-
> inson might have said the very same things but people's reaction
> depend very largely on who says those things. And also how they
> say them. Nonetheless he was looking forward to his return to
> Cambridge where the intellectual world hardly rubs shoulders
> with real life and where his family will do him a lot of good.*

In February 1964 Sarah wrote to say she was marrying a Malawian, Joe Kachingwe. 'I may have to live up north – after all, all the good people like you are gone
north!' When she went home to Dowa as a radiant bride in her late twenties her
aunts sang, 'At long last the old cow comes to the barn.' Kachingwe joined the Malawi diplomatic service which complicated my relations with Sarah because I had
fallen very foul of Banda. When Kachingwe went as Malawian envoy to Nairobi,
which I regularly visited on University of East Africa business, Sarah and I used to
meet clandestinely in remote suburbs.

Mutumba Mainga wrote to say she was marrying Theo Bull, a Beit heir, and
proprietor of the *Examiner*. She and her husband came to history conferences in

Dar. Gomo Micongwe wrote to say that life in Malawi under Banda had become impossible and that he had moved to Tanzania as a teacher. He was writing a school history text largely based on my edited collection, *Aspects of Central African History*.

Since her return to Southern Rhodesia Sarah had been teaching at Nyatsime College, which had been founded by Stanlake Samkange. She found it a marvellous relief after the tyrannies of school life at Goromonzi. Meanwhile Stanlake was turning himself into an academic historian during the 1960s and becoming as much part of the African recovery of Zimbabwean history as I was myself.

In August 1964 I had received an astonishing letter from Stanlake, writing from Highfield:

> *I appear to have come to the conclusion that one of the most im-*
> *portant principles my father taught me – that of love of one's fellow*
> *men and sacrifice and service towards other people – is not worth it*
> *and is plain rubbish. I mean every word I say, Terry, and I believe*
> *that Number One is the most important thing in life and to hell*
> *with everybody, particularly in Southern Rhodesia … Can I contin-*
> *ue as if nothing has happened? African women are having their*
> *hair cut by youths in the street and African is murdering African*
> *and being proud of it. Is this sense? Is this patriotism? Terry, if I*
> *could get a job outside this country I would take it and go for many*
> *long years. There is nothing to fight for here – it is not worth it.*

I told John that, 'I can't help feeling a special emotion at the idea of Nathan in flight and Stanlake migrating to America … With Chik and George this sort of thing was willed and chosen, whereas with Nathan and Stanlake it was not. That, of course, was precisely why they did not offer a convincing alternative to the People's Caretaker Council.'

Early in 1965 Stanlake came to see us in Dar before he set off to America. Much later, in March 1967, he wrote from Bloomington, Indiana:

> *It seems like ages ago when I said goodbye to you and Shei-*
> *la and the kids, promising to tell the CID that I had been on*
> *a job hunting trip to Dar. The CID never even bothered to*
> *meet me at the airport, let alone inquire on what business I*
> *had gone to Dar. How disappointing! They did pick me up*
> *two days before I left, and let me go. They were not at the air-*
> *port the day I left which was not a bit flattering to me.*
>
> *Anyway, I came to the States, Terry, and after a week was*
> *bored. No work to do, no nothing to do. All I did was to remain*

> home with the kids while Tommie went to work. A more unMasho-
> na position you cannot imagine and so I decided to write that
> novel [*On Trial For My Country*]. I was told that you had been
> one of two readers who O.Ked it and for some time I wondered
> whether you had not done so for 'chibururu' as we say in Shona.
> But I am told it has sold extremely well so that whatever may
> have been your reasons for okeying it they have been vindicated.
>
> I came here and started work on a Ph.D. I tell you it was
> tough. I had to get into the academic frame of mind, which was
> no easy thing to do, and academic habits were even more diffi-
> cult to cultivate. I have never, repeat never, worked so hard and
> diligently in my life as I did from September 65 to June 66.

Then Stanlake casually announced that he had written a book which was as yet unpublished but which went on to win America's premier Africanist award, the Herskovits Prize of the American African Studies Association:

> I have, incidentally, written another book – Origins of Rhode-
> sia. I wrote this book in the summer of last year. Terry, I have
> never had so much fun. Perhaps Heinemann have already passed
> it on to you as their expert. They have told me that it received a
> favourable report … I hope they will publish it because I really
> enjoyed writing it. I just put my tongue in my cheek, in most cases.
> And let go … I propose to write [my thesis] on my age old topic
> of African land during the BSAC period only. There is nothing
> exciting about the topic and I expect it will be as dull as ditch
> water but I suppose this is how an academic subject is supposed to
> be written so that no one can stand it … Some say your book on
> Chimurenga is out; others say no. I would like to get a copy of it.

By the time he wrote again on 29 March 1968 Revolt was out and Stanlake had read it:

> I was glad to hear that more books are on the production line. If
> they are anything like as good as the first one you will be in danger
> of becoming the leading authority on Central African history.

And Stanlake meant his praise. Years later he based his novel about the 1896-7 uprisings very closely on *Revolt*. But the main aim of this letter was to warn me off accepting a job in the United States:

> Terry, you will never know what I have had to put up with these
> past two years. I never thought I would have to put up with so

> *much arrogance and take in so much insult in my life … What*
> *the Americans have put me through, I tell you, defies description.*

His doctoral thesis, though approved by the Central Africanist, James Hooker, had been obstructed so much by his formal doctoral chair that he nearly gave it up. He ended:

> *The [job] offers you are getting are an indication of the high rep-*
> *utation you have built yourself. It is a wonderful thing to be able*
> *to do or to have got there although you probably do not realize or*
> *care to realize that you have got there. I am really glad for you. If*
> *I were you I would set my eyes on Cambridge first. As for UCLA,*
> *Wisconsin or Berkeley I would consider them as only temporary*
> *appointments. If I were you I would not take a job permanently*
> *at UCLA … I doubt very much if, in the end, you will enjoy the*
> *experience even. You see, I am not really in love with America.*

I did not heed his advice and accepted an offer from UCLA for a job which I much enjoyed.

Other old acquaintances also wrote to me. On 20 May 1965 Tranos Makombe wrote from Gonakudzingwa Restriction Area. Tranos had been my student at UCRN, had chaired the inaugural meeting of the NDP, had represented ZANU before the Liberation Committee, but then had switched to ZAPU because everyone in his home area supported Nkomo. Now he was restricted together with the other ZAPU leaders. He wrote to me:

> *Your remarks concerning the split and my subsequent decision are*
> *well taken. Perhaps it is time to regard the matter as closed, as it*
> *does indeed seem to be regarded by the majority of people here. I*
> *found your description of the attitude of the British people to our*
> *political problems most illuminating. It is a pity that despite our*
> *efforts to interest outside opinion – particularly British – in our*
> *case, and despite the savage repression by the Smith regime of the*
> *majority opinion here at home, there should be an appearance of*
> *accommodation in Britain with the status quo. Let me assure you*
> *that there is no question of capitulating to white supremacy on the*
> *part of the African masses here. What we are witnessing here are*
> *frantic efforts to silence the African nationalist opinion and voice*
> *by every available means, while carrying out a Nazi-like brain*
> *washing campaign among the population. Recently the regime has*
> *been trying to buttress the African chiefs as a substitute for the true*

*leaders of the people ... You can rest assured that the majority of
the people here are still dedicated to the struggle, but their aspirations and their efforts are no longer permitted any publicity.*

A much less optimistic report came from Lovemore Chimonyo, who had worked with me closely in CACBA and with John Reed in the Salisbury City branch. On 11 April 1966 Lovemore wrote to me from the University of Zambia where he had been accepted as a student – and found himself in John Reed's first year English class:

*Since you left Rhodesia I have been in and out of restriction. I
came here to Zambia in August last year soon after detention in
Whawha. I was arrested on 26 August 1964 and released from
detention in May 1965. I then decided to jump across the border into Zambia ... The political situation at home is the same
if not worse. The nationalists, both at home and abroad, have
reverted to armchair and radio politics. Their main job is to
listen to what the outside world has got to say and then say the
same. None of the nationalist organizations at home is prepared
to take the initiative to liberate our people. They are all talking of having been sold out by Britain and yet they themselves
are indirectly subscribing to the situation by sitting idle in some
foreign pubs and hotels. Most of the energy is spent on throttling
and mud-slinging each other. The trouble with our people is that
they are too sophisticated and love luxury too much, unaware
that the longer we postpone it the longer we keep going in and
out of prison. It is a depressing affair. Their biggest excuse is that
they are still planning and will still plan to no end. I feel I could
have done a better job if I were in the upper room of the whole
thing or if I had enough influence on them. We are constantly
embarrassed when we meet people from other countries who
always ask 'Why, you Rhodesian Africans, don't do something?'*

When Lovemore finished his degree he joined the Zambian Prosecutor's office. In that capacity he helped me when I visited Lusaka prison and found poor, con-fused Mr Mhizha illegally detained there because neither ZAPU nor ZANU would vouch for him. Lovemore got him released. Mutumba, by now a staunch UNIP member, rebuked me for meddling in Zambia's affairs.

So there were plenty of echoes in Dar of the increasingly grim Rhodesian situa-tion. But there was nothing that I could do about the situation. And as my interac-tion with Zimbabwe declined, so the contrast between Salisbury and Dar became more starkly evident. Coming from Salisbury to Dar was like going out of a crowded room, full of people and conversation, into an empty space. In Salisbury I knew dozens of Africans and visited their homes. During six years in Dar I made almost no Tanzanian friends. (The Dean of Law, A.B. Weston, had his own solution, frequenting Swahili night-clubs and brothels and becoming so integrated that he ran off in his yacht with a Swahili teenager and was intercepted at sea in a rare exploit by the Tanzanian navy. But such bravado was not my style.) An enlightened foundation grant meant that the first professors at the University College had a year to devise syllabi and order books for the library before beginning to teach. I invented a splendid syllabus. As well as African history it included all my old enthusiasms. There was a course on the historiography of revolutions which coupled the English revolution of the 1640s, which I taught, with the Russian revolution of 1917, which came to be taught by Walter Rodney. There was a comparative nationalism course which coupled Ireland, which I taught, and India, which was taught by John Mc-Cracken. I built up the library. But for a year I had no students to teach. When the first students arrived on campus in July 1964 I was so anxious to talk to somebody that I rushed out and dragged students in to tea. In Tanzania, of course, it cut no ice that one accepted African rule. But when teaching began I found it enormously stimulating. And I was writing *Revolt*. So I began to see my Rhodesian days differently.

In 1967 Roland Oliver wrote to me to say that a search was on for a successor to Philip Mason as Director of the Institute of Race Relations. He was on the selection committee. Would I allow my name to go forward? On 20 July, on the eve of the publication of *Revolt*. I replied:

> *After thinking it over carefully I have decided not to ask that my*
> *name be considered for the Directorship. I was attracted to the*
> *idea of being thus centrally committed to the question of race*
> *relations and also the opportunity to develop new ideas and forms.*
> *But I have become too deeply attached to writing and teaching*
> *to contemplate even a four or five year period away from them.*
> *I should certainly have answered differently immediately after*
> *my departure from Rhodesia, when I could not imagine that the*
> *academic life could hold out prospects of as much excitement as*
> *the public life of controversy I had been leading. But I have found*
> *at Dar that the excitement of research and teaching is equal in*
> *intensity and in many ways more satisfying in achievement.*

Having at last discovered how to be an African historian I wanted to go on being one. When I wrote to John Reed to urge him not to follow the example of Richard

Brown and Eric Stokes and to leave Africa, I did so in intellectual rather than political terms, urging him not so much to stay and agitate but to stay in order to maintain academic standards in a period when I foresaw a decline in expatriate commitment and ability.

Meanwhile there was no such decline in the department I began to found in Dar. It became, indeed, remarkably well equipped to study and teach Africa. John Sutton was an archaeologist; Andrew Roberts was an oral historian; Edward Alpers was fluent in Portuguese; John Iliffe had worked on the German colonial archives; John Lonsdale was expert in the history of Kenya, John McCracken in the history of Malawi. The extraordinary and charismatic Walter Rodney added a radical perspective to his West African expertise. Isaria Kimambo and Arnold Temu had carried out detailed Tanzanian case studies. These historians interacted intensely with each other, attending each others' lectures, giving research seminars, collaborating in the Maji Maji research project, travelling into the interior to give Historical Association courses. This 'Dar es Salaam school of history' was my main contribution during my Dar years. I had other impacts on the University College. I chaired most of the public lectures. I chaired the conference on the role of the university in a socialist Tanzania. But I played no part in Tanzanian public life. Of course there were plenty of exciting public events – the Zanzibar Revolution, the army mutiny, its suppression by a British aircraft carrier moored below the university college, the dismissal of all the Tanzanian university students for protesting against 'the bureaucratic bourgeoisie', the Arusha Declaration, villagization. And there were important private events in those six Tanzanian years.

We adopted a further two daughters – Margaret Mary, a Tanzanian, and Jane, a Kenyan. But all these are subjects for another book. Here I want only to finish the story of the writing of *Revolt*.

# History

I wrote to my parents on 1 December 1963 that, 'if I can make reasonable arrangements I should have the time to get a lot of writing done before July. I should be able to spend half of every day on the book.' On 21 December I told them that 'I spend most mornings in my town office and afternoons at home working on the book and this works very well except that I am frequently seduced out to sit on the patio with a cool breeze and a cool drink and bright blue sea.' I described to them the overall situation for research in Tanzania. 'The only snag as far as prospects for historical research are concerned is the poverty of the Tanganyika government and its reluctance at some levels to concern itself much with things like archives or ancient monuments. I am hoping that I may be able to excite the interest of Nyerere himself in the idea of a co-ordinated research attack on Tanganyikan history so that he orders more support to be given to archivists and archaeologists. The College library is quite good on African history and anthropology ... There is nothing much, though, on anything else.'

Nyerere did become interested enough to give support to the international conference which led to the publication of *Emerging Themes in African History*. Largely due to the heroic efforts of Marcia Wright, the National Archives began to grow and I did some work on them. But gradually a divide opened up between my researching and my writing. My writing was processing the nationalist history I had collected in Rhodesia. 'I have been writing away,' I told my parents on 22 March 1964, 'interrupting the book to do a revision of an article on Rhodes and writing another article on the independent churches ... This makes five articles written and published since I left Southern Rhodesia together with the bulk of the book: by far the most fertile period of my academic existence.' On 6 May I reported a fruitful trip to Lusaka, where 'I was able to do some good work in the Archives and to open up all sorts of lines of further research'. (I also reported the terrible interparty violence in Southern Rhodesia. 'I feel guilty at my present remoteness from the struggle but I cannot bring myself to join either side when things like this are happening.') On 24 June 1964 I boasted that, 'I have written two more articles since I got back from Lusaka, both on Barotseland, which brings my article total up to 10 since I left Salisbury, not to mention two thirds of the great book in final form.'

But while I was writing up my nationalist history my new research was very differently directed. Tanzania offered analogues to Rhodesia. The 1905 Maji Maji rising rivaled 1896; the rise of TANU paralleled the slow growth of Zimbabwean nationalism. But there were people already working on these subjects and I did not wish to replicate their research. Instead I decided to take advantage of my familiarity with a number of African archives. I knew the Salisbury ones very well, of course; I had also worked in Lusaka. After my arrival in Dar I worked in the Tanzanian archives. I employed a Kenyan history student, Nereas Gicuru, to work in Nairobi. I paid particular attention to phenomena which were reported in all these archives – transnational phenomena like witchcraft eradication movements, dance societies, the Watch Tower church. I began to work not on national or nationalist themes but on supra-national ones. This led to my book *Dance and Society in Eastern Africa* and to a frustrated project on 'The Problem of Evil in Eastern Africa'. At the same time I began to work on local rather than national topics. When we visited Masasi in south-eastern Tanzania to give a Historical Association conference, Bishop Trevor

Huddleston gave into my custody dozens of the daily logbooks which clergy and staff of the Universities Mission to Central Africa had to keep. I began to work on these, producing a number of articles and aiming at a book on the interaction of mission with African society. At that time there were grants available for history students to undertake vacation research and I was able to employ them to carry out interviews on eradication movements, dance societies and the history of Masasi. Together with my own fieldwork all this resolved the problem of the oral evidence missing from my research on 1896.

But all the while I was writing up *Revolt*. Then in April 1966 we arranged to exchange our house on campus with the house occupied by the Adult Education officer in Mbeya. I wrote to my mother on 23 April: 'We find Mbeya everything that was promised. The house is a capacious one, on the slopes of the mountain, with a big garden and at the bottom of that a nursery school and playground in which we hope to introduce Franny and Margaret next week. There is a path at the back of the house which leads right up the mountain and takes one very quickly into the most attractive open scenery, and yet the house is only five minutes away from the Mbeya shops. Even in Mbeya one sees plenty of signs of the Rhodesian crisis because it is on the oil-lift road to Zambia.' And in Mbeya too were the representatives of the Zimbabwean nationalist movements, so that I finished *Revolt* once again in dialogue with ZAPU and ZANU. On 2 May I told my mother:

> I have done a fair amount of writing so far and finished off var-
> ious articles and reviews. Today I am again able to turn to the
> book. I find my mind much livelier than in Dar. Mbeya is really
> a wonderful place for drives and walks and I manage to get a
> small drive or walk in every day even when my flow is going well.
> On Sunday we all go for family excursions. It is as beautiful as
> any of the places we have been in Africa. There is a remarka-
> ble variety of climate – one can get peaches and strawberries as
> well as bananas and oranges, there are some stark, sun-baked
> mountains and some lush, rain-fed ones, and splendid views all
> round. At this time of year the grass is full everywhere of flowers
> of all kinds … I have had long talks with the ZANU men here
> and get the impression that they have become much more active.

On 9 May I wrote that, 'last week I completed two chapters of the book – a record – and hope to have the thing very nearly complete by the time we leave in three weeks time. I think I have been doing some good writing here … Yesterday I went and climbed the mountain behind the house – rather like Savoy since the cows all have bells and the churches in Mbeya are busily ringing throughout Sunday.' On May 26 I wrote to John Iliffe: 'You told me not to come back from Mbeya until I had finished the book and I have taken you at your word. I have 5 or 6 pages more to do today and that will be it – 10 chapters, introduction, note on sources and the lot. I shall carry it with me to Europe and read it there to see whether the air of Mbeya has had the same effect as a stimulant drug and that all this stuff is not gibberish. If not I shall give it to my publishers in London. It is a great relief to have it done. Now for the documents volume.' And on 16 June I was able to write to my mother that, 'I finished my book in Mbeya and am bringing it to London to hand to Alan Hill.'

When I was deported in 1963 many publishers had written to me asking to see the book I was writing. They expected an 'I was a teenage terrorist' kind of book. They would have been pleased if Shelagh had offered them her accessible account of the Inkomo trials. But when they heard I was writing a history they became much less interested. I had met Alan Hill of Heinemann Educational Books when he visited Rhodesia and liked him very much. I knew he was publishing the African Writers Series and had done business with John Reed and Clive Wake. So in 1963 I wrote offering him *Revolt*. He accepted, planning to make it the first in an African history series. He had to wait three years, but now in 1996 he received the manuscript and promised rapid publication.

In October 1966 I wrote to my mother: 'I gather from my publishers that the book is now being set up so the time-table seems to be being kept.' At Easter 1967 I received the first page proofs and 'a copy of the dust-jacket which I like very much'. In September Alan Hill visited Dar and spent a week with us. On 9 September I told my mother that 'my rebellion book is definitely (they say) coming out in October. To make up for their slowness on this they are still aiming at getting my edited *Aspects of Central African History* out by the end of the year. Two in three months!' (*Aspects* was a collective production by the Dar department which included two chapters by me which in effect summarized the two books I was writing.) On 6 October, by which time my mother had received an advanced copy, I was writing to say that the publication date was 23 October. 'They have certainly produced it very handsomely and the maps and illustrations have come up very clearly.'

I sent off copies to John and Clive, to Richard Brown, Eric Stokes, Stanlake Samkange and Nathan Shamuyarira. I sent copies to Salisbury prison for Maurice Nyagumbo and Ndabaningi Sithole. Then I sat back to wait for reviews. I did not have to wait long. For the only time in my career, a book of mine was reviewed in the Sunday papers. I wrote jokingly to my mother on November 21. 'I see my book has been reviewed at last in the *Observer* of November 19 by my old acquaintance,

Cyril Dunn. He doesn't say that it is the masterpiece of all time or even that people should rush out and buy it, but I suppose I shall have to rest content with "timely", "remarkably objective", "vivid narrative" and "splendidly illustrated" until a truly perceptive reviewer comes along! I didn't like his 'didactic' bit though.' This review was banned in Southern Rhodesia, as was the dust-jacket. The book itself was not, though, and copies were made available to every Native Commissioner as a guide-book to African revolt!

Much later, on 16 September 1968, came the first significant academic review. I told my mother: 'I am delighted with a review of *Revolt* in the Africanist Bible, the *Journal of African History* by the Africanist, 'Pope' Roland Oliver. He writes of the book as "one of those very rare and precious books that tell us something of the African reaction … It had the pace and clarity of a best-seller and deserves to be one"', though as I told my mother, 'Shelagh has not managed to get through it yet'. Oliver also commented that the book was written during my 'distinguished tenure of the Chair of History at Dar es Salaam where he has gathered around him some of the best minds at work on modern African History'. I told my mother that 'this pleased my whole department. I regard *Revolt* as having had the seal of approval set upon it.' The book was presented to the Tanzanian papal figure, Julius Nyerere, through our good friend, his personal assistant Joan Wicken, who suggested that I accompany it with a letter detailing all the other things which were about to appear. And another papal endorsement came later from Ndabaningi Sithole, writing from Salisbury jail in January 1972:

> *I have had the opportunity of reading and studying your excellent Revolt in Southern Rhodesia, 1896-7. You deserve a good Zimbabwean heifer for having written this book. I like the comprehensiveness and its wide range of documentation. This is one of the few books on Rhodesia that I would feel students must be compelled to read and no student of Rhodesian history would not find it invaluable, Thank you very much for it. How is Sheila? Tell her I still admire her tireless energies in trying to help us in various ways when you and she were in this country, almost a century ago it now seems.*

There was an even more enthusiastic endorsement from the young Zimbabwean historian, Frank Chiteji. Writing from Michigan State University, he told me that 'your works, in my opinion, should be the only sources for the study of East and Central African history'.

Such excessive praise helped me to keep my balance. It was never my intention to produce a single authoritative version of Central African history. I aimed to correct an imbalance in the existing literature rather than to replace it altogether. But I could not resist Maurice Nyagumbo's enthusiasm. For several years I had not heard from Maurice – as he confessed when a letter finally did arrive, his letters had been so intemperate that the censor had suppressed them. He had read *Revolt* though. In 1974 he wrote to Shelagh asking her to send him Lewis Gann's history of Southern Rhodesia and other conservative books so that 'I can be able to contrast their observations with Terry's.' But *Revolt* made more and more sense to him, and as the guerrilla war in Rhodesia intensified it seemed to him that the book was about the present. He wrote to us from Salisbury prison on 8 May 1973. 'It is a long time since I heard from you. It is indeed wonderful to be in our peculiar and rare world as it is so thrilling to witness what is actually happening in our days. All that you wrote about is not ancient history, but is something which is actually occurring in our days. Your description of what happened in a cave near Marandellas [in fact Makoni] is what is now happening daily and this time not in caves but in houses. The most horrifying part of it is that such activities are carried out at night when everyone is asleep and this is done in the name of "Western Civilization". In fact, the world will never know the truth about everything.' In a letter of 24 August 1964, written from Que Que prison, he told me that in the past years he had been through 'a very depressing period' in the struggle. 'It looked as though the settlers were having it their way. From time to time we were hearing of quarrels among our friends in Lusaka and Dar. It actually appeared as if we were heading for a complete breakdown in our struggle.' In June 1970, he told me, Leopold Takawira had died in prison from untreated diabetes. In early 1972 Maurice was abused by the prison doctor – 'as you are aware of my character, I just could not stand that arrogance and decided to lynch this man'. He was barred from all studies for two years. 'Without any radio or any kind of newspaper to inform us what was happening in the north-east, we remained curious. However, in July 1973, we saw eight of the arrested freedom fighters. This was just before they were hanged. I can tell you we were shocked by the bravery of these boys as they appeared absolutely unconcerned with the death they were now facing. It was also interesting to hear that they are being guided by the Mwari cult just as you mention in *Revolt*. This raised our spirits very high.'

Responses to *Revolt* were not universally enthusiastic, however. Early in 1968 Stokely Carmichael [Trinidadian-American civil rights activist] visited the College to give a lecture under the auspices of the Student Revolutionary Front. As the frogs croaked loudly in the pool outside, Stokely held his audience spellbound inside. A master orator, he could do more with a whisper than anyone else with a shout. He had three messages. The first was that the African students were the true proletariat and that they, guns in hand, must spearhead the revolution. The second was that the major liberation movements could not be trusted. He attacked particularly the so-called 'authentic' movements, recognized as such by Soviet Russia – ZAPU, FRE-LIMO, the MPLA. He offered to chair a debate between their representatives and spokesmen of the rival parties, ZANU included. (Wisely none of them took up the challenge.) Giovanni Arrighi, now teaching in Dar and a strong supporter of ZAPU, was incandescent with rage, hissing to me that Stokely must be an agent of the CIA. The third message was that it was necessary, but hard, to hate the whites. It was easy to hate Asians, he said, but whites were so much admired and so dominant that one had to work really hard to hate them. It has taken him all his life to manage it. The students were enraptured and only too ready to bask in the proletarian role he had allocated to them. At one stage he was interrupted while students came up and mopped his brow with a large handkerchief. A history student sitting next to me was shouting 'I do hate the whites, I do hate the whites,' pausing to whisper to me, 'I don't mean you, Professor Ranger.' Stokely's then wife, Miriam Makeba, sang 'Nkosi Sikelele Afrika', a moment of true emotion. It was the only meeting I have ever been to at which it was impossible for me to raise a question or to make an objection.

The next day I was to visit the Refugee School, where the teachers thought their students would be interested to hear about 1896. I took *Revolt* with me. It turned out that Stokely had been there the day before. He had told the students that he was pleased they were passing exams but they must not take this white knowledge seriously. They must always be suspicious of whatever whites told them, and be most suspicious when a white told them something they liked to hear. They must always ask themselves what the motive was. So I encountered a very critical audience. The first questioner told me that he had understood what I had said but that what he wanted to know was the function of it. Fortunately for me, he gave an example by adding: 'I think you have told us about 1896 because the Africans were defeated in the end and you want to discourage us.' I determined not to knuckle under and fought back, grasping a convenient hammer which was lying on the desk. I asked whether Nyerere talked of Maji Maji because it had been defeated in the end and he wanted to discourage Tanzanians. When they refused to believe that some Africans served on the white side in 1896, I showed them photos in the book. 'But who took the photos?' they asked. Would that all audiences were so critical! A very different repudiation of the book came when I arrived at UCLA in 1969. As I entered the elevator in the Bunche building, Donald Abraham wheeled himself out. 'I hold you personally responsible for the death of spirit mediums in Mozambique,' he said in passing.

Nor were the academic reviews all positive. Robert Rotberg wrote a particularly disobliging one for *African Historical Studies*. In a rather pot and kettle way he accused me of 'a leaden style redolent of the classroom'. He objected, perfectly justifiably, to my 'idiosyncratic and occasionally bizarre references'. I have been trying to perfect them ever since. And he thought I did not answer the main questions or provide what a reader needed:

> *Could the physical calamities alone and not the accumulation*
> *of white malfeasance in fact have impelled the rebellion? This is*
> *among the important questions that Professor Ranger has failed*
> *even indirectly to raise. It might have been especially fruitful to*
> *raise a number of questions over the causal as well as the co-ordi-*
> *nating role of the religious leaders. Were they simply articulating*
> *the grievances of the masses, as is implied, or was the rebellion*
> *a projection of rivalries among divines, or a reaction by a reli-*
> *gious oligarchy to an erosion of their collective and individual*
> *significance? Was the rebellion additionally, or even primarily,*
> *an instrumental expression (in the sociological sense) of spiritual*
> *discontent? Or did it result from rivalry between the religious and*
> *secular leaders of Ndebele and Shona life? Furthermore, Professor*
> *Ranger surprisingly never seems to consider whether the rebellion*
> *was in origin a popular movement or, more narrowly, a response*
> *to agitation from above by the traditional leaders of society ... It*
> *had been hoped that this would have been the definitive treatment*
> *of the rebellions. Instead ... it contains the definitive hypothesis and*
> *a fascinating explanation of many aspects of the rebellion. We still*
> *need what Professor Ranger presumably could easily have supplied,*
> *a painstaking detailed account of the actual course of the rebellion*
> *and a fuller exploration of African motivation and response.*

A more informed and balanced critique came from the anthropologist, Richard Werbner, who had himself researched in southern Matabeleland, and was convinced that the cult of the High God, Mwali, had nothing to do with war and had been concerned only with fertility. This initiated a dispute between us which ended up with Werbner as one of my closest friends and our students unable to detect the difference between us. What these critiques showed, to my pleasure, was that *Revolt* was very much an interim account and that the topic of the rebellions needed much further analysis and research, as indeed I had emphasized in the foreword to the book. They were followed by one of the great debates of Zimbabwean historiography, as David Beach and Julian Cobbing attacked the idea of the significance of the religious authorities. By the time of the second edition in 1979, *Revolt* needed a long introduction from me summarizing the arguments. In short, the publication of the book had repercussions almost commensurate with the time it had taken to arrive at the topic and to do research and write it. And as these responses were coming in I had been writing *The African Voice in Southern Rhodesia, 1898 – 1930* during another session in Mbeya and publishing it in London in 1970.

# Conclusion

The ten years in Africa between 1957 and 1967 had answered most of the questions which I had carried to Southern Rhodesia. I knew now that both I and Shelagh had moral and physical courage and that we could commit ourselves to a cause while retaining our own consciences. I knew that I could lead people in service of that cause. I had worked out, after much trial and error, a way of writing African history. Shelagh had received many letters from Africans telling her what a remarkable man I was. I was no longer a very ordinary boy. All this was – and is – good to know.

And yet when I look back at the story told in this memoir – and at the work which emerged from it – I find two things extraordinary. My enemies in Rhodesia, and sometimes my friends, used to say I was arrogant. Looking back, I don't think I was. There is too much evidence of humble compassion and loving friendship for this. But I am disconcerted at my total self-confidence. I was as certain that I was right in the correctness of my liberalism as any Marxist could have been in the inevitability of the dialectic. This led to a massive simplicity both in life and in historical analysis. Gradually in Tanzania and thereafter my attitude and my history became more complex and ambiguous. That is why my 1999 book, *Voices From the Rocks*, which returns to many of the questions raised in *Revolt*, is a much better book, reflecting as it does the full range of the complexities and ambiguities of African response to colonial invasion and dominance. It also embodies enough African testimony to enable me to escape from the constraints of the colonial archive. It had taken me fifty years rather than ten to arrive at a satisfactory account of Zimbabwean history.

But the second thing that strikes me is that although my attitude was simple I don't think it was authoritarian. John Reed records in his diaries one of Bernard Chidzero's visits. John and I and Herbert Chitepo were driving him to the airport. John records that the atmosphere was relaxed and warm. Herbert and Bernard jestingly foresaw the future. Bernard would be Prime Minister, Herbert would be Minister of Justice – and I would be in Khami prison. It was a good joke because of the truth it contained. It is clear that I was a natural dissident. I was committed to nationalism but to a liberal nationalism. Here I think that the key document I have quoted is my letter to the *Malawi News* in defence of Sarah. In it I argued that after the achievement of secure majority rule there would be no need for repression and that varying opinions could and should be tolerated. Even at the time this did not seem very convincing for Banda's increasingly authoritarian Malawi. Sarah, coming back to Southern Rhodesia at the end of 1962, wrote to me that as she crossed over the border she felt a great cloud of repression and depression lift. The struggle with white minority rule seemed much more straightforward than the stifling conformity of independent Malawi. Now she would not have to watch her every word. Nevertheless, I had been expressing my core belief. It was the same message that I had conveyed in my barefoot speech to the great NDP rally at the end of 1961 – that the nationalist movement aimed at unity, but not at a coerced unity.

In Southern Rhodesia too this idea seemed increasingly improbable – as Stanlake's letter of August 1964 revealed, mourning as it did the death of his father's inclusive and tolerant nationalism. Yet my ideal was shared by many others. It was Sketchley Samkange's vision, and Sarah's, and even Maurice Nyagumbo's, though he worried that the die-hard whites would make it impossible. As for me, I genuinely felt that authoritarian intolerance was worse within an African movement or an African state than it was in the repressive settler regime against which most of my dissidence was directed. So this memoir is dotted with examples of my expressions of freedom of conscience and dissidence against the African majority view. It shows in my visit to give Michael Mawema support just as he had been deposed. It shows in my support for Sarah. It shows in my indignation at the libels against Nathan Shamuyarira. It shows in my intervention to get Mhizha released from Lusaka prison. What strikes me now is for how long I was able to get away with this dissidence so that even Chikerema in 1963 told objectors that if they wanted me in the nationalist movement they had to accept that I would speak my mind. But in the end, and after the split, attitudes hardened and I was cast off as a traitor by Chikerema himself.

It was time, as I wrote to Roland Oliver, for me to abandon politics and to seek to defend freedom of thought within the university and in my writings. Tanzania was a good, if difficult, setting for this kind of dissidence. And I have come to think that my nationalist dissidence of the 1960s foreshadowed my present criticism of Mugabe's authoritarianism. I don't see this as a repentance from earlier nationalist conformity, but as a continuation of the ideals and practice of the 1960s.

# Appendix of Names

**Adams, Walter** (1906–1975) British historian who studied at University College London. Principal of the University College of Rhodesia and Nyasaland (UCRN) between 1955 and 1967, and Director of the London School of Economics and Political Science, 1967–74.

**Arrighi, Giovanni** (1937–2009) Italian-born Marxist, and theorist of under-development, who taught at UCRN in the 1950s. Deported from Rhodesia for his support to the nationalist movement, he went on to teach at the University of Dar es Salaam in Tanzania and at several universities in the United States.

**Beadle Tribunal** Chaired by Justice Beadle, it was set up to review the continued detention of 100 nationalists following the state of emergency in Southern Rhodesia in 1959. Its report vindicated the government's actions and also challenged the findings of the Devlin Report.

**Bull, Theodore** (?–2003) An heir to part of the Beit fortune who bought the *Central African Examiner* in 1960. The journal's editorial stance became increasingly critical of the government and sympathetic towards the nationalists, which led to its being forced out of business by the Smith government in 1965. Married Mutumba Mainga in 1969 and settled in Zambia.

**Benjamin Burombo** (*c*.1909–1958) Prominent trade unionist who founded the African Workers Voice Association in 1947 and was one of the key leaders of the 1948 strike in Southern Rhodesia. In the 1950s worked to challenge the Native Land Husbandry Act.

**Cameron, Colin** (1933– ) Studied law at Glasgow University and worked as a solicitor in Nyasaland where he represented Africans arrested and detained during the 1959 Emergency. After independence was appointed to Banda's first cabinet but was subsequently deported in 1964 after representing Henry Chipembere in a constitutional case against Banda.

**Carr Saunders Hall** UCRN residence named after Sir Alexander Carr Saunders

183

(1886–1966), an English biologist and sociologist who chaired the 1953 Committee on Higher Education in Central Africa. The committee recommended that a university be established to serve Southern Rhodesia, Northern Rhodesian and Nyasaland.

**Chambati, Ariston Maguranyanga** (1935–1995) Studied at Princeton, Oxford, and New York Universities in the 1960s. Founder member of the National Democratic Party; become a member of ZAPU and remained with the party after 1963. In the 1970s worked with the Commonwealth Secretariat and the University of Rhodesia. After independence joined the corporate sector before being appointed Minister of Finance in 1995.

**Chavunduka, Sarah** (1936–2012) The first African woman to be enrolled at the UCRN, in 1957. Worked as a teacher in Malawi after graduating, and married Joe Kachingwe, a Malawian diplomat. Joined the Zimbabwean civil service after 1980 and rose to the position of Permanent Secretary in the Ministry of Information.

**Chidzero, Bernard** (1927–2002) Graduated with a PhD from McGill University and held a Postdoctoral Fellowship at Nuffield College, Oxford. In the 1960s and 1970s he worked with the United Nations. Appointed Minister of Economic Planning and Development in 1980. The Ministry of Finance was added to his ministerial portfolio in 1983 and he held this post until he resigned in 1995.

**Chikerema, James Robert** (1925–2006) The first African teacher at Kutama Roman Catholic Mission; in 1956 became the founding president of the Salisbury City Youth league. Held leadership roles in the SRANC, NDP, ZAPU and FROLIZI. Joined the Internal Settlement Government under Muzorewa's UANC and served as co–Minister of Transport and Power. Efforts to return to active politics after 1980 were unsuccessful.

**Chitepo, Herbert** (1923–75) The first African lawyer in Southern Rhodesia and a prominent nationalist politician. In the late 1950s and early 1960s, provided legal advice and legal representation for the leadership of NDP, ZAPU and later ZANU. Resigned from his post as the Director of Public Prosecutions in Tanzania in 1966 and moved to Lusaka from where he spearheaded the armed struggle on the ZANU side until he was killed by a car bomb in March 1975.

**Chitepo, Victoria** (1928– ) Married to Herbert Chitepo, whom she met at Fort Hare. Active in the Southern Rhodesia Detainees Legal Aid and Welfare Fund. After independence, elected to Parliament and served in the first cabinet as Deputy Minister of Information and Tourism. Later appointed Minister for Post and Telecommunications; retired from government in 1992.

**Clutton–Brock, Arthur Guy** (1906–1995) Came to Southern Rhodesia with his wife Molly in 1949 and was actively involved in the co–operative farming scheme at St Faith's Mission Farm. Later co–founded Cold Comfort Farm, a multiracial co–operative on the outskirts of Salisbury. In 1971 Cold Comfort was declared an unlawful organisation by the Smith administration and he was expelled from Rhodesia. In 1995, became the first white person to be declared a Zimbabwean National Hero.

**Cole, George Douglas Howard** (1889–1959) English academic and an active member of the Fabian Society. Taught at Oxford from the 1920s to the 1950s and published extensively on history and economics.

**Collins, John** (1905–1982) Anglican priest and Canon of St Paul's Cathedral in London. Helped to found Christian Action and later spearheaded efforts to raise funds for political prisoners and their families in southern Africa. This initiative led to the establishment of the International Defence and Aid Fund.

**Conradie, John Andrew** (1937–1998) Born in Pretoria; lectured in the UCRN History Department. Became deeply involved with ZAPU, and in 1967 was imprisoned for 20 years under the Law and Order Maintenance Act. Released in 1978 on condition of leaving Rhodesia, he took up a fellowship at Churchill College, Oxford. Worked for the Zimbabwe Project in London, returned to Zimbabwe in 1983, and managed the Kushanda pre-school project until his death. Declared a Provincial Hero, and given a state funeral.

**Courtauld, Sir Stephen** (1883–1967) English businessman who moved to Rhodesia in 1951. His family settled on La Rochelle, an estate near Mutare. Served as a board member of the *Central African Examiner* during the early 1960s.

**Devlin Commission** A Commission of Enquiry appointed by the British government to enquire into the Nyasaland colonial government's handling of the 1959 Emergency. It produced a critical report on the colonial government's heavy-handed action, describing the colony as having been transformed into a 'police state' during the emergency.

**Dumbutshena, Enoch** (1920–2000) Graduated in History and Politics at the University of South Africa and studied law at Gray's Inn, London. Went to Lusaka in the late 1960s and worked in the Zambian Ministry of Justice. Appointed the first black judge in the Zimbabwean High Court and served as the Chief Justice from 1984 to 1990.

**Field, Winston Joseph** (1904–1969) Rhodesian tobacco farmer and politician who began his political career as a member of the Federal Parliament in 1957. Became the Southern Rhodesian Prime Minister in 1962 but was forced to resign by his cabinet in 1964, on the grounds that he had not fought hard enough for independence, and was replaced by Ian Douglas Smith.

**Fletcher, Sir Patrick Bisset** (1900–1981) Rhodesian politician who served as Minister of Agriculture, Minister of Native Affairs and later Minister of Health. Became Garfield Todd's Deputy Prime Minister and was amongst the cabinet members who resigned declaring that they had lost confidence in him.

**Fortune, George** (1915–2012) British linguist, and Catholic priest. Taught at the

University of Cape Town, and became the first Chair of African Languages at UCRN in 1962, a position he retained until his retirement in 1980. Published extensively on African languages and played a key role in promoting Shona literature.

**Foy, Whitfield** Methodist missionary who edited the periodical *Dissent* along with Terence Ranger and John Reed. Clashed with his European congregation due to his critical views on settler racial attitudes, as well as his support for African nationalist aspirations, and was transferred back to England in 1960.

**Garbett, Kingsley** (1935–2006) British anthropologist who worked at UCRN. Left Rhodesia after UDI and was barred from returning due to his critical views about the Rhodesian government. Went on to teach at the Universities of Manchester and Adelaide.

**Ginwala, Frene Noshir** (1932– ) South African journalist and ANC activist who completed her D.Phil at Linacre College, Oxford. Spent two periods in Tanzania as editor of *The Nationalist*. Served as Speaker of the South African National Assembly between 1994 and 2004 and was appointed Chancellor of the University of KwaZulu-Natal in 2005.

**Graham, Lord James Angus** (1907–1992) Rhodesian farmer and politician who served as Smith's Minister of Agriculture and was amongst those who signed the Unilateral Declaration of Independence. Left Rhodesia in 1979 and lived in South Africa before settling in Scotland.

**Haddon, Eileen** (1921–2003) South African-born journalist and activist. Moved to Southern Rhodesia with her family after the National Party won the elections in South Africa in 1948. She and her husband supported several progressive causes during the 1950s and 1960s. She joined the *Central African Examiner* in 1960 and went on to become its editor until it closed in 1965.

**Haddon, Michael** (1915–1996) Born in Southern Rhodesia and went on to study at the Royal School of Mines in London. In 1963 he and his wife offered the use of their Cold Comfort Farm to the People's Caretaker Council for its inaugural Congress. They later donated the farm to the multiracial co-operative initiated by Didymus Mutasa, Guy Clutton-Brock and others. Arrested in 1965 and imprisoned for three years, he left the country in 1969 and settled in Zambia. Returned to Zimbabwe after independence and assisted in setting up the Zimbabwe Mining Development Corporation.

**Hamadziripi, Henry** (?–2005) Nationalist politician and founder member of ZANU. Member of the Dare re Chimurenga, and central to the formation of the Crocodile Commando. In 1978 he was arrested by ZANLA, along with Rugare Gumbo, Joseph Taderera and Cletus Chigove, on charges of plotting a coup against Mugabe. Left active politics after independence.

**Jamela, Reuben Thomas** Prominent trade unionist who led the Southern Rhodesia

Trade Union Congress. In the early 1960s fell out with ZAPU because of the party's desire to influence the labour movement, and his support for the International Confederation of Free Trade Unions. Later formed the short-lived Pan-African Socialist Union.

**Loft, George** (1915–?) Quaker activist, born in New York. Appointed by the American Friends Service Committee as a special representative in southern Africa and based in Salisbury. He left Salisbury in 1960 but continued to be engaged with the political developments as well as development projects in southern Africa.

**Mackay, Peter** (1926–) Served in the British army before migrating to Southern Rhodesia where he became involved with the Capricorn Africa Society. Later engaged in the nationalist struggle in Nyasaland, where he edited the anti-colonial journal *Tsopano,* and in Rhodesia, where he supported ZAPU. After independence, was actively involved in humanitarian efforts in the Omay communal lands in north–western Zimbabwe. Now lives in Marondera.

**Madzimbamuto, Daniel** (1930–?) Joined the SRANC and supported opposition to the Native Land Husbandry Act between 1957 and 1959. Between 1959 and 1974 spent much time in detention, where he gained several qualifications including a law degree. His legal challenge against his detention in 1966 was one of the prominent constitutional cases which challenged the legality of the Smith government.

**Mainga, Mutumba** Zambian historian who completed her PhD at the University of London in 1969 and taught at the University of Zambia between 1969 and 1973. Between 1973 and 1991 she was involved in active politics and served as Member of Parliament in Zambia as well as a cabinet minister. After her political career she took up a post at the University of Zambia.

**Makombe, Tranos Amos Gono** (?–2004) Nationalist politician who presided over the meeting in Highfield to form the NDP on 1 January 1960. In 1963 he joined ZANU but later switched back to ZAPU. Served as the Governor of Midlands Province 1986–1992. Subsequently appointed Zimbabwean Ambassador to Tanzania and later Ethiopia, during which time he also served as representative to the Organisation of African Unity.

**Morton Malianga** (1930– ) Nationalist politician who was elected Vice–President of the NDP. Later joined ZANU and was detained between 1964 and 1974. After independence, was appointed Deputy Minister of Finance and later Deputy Minister of Industry and Commerce.

**Maluleke, Josiah Terry** (1928–?) Trade unionist who organised the African Commercial and General Workers Union and became the Secretary General in 1953. In 1962 he and Thomas Mswaka broke away from the Southern Rhodesia Trade Union Congress and formed the African Trade Union Congress. Restricted to Gonakudzingwa but escaped and ultimately found his way to London where he completed an economics degree and began working with the Zimbabwe Students Union.

**Manfred Hodson Hall** UCRN hall of residence named after a member of the Southern Rhodesia Legislative Assembly who was instrumental in the establishment of the university.

**Matimba, Patrick** Nationalist politician who studied in England in the 1950s and married a Dutch woman, Adri van Hoorn. When his wife joined him in Southern Rhodesia, their inter-racial marriage created a furore within the settler community. In 1959 he was detained and released on condition that he leave the country. He later returned and joined Michael Mawema, Paul Mushonga and Edson Sithole in their split from NDP to form the Zimbabwe National Party but was later expelled from the party. He went on to edit the *Zimbabwe Newsletter* from London in the 1970s and later established a publishing company.

**Mawema, Michael** (1928–2000) A teacher, whose entry into politics came through working as a trade union leader. He was elected NDP President, but resigned over internal squabbles. He formed the Zimbabwe National Party but joined ZANU after 1963 and was elected the party's organising secretary.

**Moyo, Jason Ziyapapa** (*c.*1927–1977) A nationalist politician who cut his teeth as a trade unionist. He served as the General Secretary of the African Artisans' Union in Bulawayo and was later was active in the SRANC, NDP and ZAPU. He remained with ZAPU after the split and became its Vice–President in charge of external affairs. Killed by a parcel bomb delivered to the ZAPU offices in Lusaka.

**Mtambanengwe, Simpson** (1930–) After qualifying as a barrister in London, went to Lusaka and worked alongside Herbert Chitepo. He later joined the Muzorewa UANC. After independence, appointed to the Zimbabwean High Court bench and later seconded to Namibia in 1994. Currently chairs the Zimbabwe Electoral Commission.

**Musarurwa, Willie** (1927–1990) Editor of several newspapers, including the *African Weekly*, *Bantu Mirror*, *African Parade* and the *African Daily News*. Joined the SRANC in 1957 and was a founding member of the NDP. Stayed with ZAPU after the split and was detained between 1964 and 1974. After independence, appointed the editor of the *Sunday Mail* but was dismissed in 1985 for being critical of the government.

**Mushonga, Paul** (?–1962) Businessman who supported the NDP financially. Joined ZAPU but later broke away and became the leader of the Zimbabwe National Party. Died in a car accident.

**Mutsvairo, Solomon** (1924–2005) Taught at Goromonzi Secondary School and later became headmaster of Sanyati Baptist Mission School. Wrote several novels in Shona and English, including *Feso* which became popular within nationalist circles. Completed his PhD at Howard University in 1978 and later joined the University of Zimbabwe. In 1991, wrote the lyrics for the Zimbabwean national anthem.

**Nkala, Enos (1932–)** Founder member of ZANU and served on the Dare re Chimurenga. After independence, appointed Minister of Finance and later Minister of National Supplies, Home Affairs and Defence; spearheaded the government–directed violence against ZAPU supporters in Matabeleland.

**Nyabadza, Basil (?–1977)** Pastor of an independent African church in Manicaland Province, and a rural entrepreneur. His support for the guerrillas earned him the suspicion of government officials and he was killed by Criminal Investigation Department agents.

**Nyagumbo, Maurice (1924–1989)** Founder member of the Salisbury City Youth league in 1956; active in the SRANC, NDP and ZAPU. Spent very little time outside prison between 1959 and 1979. After independence, elected to Parliament and held several cabinet appointments. Resigned from government in April 1989, and committed suicide after being charged with perjury following the publication of the Sandura Commission report into corruption amongst senior government officials.

**Nyandoro, George (1926–1994)** Nationalist politician, involved in several African associations and unions and in campaigns against the Native Land Husbandry Act from the early 1950s. A founder of the City Youth League and later elected Secretary General of the SRANC. Remained with ZAPU until 1971 when he switched to FROLIZI and later joined Muzorewa's UANC. Withdrew from politics after independence and went into business.

**Prestwich, John (1914–2003)** British historian of the medieval period. A fellow of Queen's College, Oxford from 1937 until retirement in 1981.

**Rubadiri, David (1930– )** Malawian academic and acclaimed poet. Malawi's first ambassador to the United States of America and the United Nations, but left Malawi after a falling out with President Banda. Taught at universities in Nigeria, Kenya and Botswana, and in 2002 was appointed Vice-Chancellor of the University of Malawi.

**Savanhu, Jasper (1917–?)** Journalist and politician. Rose to prominence during the 1945 railway strike and went on to lead the Federation of Bulawayo African Workers Trade Union. He and Masotsha Mike Hove were the first two Africans from Southern Rhodesia to become members of the Federal Parliament. In 1959, became the first African to be appointed Parliamentary Secretary to the Federal Minister of Home Affairs.

**Shamuyarira, Nathan (1930– )** Nationalist politician and journalist; editor of the *African Daily News* from 1956 and became in 1959 the Editor-in-Chief of African Newspapers group, from which he resigned due to differences with the proprietors. In the 1960s he was appointed ZANU's Secretary for Foreign Affairs but left to join FROLIZI in 1972. Shamuyarira completed a doctorate at Princeton and later re–joined ZANU. After independence served as Minister of Information and of Foreign Affairs.

**Silundika, Tarcicius George Malan** (1929–1981) Secretary General of the NDP. Stayed in ZAPU after 1963 and held several senior leadership posts in Lusaka. After independence, was elected to Parliament and was appointed Minister of Roads, Road Traffic, Post and Telecommunications.

**Symonds, Jane** Secretary for the London–based Africa Bureau, founded in 1952 by Rev. Michael Scott. Involved in raising funds for political detainees and creating awareness about the political situation in Southern Rhodesia. Chaired the Africa Publications Trust and later worked as a magistrate in Nottingham.

**Swinton Hall** UCRN residence named after the Earl of Swinton (Philip Lloyd-Greame, 1884–1972), a Conservative politician and the Secretary of State for Commonwealth Relations between 1952 and 1955.

**Takawira, Leopold** (1916–1970) A teacher by profession before becoming executive officer of the Capricorn Africa Society in 1957. Later embraced nationalist politics and was central in the formation of ZANU and was elected its Vice–President. In 1964 he was detained along with many nationalists and died in Salisbury Prison.

**Vambe, Lawrence** (1917– ) Worked as a teacher before becoming a journalist. In 1953, appointed Editor–in–Chief of the African Newspapers group; awarded an MBE for services to journalism in 1958. Worked for Anglo America and its sister company Charter Consolidated in the 1960s. Author of *An Ill-fated People* (Heinemann, 1972). Lives in England.

**van Velsen, Jaap** (1921–1990) Anthropologist who studied at Oxford and Manchester Universities. Joined the UCRN in 1959 but was deported in 1966 due to his opposition to UDI. Later taught at the University of Zambia and University College of Wales, Aberystwyth.

**Wästberg, Per** (1933– ) Swedish writer, actively involved in the struggle against colonialism and apartheid. Expelled from Southern Rhodesia in 1959, and later declared *persona non grata* in Rhodesia and South Africa because of his anti-apartheid book *På Svarta Listan* (On the Black List). Chairman of International PEN, 1979–86.

**Whitehead, Sir Edgar** (1905–1971) Rhodesian politician. Elected to the Southern Rhodesian Legislative Assembly in 1939 and later served in several senior capacities in the government. Took over from Garfield Todd as Prime Minister in 1958 and held the post until 1962 when he was replaced by the Rhodesian Front's Winston Field.

# Select References

Chung, Fay. 2006. *Re-living the Second Chimurenga: Memories from Zimbabwe's Liberation Struggle* (Uppsala, Nordic Africa Institute; Harare, Weaver Press).

Etherton, Michael and John Reed. 2011. *Chikwakwa Remembered. Theatre and Politics in Zambia, 1968-1972* (Dublin, Original Writing).

Gelfand, Michael. 1978 *A Non-racial Island of Learning. A History of the University College of Rhodesia from its Inception to 1966* (Gwelo, Mambo Press).

Jeater, Diana. 2011. 'Terence Ranger: Life as Historiography', *History at Large*, July.

——. 2012. 'Stuff Happens and People Make it Happen: Theory and Practice in the work of Terence Ranger', *History Workshop Journal*, Vol. 77, No. 1.

King, Tony. 1996. 'The Central African Examiner, 1957-1965', *Zambezia*, Vol. 23, No. 2.

Limb, Peter. 2011. 'Terence Ranger, African Studies and South African Historiography', *Historia*, Vol. 56. No. 1.

Mackay, Peter. 2008. *We Have Tomorrow. Stirrings in Africa, 1959-1967*. Introduction by Terence Ranger. (Wilby, Michael Russell).

Nyagumbo, Maurice. 1980. *With the People. An Autobiography from the Zimbabwean Struggle.* Preface by John Conradie, Introduction by Terence Ranger. (London, Allison and Busby; Salisbury, Graham Publishers).

Ranger, Terence. 1960. *Crisis in Southern Rhodesia*, Fabian Commonwealth Bureau.

—— 1961. *State and Church in Southern Rhodesia, 1919-1939*, Salisbury, Historical Association of Rhodesia and Nyasaland.

—— 1963. 'Revolt in Portuguese East Africa: The Makombe Rising of 1917', in K. Kirkwood (ed.), *St Antony's Papers*, No. 15.

—— 1965. 'The "Ethiopian" Episode in Barotseland, 1900-1905', *Rhodes Livingstone Journal*, Vol. 37, No. 1.

—— 1966. 'The Role of the Ndebele and Shona Religious Authorities in the Rebellions of 1896 and 1897', in E. Stokes and R. Brown (eds), *The Zambesian Past: Studies in Central African History* (Manchester, Manchester University Press).

—— 1967. *Revolt in Southern Rhodesia, 1896-7: A Study in African Resistance* (London, Heinemann).

—— 1968. 'Nationality and Nationalism: The Case of Barotseland', *Journal of the Historical Society of Nigeria*, Vol. 4, No. 2.

—— 1968.'Introduction', 'The Nineteenth Century in Southern Rhodesia' and 'African Politics in Twentieth-Century Southern Rhodesia', in T. Ranger (ed.), *Aspects of Central African History* (London, Heinemann).

—— 1970. *The African Voice in Southern Rhodesia, 1898-1930* (London, Heinemann; Evanston, Northwestern University Press; New York, International Publications Service; Nairobi, East Africa Publishing House).

—— 1975. *Dance and Society in Eastern Africa, 1890-1970* (London, Heinemann).

—— 1985. *Peasant Consciousness and Guerrilla War in Zimbabwe* (London, James Currey).

—— 1985. *The Invention of Tribalism in Zimbabwe* (Gweru, Mambo Press).

—— 1988. *Chingaira Makoni's Head: Myth, Mystery and the Colonial Experience*, Bloomington, Africa Studies Program, Indiana University.

—— 1999. *Voices From the Rocks: Nature, Culture & History in the Matopos Hills of Zimbabwe* (Oxford, James Currey; Bloomington, Indiana University Press; Harare, Baobab Books).

——, Jocelyn Alexander and JoAnn McGregor. 2000. *Violence and Memory: One Hundred Years in the 'Dark Forests' of Matabeleland* (Oxford, James Currey; Harare, Weaver Press; Cape Town, David Philip; Portsmouth NH, Heinemann).

—— 2011. *Bulawayo Burning: A Social History of a Southern African City* (Woodbridge, James Currey; Harare, Weaver Press).

—— 1995. *Are We Not Also Men? The Samkange Family & African Politics in Zimbabwe, 1920-64* (London, James Currey; Cape Town, David Philip; Portsmouth NH, Heinemann; Harare, Baobab Books).

Samkange, Stanlake. 1966. *On Trial For My Country* (London, Heinemann).

—— 1968. *The Origins of Rhodesia* (London, Heinemann).

—— 1978. *Year of the Uprising* (London, Heinemann).

Vansina, Jan. 1994. *Living With Africa* (Madison, University of Wisconsin Press).

White, Luise. 2011'Terence Ranger in Fact and Fiction', *International Journal of African Historical Studies*, Vol. 44 No. 2.

Zimudzi, Tapiwa. 2007. 'Spies and Informers on Campus: Vetting, Surveillance and the Deportation of Expatriate University Lecturers in Colonial Zimbabwe, 1954-1963', *Journal of Southern African Studies*, Vol. 33, No. 1.

# TERENCE RANGER

# Bibliography

The 'Ranger Papers' are held under that name at Rhodes House Library in Oxford. They may be consulted with permission from Terence Ranger and on the advice of the librarian-archivist, Lucy McCann, who knows the contents well although they have not been catalogued. Lucy. mccann@bodleian.ox.ac.uk 270508

T. Ranger. 1959. The Career of Richard Boyle, first Earl of Cork in Ireland, 1588-1643, (University of Oxford, D. Phil. Thesis).

## BOOKS

T. Ranger. 1967. *Revolt in Southern Rhodesia, 1896-7: A Study in African Resistance* (London, Heinemann).

—— 1969. *The African Churches of Tanzania* (Nairobi, East African Publishing House).

—— 1970. *The African Voice in Southern Rhodesia, 1898-1930* (London, Heinemann; Illinois, Northwestern University Press; New York, International Publications Service; Nairobi, East Africa Publishing House).

—— 1975. *Dance and Society in Eastern Africa, 1890-1970* (London, Heinemann).

—— 1979. (2nd edn) *Revolt in Southern Rhodesia, 1896-97: A Study in African Resistance* (London, Heinemann).

—— 1985. *The Invention of Tribalism in Zimbabwe,* (Gweru, Mambo Press).

—— 1985. *Peasant Consciousness and Guerrilla War in Zimbabwe* (London, James Currey).

—— 1995. *Are We Not Also Men? The Samkange Family & African Politics in Zimbabwe, 1920-64* (London, James Currey; Cape Town, David Philip; Portsmouth NH, Heinemann; Harare, Baobab Books).

—— 1999. *Voices From the Rocks: Nature, Culture & History in the Matopos Hills of Zimbabwe* (Oxford, James Currey; Bloomington, Indiana University Press; Harare, Baobab Books).

——, Jocelyn Alexander and JoAnn McGregor. 2000. *Violence and Memory: One Hundred Years in the 'Dark Forests' of Matabeleland* (Oxford, James Currey; Harare, Weaver Press; Cape Town, David Philip; Portsmouth NH, Heinemann).

—— 2011. *Bulawayo Burning: A Social History of a Southern African City* (Woodbridge, James Currey; Harare, Weaver Press).

## EDITED COLLECTIONS

——, W. Foy and J. Reed (eds) *Dissent,* periodical published in Salisbury from c. 1959-1961.

—— (ed.). 1968. *Aspects of Central African History* (London, Heinemann).

—— (ed.). 1968. *Emerging Themes in African History* (London, Heinemann).

—— and I. Kimambo (eds). 1972. *The Historical Study of African Religion* (London, Heinemann).

—— and M. Hlashwayo (eds) *African Religious History: a newsletter for the historical study of African religious systems in East, Central and Southern Africa,* from 1971-1975.

—— and J. Weller (eds). 1975. *Themes in the Christian History of Central Africa* (London, Heinemann).

—— and W. Shiels (eds). 1982. *The Church and Healing* (Oxford, Basil Blackwell).

—— and J. Peel (eds). 1982. *Past and Present in Zimbabwe* (Manchester, Manchester University Press).

—— and E. Hobsbawm (eds). 1983. *The Invention of Tradition* (Cambridge, Cambridge University Press).

—— and P. Slack (eds). 1992. *Epidemics and Ideas: Essays on the Historical Perception of Pestilence* (Cambridge, Cambridge University Press).

——, W. Beinart and R. Turrell (eds). 1992. *Journal of Southern African Studies,* Vol. 18, No. 3: Special Issue on Violence.

—— and N. Bhebe (eds). 1995. *Soldiers in Zimbabwe's Liberation War* (London, James Currey; Portsmouth NH, Heinemann; Harare, University of Zimbabwe Publications).

—— and O. Vaughan (eds). 1993. *Legitimacy and the State in Twentieth Century Africa* (London, MacMillan).

——, Y. Samad and O. Stuart (eds). 1996. *Culture, Identity and Politics: Ethnic Minorities in Britain* (Aldershot, Avebury).

—— and N. Bhebe (eds). 1996. *Society in Zimbabwe's Liberation War* (London, James Currey; Portsmouth NH, Heinemann; Harare, University of Zimbabwe Publications).

—— and R. Werbner (eds). 1996. *Postcolonial Identities in Africa* (London, Zed Books).

—— and N. Bhebe (eds). 2001. *The Historical Context of Human Rights and Democracy in Zimbabwe: Pre-colonial and Colonial Legacies* (Harare, University of Zimbabwe Publications). Awarded prize for non-fiction at the Zimbabwe Book Publishers' Awards, August 2002.

—— and N. Bhebe (eds). 2003. *The Historical Context of Human Rights and Democracy in Zimbabwe: Nationalism, Democracy and Human Rights* (Harare, University of Zimbabwe Publications; Oxford, Africa Books Collective). Awarded first prize for non-fiction in the Zimbabwe Book Publishers' Awards, August 2004.

—— (ed.). 2008. *Evangelical Christianity and Democracy in Africa* (New York, Oxford University Press).

## ARTICLES

T. Ranger. 1957. 'Richard Boyle and the Making of an Irish Fortune, 1588-1614', *Irish Historical Studies,* Vol. 10, No. 39.

—— 1961. 'Stafford in Ireland: A Revaluation', *Past and Present,* Vol. 19. Reprinted in T. Ashton (ed.). 1967. *Crisis in Europe, 1560-1660* (London, Routledge and Kegan Paul).

—— 1963. 'Revolt in Portuguese East Africa: The Makombe Rising of 1917', in K. Kirkwood (ed.), *St Antony's Papers,* No. 15.

—— 1964. 'The Early History of Independency in Southern Rhodesia', in W. Montgomery Watt (ed.), *Religion in Africa* (Edinburgh, mimeo).

—— 1964. 'The Last Word on Rhodes?', *Past and Present,* No. 28.

—— 1965. 'The "Ethiopian" Episode in Barotseland, 1900-1905', *Rhodes Livingstone Journal,* 37.

—— 1966. 'Roger Casement and Africa', *Transition,* Vol. 26, No. 3.

—— 1966. 'The Role of the Ndebele and Shona Religious Authorities in the Rebellions of 1896 and 1897', in E. Stokes and R. Brown (eds), *The Zambesian Past: Studies in Central African History* (Manchester, Manchester University Press).

—— 1966. 'Traditional Authorities and the Rise of Modern Politics in Southern Rhodesia 1898-1930', in E. Stokes and R. Brown (eds), *The Zambesian Past: Studies in Central African History* (Manchester, Manchester University Press).

—— 1968. 'Nationality and Nationalism: The Case of Barotseland', *Journal of the Historical Society of Nigeria,* Vol. 4, No. 2.

—— 1968. 'Connexions Between "Primary Resistance" Movements and Modern Mass Nationalisms in East and Central Africa. Part One', *Journal of African History,* Vol. 9, No. 3.

—— 1968. 'Connexions Between "Primary Resistance" Movements and Modern Mass Nationalisms in East and Central Africa. Part Two', *Journal of African History,*

Vol. 9, No. 4.

—— 1968. 'Introduction', in *Aspects of Central Africa History* (London, Heinemann).

—— 1968. 'African Politics in Twentieth Century Southern Rhodesia', in *Aspects of Central African History* (London, Heinemann).

——. 1968. 'The Nineteenth Century in Southern Rhodesia', in *Aspects of Central African History* (London, Heinemann).

—— 1971. 'The Historiography of Southern Rhodesia', *TransAfrican Journal of History*, Vol. 1, No. 2.

—— 1972. 'Missionary Adaptation of African Religious Institutions: The Masasi Case', in T. Ranger and I. Kimambo (eds), *The Historical Study of African Religion* (London, Heinemann).

—— 1973. 'The Apostle: Kolumba Msigala', in J. Iliffe (ed.), *Modern Tanzanians* (Nairobi, East African Publishing House for the Historical Association of Tanzania).

—— 1973. 'Territorial Cults in the History of Central Africa', *Journal of African History*, Vol. 14, No. 4.

—— 1974. 'The Meaning of Mwari', *Rhodesian History*, Vol. 5.

—— 1975. 'The Mwana Lesa Movement of 1925', in T. Ranger and J. Weller (eds), *Themes in the Christian History of Central Africa* (London, Heinemann).

—— 1976. 'From Humanism to the Science of Man: Colonialism in Africa and the Understanding of Alien Societies', *Transactions of the Royal Historical Society*, Vol. 26.

—— 1977. 'The People in African Resistance: A Review', *Journal of Southern African Studies*, Vol. 4, No. 1.

—— 1978. 'Reflections on Peasant Research in Central and Southern Africa', *Journal of Southern African Studies*, Vol. 5, No. 1.

—— 1978. 'Faction-Fighting, Race Consciousness and Worker Consciousness: A Note on the Jagersfontein Riots of 1914', *South African Labour Bulletin*, Vol. 4, No. 5.

—— 1978. 'Summary Report of the Situation of Refugees in Zambia and Botswana', *Zimbabwe Revolution*, Vol. 7, No. 516.

—— 1979. 'European Attitudes and African Realities: The Rise and Fall of the Matola Chiefs of South East Tanzania', *Journal of African History*, Vol. 20, No. 1.

—— 1979. 'Foreword', to J.M. Schofeleers (ed.), *Guardians of the Land: Essays on Central African Territorial Cults* (Gweru, Mambo Press).

—— 1979. "The Mobilisation of Labour and the Production of Knowledge: The Antiquarian Tradition in Rhodesia', *Journal of African History*, Vol. 20.

—— 1979. 'White Presence and Power in Africa', *Journal of African History*, Vol. 20, No. 4.

—— 1980. 'Making Northern Rhodesia Imperial: Variations on a Royal Theme, 1924-1938', *African Affairs,* Vol. lxxix, No. 316.

—— 1980. 'Foreword', to M. Nyagumbo, *With the People: An Autobiography from the Zimbabwean Struggle* (London, Allison and Busby; Salisbury, Graham Publishers).

—— 1980. 'The Changing of the Old Guard: Robert Mugabe and the Revival of ZANU', *Journal of Southern African Studies,* Vol. 7, No. 1.

—— 1981. 'Kolonialismus In Ost-Und Zentral Afrika', in J.H. Grevemeyer (ed.), *Traditionale Gesellschaften Und Europaischer Kolonialismus* (Frankfurt, Syndikat Publishers).

—— and C. Murray. 1981. 'Introduction', *Journal of Southern African Studies,* Vol. 8, No. 1.

—— 1982. 'The Death of Chaminuka: Spirit Mediums, Nationalism and the Guerrillas in Zimbabwe', *African Affairs,* Vol. 324, No. 81.

—— 1982. 'Guerrilla War and Peasant Violence: Makoni District, Zimbabwe', *Political Violence,* Institute of Commonwealth Studies, London, Collected Seminar Papers, No. 30.

—— 1982. 'Medical Science and Pentecost: The Dilemma of Anglicanism in Africa', in T. Ranger and W. Shiels (eds), *The Church and Healing* (Oxford, Blackwell).

—— 1982. 'Race and Tribe in Southern Africa: European Ideas and African Acceptance', in R. Ross (ed.), *Racism and Colonialism* (Leiden, Martinus Nijhoff).

—— 1982. 'Revolutions in the Wheel of Zimbabwean History', *Moto,* Vol. 1, No. 8.

—— 1982. 'Tradition and Travesty: Chiefs and the Administration in Makoni District, Zimbabwe, 1960 to 1980', *Africa,* Vol. 52, No. 3.

—— 1983. 'The Church and War: Holy Men and Rural Communities in Zimbabwe, 1970-1980', in B. Shiels (ed.), *The Church and War* (Oxford, Blackwell).

—— 1983. 'Literature and Political Economy: Arthur Shearly Cripps and the Makoni Labour Crisis of 1911', *Journal of Southern African Studies,* Vol. 9, No. 1.

—— and D. Birmingham. 1983. 'Settlers and Liberators in the South, 1953-1980', in D. Birmingham and P. Martin (eds), *History of Central Africa, Volume Two* (London, Longman).

—— 1984. 'Religions and Rural Protests: Makoni District, Zimbabwe, 1900 to 1980', in J. Bak and G. Benecke (eds), *Religion and Rural Revolt* (Manchester, Manchester University Press).

—— 1985. 'Rendre Present Le Passe Au Zimbabwe', *Politique Africaine,* No. 1.

—— 1986. 'Religion, Development and African Christian Identity: The Case of Zimbabwe', *Neue Zeitschrift für Missionswissenschaft,* Vol.42, No. 1.

—— 1986. 'Religious Movements and Politics in Sub-Saharan Africa', *African Studies*

*Review*, Vol. 29, No. 2.

—— 1986. 'Religious Studies and Political Economy: Mwari Cult and The Peasant Experience in Southern Rhodesia', in W.M.J. Van Binsbergen and M. Schoffeleers (eds), *Theoretical Explorations in African Religion, Politics and Patriarchy* (London, Routledge).

—— 1986. 'Resistance in Africa: From Nationalist Revolt to Agrarian Protest', in G. Okihiro (ed.), *In Resistance: Studies in African, Afro-American and Caribbean History* (Amherst, University of Massachusetts Press).

—— 1987. 'From Commaid to Service: Trevor Huddleston in Masasi, 1960-1968', in D.D. Honore (ed.), *Trevor Huddleston: Essays on his Life and Work* (Oxford, Oxford University Press).

—— 1987. 'An Africanist Comment', *American Ethnologist*, Vol. 14, No. 1.

—— 1987. 'Concluding Summary', in K. Holst-Petersen (ed.), *Religion, Development and African Identity* (Uppsala, Scandinavian Institute of African Studies).

—— 1987. 'Pilgrimages and Holy Places in Twentieth Century Zimbabwe', *Past and Present*, No. 117, November.

—— 1987. 'Pugilism and Pathology: African Boxing and the Black Urban Experience in Southern Rhodesia', in W.J. Baker and J.A. Mangan (eds), *Sport in Africa: Essays in Social History* (New York, Africana Publishing Company).

—— 1987. 'Religion in the Zimbabwean Guerrilla War', in J. Obelkevich et al. (eds), *Disciplines of Faith: Studies in Religion, Politics and Patriarchy* (London, Routledge).

—— 1988. 'African Traditional Religion', in S. Sutherland and P. Clarke (eds), *The Study of Religion, Traditional and New Religion* (London, Routledge).

—— 1988. 'The Influenza Pandemic in Southern Rhodesia: A Crisis of Comprehension', in D.A. Arnold (ed.), *Imperial Medicine and Indigenous Societies* (Manchester, Manchester University Press).

—— 1988. 'Introduction: Penetrating Appearances', *Journal of Southern African Studies*, Vol. 14, No. 2.

—— 1988. 'Review Articles: Africa Looks at Southern Africa: A Review of Journals', *Journal of Southern African Studies*, Vol. 14, No. 3.

—— 1989. 'Missionaries, Migrants and the Manyika: The Invention of Ethnicity in Zimbabwe', in L. Vail (ed.), *The Creation of Tribalism in Southern Africa* (London, James Currey).

—— 1989. 'Whose Heritage? The Case of the Matobo National Park', *Journal of Southern African Studies*, Vol. 15, No. 2.

——. 1989. 'Matabeleland Since the Amnesty', *African Affairs*, Vol. 351, No. 88.

—— 1991. 'Ethnicity and Nationality: The Case of Matabeleland', Institute of Commonwealth Studies, London, Collected Seminar Papers.

—— 1992. 'Plagues of Beasts and Men; Prophetic Responses to Epidemics in Eastern and Southern Africa', in T. Ranger and P. Slack (eds), *Epidemics and Ideas: Essays on the Historical Perception of Pestilence* (Cambridge, Cambridge University Press).

—— 1992. 'Power, Religion and the Community: The Matobo Case', *Subaltern Studies*, Vol. 7.

—— 1992. 'War, Violence and Healing in Zimbabwe', *Journal of Southern African Studies*, Vol. 18, No. 3.

—— 1993. 'The Invention of Tradition Revisited: The Case of Colonial Africa', in T. Ranger and O. Vaughan (eds), *Legitimacy and the State in Twentieth Century Africa* (London, Macmillan).

—— 1993. 'The Communal Areas of Zimbabwe', in T. Bassett and D. Crummey (eds), *Land in African Agrarian Systems* (Madison, University of Wisconsin Press).

—— 1993. 'The Local and the Global in Southern African Religious History', in R.W. Hefner (ed.), *Conversion to Christianity* (Berkeley, University of California Press).

—— 1994. 'African Identities: Ethnicity, Nationality and History. The Case of Matabeleland, 1893-1993', in J. Heidrich (ed.), *Changing Identities. The Transformation of Asian and African Societies Under Colonialism* (Berlin, Centre for Modern Oriental Studies).

—— 1994. 'Protestant Missions in Africa: The Dialectic of Conversion', in T.D. Blakely, W.E.A. Van Beek and D.L. Thomson (eds), *Religion in Africa: Experience and Expression* (London, James Currey).

—— 1994. 'Tribalisation of Africa. Retribalisation of Europe', *The Woodstock Road Editorial. An Oxford Magazine of International Affairs*, Vol. 16.

—— 1994. 'Studying repatriation as part of African Social History', in T. Allen and H. Morsink (eds) *When Refugees go home: African Experiences* (London, James Currey).

—— 1995. 'Concluding Remarks', in A.H.M. Kirk-Greene (ed.), *The Emergence of African History at British Universities* (Oxford, WorldView Publications).

—— 1996. 'The Moral Economy of Identity in Northern Matabeleland', in L. de la Gorgendiere et al. (eds), *Ethnicity in Africa* (Edinburgh, Centre of African Studies).

—— 1999. 'The Nature of Ethnicity: Lessons from Africa' in E. Mortimer (ed.), *People, Nation and State* (London, I.B. Tauris)

—— and J. Alexander. 1998. 'Competition and Integration in the Religious History of North-Western Zimbabwe', *Journal of Religion in Africa*, Vol. 28, No. 1.

—— and J. McGregor. 2000. 'Displacement and Disease: Epidemics and Ideas about Malaria in Matabeleland, Zimbabwe, 1945-1996', *Past and Present*, Vol. 167.

—— 2000. 'The Reception of Mau Mau in Southern Rhodesia, 1952-1961' in Piet Konings et al, (eds). *Trajectoires de liberation en Afrique contemporaine* (Paris, Karthala).

—— 2001. 'Priestesses and Environment in Zimbabwe', in Alaine Low and Sonya Tremayne, (eds), *Women as Sacred Custodians of the Earth?* (New York and Oxford, Berghahn Books).

—— 2001. 'Pictures Must Prevail: Sex and the Social History of African Photography in Bulawayo, 1930-1960', *Kronos*, Vol. 27.

—— 2002. 'Zimbabwe. Cultural Revolution', *The World Today*, Vol. 58, No. 2.

—— 2002. 'African Local Historiographies: A Negative Case', in Axel Harneit-Sievers (ed.), *A Place in the World: New Local Historiographies from Africa and South-Asia* (Leiden, Brill).

—— 2002. 'Kulturlandschaften und Afrikanische Heschichte am Beispiel Zimbabwes,' in Bernd Busch, (ed.), *Erde* (Köln, Wienand).

—— 2002. 'Taking on the Missionary's Task: African Spirituality and the Mission Churches of Manicaland in the 1930s', in David Maxwell (ed.), *Christianity and the African Imagination* (Leiden, Brill).

—— 2002. 'History has its ceiling. The Pressures of the past in *The Stone Virgins*', in R. Muponde and M. Taruvinga, (eds), *Sign and Taboo: Perspectives on the Poetic Fiction of Yvonne Vera* (Harare, Weaver Press; Oxford, James Currey).

—— 2002. 'The Zimbabwe Elections: A personal experience', *Transformation*, Vol. 19, No. 3.

—— 2002. 'Evangelical Christianity and Democracy in Africa', *Transformation*, Vol. 19, No. 4. (Also Published in the *Journal of Religion in Africa*, Vol. 33, No. 3, 2003).

—— 2002. 'Peeling Back the Layers of Yoruba Religion', *Politique Africaine, 'Les Sujects de Dieu'*, 87.

—— 2003. 'Women and Environment in African Religion', in William Beinart and JoAnn McGregor (eds), *Social History and African Environments* (Oxford, James Currey).

—— 2003. 'A Historian's Foreword', in Howard Phillips and David Killingray (eds), *The Spanish Influenza Pandemic of 1918-19* (London, Routledge).

—— 2003. 'Christianity and Indigenous Peoples: A Personal Overview', *Journal of Religious History*, Vol. 27, No. 3.

—— 2003.'Commentary' in J. A. Draper, (ed.), *Orality, Literacy and Colonialism in Southern Africa* (Atlanta, Society of Biblical Literature).

—— 2004. 'Zimbabwe', in Gabriel Palmer-Fernandez (ed.), *Encyclopaedia of Religion and War* (London, Routledge).

—— 2004. 'Dignifying Death: The Politics of Burial in Bulawayo, 1893 to 1960', *The Journal of Religion in Africa,* Vol. 34, No. 1.

—— 2004. 'Bicycles and the Social History of Bulawayo' in Jane Morris (ed.), *Short*

*Writings from Bulawayo,* (Bulawayo, 'amaBooks). Awarded first prize for work in English, Zimbabwe Publishing Awards, 2005.

—— 2004. 'Nationalist History, Patriotic History and the History of the Nation: the struggle over the past in Zimbabwe', *Journal of Southern African Studies,* Vol. 30, No. 2.

—— 2005. 'The Narratives and Counter-Narratives of Zimbabwean Asylum: female voices', *Third World Quarterly* Vol. 26, No. 3.

—— 2005. 'Christianity and the First Peoples: Some Second Thoughts', in Peggy Brock (ed.), *Indigenous Peoples and Religious Change* (Leiden, Brill).

—— 2005. 'Chimurengas', in Prem Poddar and David Johnson, (eds), *A Historical Companion to Postcolonial Literatures in English* (Edinburgh, Edinburgh University Press).

—— 2005. 'Rule by historiography: the struggle over the past in contemporary Zimbabwe', in Robert Muponde and Ranka Primorac (eds), *Versions of Zimbabwe: New Approaches to Literature and Culture* (Harare, Weaver Press).

—— 2005. 'Postscript' in Ton Otto and Paul Pedersen (eds), *Tradition and Agency: Tracing cultural continuity and invention* (Aarhus, Aarhus University Press).

—— 2005. 'Zimbabwe: Spirit Mediums, Guerrillas, and Nature' and 'Zimbabwe's Matopo Hills' in B. Taylor (ed.), *Encyclopaedia of Religion and Nature* (London, Continuum).

—— 2005. 'The Uses and Abuses of History in Zimbabwe', in Mai Palmberg and Ranka Primorac (eds), *Skinning the Skunk – Facing Zimbabwe Futures* (Uppsala, Nordic Africa Institute).

—— 2005. 'Christian Mission, Capitalism and Empire: The State of the Debate', *Le Fait Missionaire: Social Sciences and Missions,* No. 17.

—— 2005. 'The Rise of Patriotic Journalism in Zimbabwe and its Possible Implications', *Westminster Papers in Communication and Culture: Special Issue,* 'The Media and Zimbabwe'.

—— 2006. 'The Meaning of Urban Violence in Africa: Bulawayo, Southern Rhodesia, 1890-1960', *Cultural and Social History,* Vol. 3, No. 2.

—— 2006. 'African Religion, Witchcraft and the Liberation War in Zimbabwe', in B. Nicolini (ed.), *Studies in Witchcraft, Magic, War and Peace in Africa: Nineteenth and Twentieth Centuries* (Lampeter, Mellen Press).

—— 2006. 'From Ireland to Africa; a personal memoir', *History Ireland,* Vol. 14, No. 4.

—— 2006. 'Storiografia nazionalista, storia patriotitica e storie della nazione. Il confliction sul passato nello Zimbabwe', *Passato e Presente,* 69.

—— 2007. 'Reconstructing Zimbabwe's Past: The Professional Historians Return', *Safundi,* Vol. 8, No. 2.

—— 2007. 'Scotland Yard in the Bush: Medicine Murders, Child Witches and Deconstructing the Occult: A Literature Review', *Africa*, Vol. 77, No. 2.

—— 2007. 'City versus State in Zimbabwe: Colonial Antecedents of the Current Crisis', *Journal of Eastern African Studies*, Vol.1, No. 2.

—— 2007. 'Going to Extremes in Zimbabwe and Britain: Reflections on the Scholar Activist. The first biannual Marja-Liisa Swantz Lecture', *Finnish Journal of Ethnicity and Migration*, Vol. 2, No. 2.

—— 2007. 'Living Ritual and Indigenous Archaeology: The Case of Zimbabwe', in Evangelos Kyriakidis (ed.), *The Archaeology of Ritual*, 3 (Los Angeles, Cotsen Institute, UCLA).

—— 2008. 'Myth and Legend in Urban Oral Memory: Bulawayo, 1930-60', *Journal of Post-colonial Literature*, Vol. 44, No. I.

—— 2009. 'Myth and Legend in urban oral memory: Bulawayo, 1930-60', in Ranka Primorac (ed.), *African City Textualities* (London, Routledge).

—— 2009. 'The Politics of Memorialisation in Zimbabwe', in Susana Carvalho and Francois Gemenne (eds), *Nations and Their Histories: Constructions and Representations* (Basingstoke, Palgrave Macmillan).

—— 2010. 'Reclaiming the African City: The World and the Township', in Achim von Oppen and Ulrike Freitag (eds), *Translocality: The Study of Globalising Processes from a Southern Perspective* (Leiden, Brill).

—— 2011. 'Dignifying Death: The Politics of Burial in Bulawayo', in Michael Jindra and Joel Noret (eds), *Funerals in Africa: Death, a Focal Institution and Social Change* (New York, Berghahn Books).

—— 2012. 'Caves in Black and White; The Case of Zimbabwe', in Holley Moyes (ed.), *Sacred Darkness: A Global Perspective on the Ritual Use of Caves* (Boulder, University of Colorado Press).

—— 'Religion and Landscape at Cyrene Mission', in Anne and Garry Charnock (eds), *Catalogue of the Cyrene Paintings*, forthcoming.

## PAMPHLETS AND OTHER PUBLICATIONS

T. Ranger. 1960. *Crisis in Southern Rhodesia*, Fabian Commonwealth Bureau.

—— 1961. *State and Church in Southern Rhodesia, 1919-1939*, Salisbury, Historical Association of Rhodesia and Nyasaland.

—— 1962. *The Inglorious age: Review article: The navy and commerce under the early Stuarts*, Salisbury, Historical Association of Rhodesian and Nyasaland.

—— 1969. *The Recovery of African Initiative in Tanzanian History*, University College, Dar es Salaam.

—— 1971. *The Agricultural History of Zambia,* (Lusaka, National Educational Company of Zambia, for the Historical Association of Zambia).

—— 1981. *Towards a Radical Practice of Academic Freedom: The Experience of East and Central Africa,* Cape Town, University of Cape Town.

—— 1988. *Chingaira Makoni's Head: Myth, Mystery and the Colonial Experience,* Bloomington, Africa Studies Program, Indiana University.

—— 1989. *Rhodes, Oxford and the Study of Race Relations,* (Oxford, Clarendon).

—— 2002. *Christianity and Indigenous People's: A personal overview,* (Basel, Basler Afrika Bibliographien).

—— 2003. 'Zimbabwean Diasporas', Report for the Britain Zimbabwe Society.

—— 2004. 'What History for Which Zimbabwe', A report on the Britain Zimbabwe Society Research Days.

—— 2008. 'Introduction' to Peter Mackay, *We Have Tomorrow: Stirrings in Africa, 1959-1967,* (Wilby, Michael Russell).

—— 2009 'Preface' to the on-line publication of *The Rose of Rhodesia.*

# Index of Names